THE *Pioneer* AND THE *Innkeeper*

ADVENTURES IN UNCERTAINTY
AND FAITH AROUND THE WORLD

THE

Pioneer

AND THE

Innkeeper

Adventures in UNCERTAINTY
and FAITH *around the* WORLD

DR. CALVIN & MIMI WILSON

RETELLING, LLC

ISBN 978-1-7369457-9-7

PUBLISHED IN ASSOCIATION WITH Retelling | retelling.net

COVER DESIGN BY Cynthia Young | youngdesign.biz

DISCLAIMER

*T*he events, dates, and details included in this story are primarily taken from the joint memories of Cal and Mimi and may differ somewhat from the details recalled by those mentioned or involved in the story. Cal and Mimi mean no offense and have no agenda if such is the case. They do acknowledge that over time, and with their accumulated ages, some discrepancies or errors may have crept into their memories and for this they humbly apologize in advance. They ask that if significant discrepancies are found, especially by those who are mentioned or were involved, to please bring it to their attention, both to correct their memory and so that a proper apology can be given.

Cal and Mimi are also increasingly aware that their memory and age will almost inevitably lead to failing to mention some individuals who were truly key influences in their lives at some point. Again, they mean no offense in this, and apologize in advance.

Contents

Beginnings

1967 - 1974

CAL AND MIMI IN LOVE

SPEES FAMILY, 1960

SPEES FAMILY, 1965

CAL AND MIMI'S WEDDING, JUNE 13, 1968

CAL AND MIMI'S WEDDING, JUNE 13, 1968

CAL & MIMI IN THEIR FIRST HOME —
A MOBILE HOME

FOUR GENERATIONS OF WILSONS, 1978

MIMI'S PARENTS, BILL AND ELLA SPEES, 1986

MIMI AND
CHRIS WILSON

CHAPTER I

Finding a Wife

*C*al Wilson traveled to Chicago for a Young Peoples' Missions Conference in 1966 during a Christmas break from college. He was on a two-fold mission. He had grown up reading biographies of missionary physicians and envisioned himself in that role, pioneering among people hidden from the developed world. For now, he was a college student focused on studying medicine, but he believed someday mission work would play a part. So, at this conference he wanted to learn more about mission work. Also, Cal wanted to find a wife.

As a freshman at Colorado College in Colorado Springs, Colorado, Cal was desperately feeling the need to have a female in his life. He was seriously looking. What safer place than a mission conference to find a suitable young woman who might be able to share some of his dreams? Several thousand young people were attending. *That was good*, Cal thought.

Cal was still considered shy. He had grown up a studious child, always curious, always reading, a bit of a recluse. He was constantly trying to understand more concepts of science. For one school science fair in junior high he created a box that you looked into to see a rotating earth, a rotating moon, and a light representing the sun. At the far end, an illuminated sign indicated when a solar eclipse occurred and when a lunar eclipse occurred. All of it was in motion, constructed and powered by an erector set.

The oldest of six children, Cal grew up on an 80-acre farm that served as an extended family compound. His grandfather owned the land and his three children had all built homes on it. With lots of land to roam and a gaggle of siblings and cousins to play with, Cal's childhood had lots of freedom. His brother Kent wrote a brief history of their childhood that mentioned in nearly every chapter something blowing up. Cal experimented with flame throwers, firebombs, and some of the big firecrackers that were available at the time. Fortunately, most of his experiments flopped. For example, he conjured up the idea to create a nifty flame thrower by filling a plastic squirt gun with gasoline, then shoot the gasoline through a candle, which he held out in his other hand. But as soon as he put the gasoline in the squirt gun, it started to melt, and the gasoline ended up pouring over his hand while he gripped a candle in the other. It occurred to him this wasn't a good idea, so he ended the experiment. His parents didn't know these kinds of experiments went on, as they were kept secret and usually attempted outside or deep in the basement.

As he entered adolescence, Cal became much more committed to his relationship with God. He had made a formal commitment to follow Jesus at age 9 while attending a Christian summer camp and had continued to read the Bible and learn from the weekly teaching at the church his family attended. As an adolescent, he began to understand how a consistent relationship with his Heavenly Father might actually work and spent a significant amount of time reading classical Christian books and praying for daily guidance in his life.

Cal's parents were also Christian believers, who had warned him against following the increasingly open and relaxed cultural attitudes toward dating and sex. His father had given him a couple of books detailing all the bad things that can happen with the wrong relationship, which made him somewhat shy in that arena. But during the last couple of years of high school he began to date a little and experienced some heartbreak a couple of times—only lightly, but enough to let him know he wasn't the only person in the world.

So here Cal was near the end of the mission conference, and frankly, still being somewhat shy and introverted, he had not met anybody who looked like she might be appropriate to date. Feeling discouraged, he had a serious, tearful talk with the Lord. "Lord, why am I not finding a woman that I feel comfortable with? Do you want me to remain single?" After a long struggle, he capitulated and said, "God, well, if you want me to remain single all my life then I will try to accept that." He was 18.

As the mission session ended and Cal rose from his chair, his eye caught a glimpse of bright red hair and hazel eyes two seats behind him. *Hmm.* There was Mimi Spees! He knew that girl! He winced a bit, embarrassed at the memory of their first meeting.

Mimi was a nursing student in Colorado Springs, the daughter of Christian missionaries in what was then Zaire (now Democratic Republic of Congo). She was living with a family friend, Dorothy Brown, who had accompanied her husband to Africa for big game hunting with Mimi's father. "If you ever need a place for Marilyn, my home is your home," she had said to Mimi's mother. Mrs. Brown was also a friend of Cal's extended Wilson family. Since Cal and Mimi were both students in Colorado Springs, Mrs. Brown had the bright idea to get them together, so she arranged a party. Mimi could invite whomever she wanted, but Cal would be the Master of Ceremonies. Mimi didn't like the feel of the arrangement, so she brought an Air Force Academy cadet with her to the party. The event did not go well, and neither she nor Cal had been very impressed with each other. But this time Mimi looked ... different.

As I live and breathe, thought Mimi, who had come to the conference because her uncle was one of the primary speakers. There was Cal Wilson! And he looked pretty good! They talked for a while and then Cal accompanied Mimi to the Chicago train station to wait for the train that would take Mimi back to Colorado Springs. It was New Year's Eve, and as the train pulled in, it was filled with soldiers returning to Fort Carson. Drunk and rowdy ones kept grabbing at Mimi to pull her into their train car. The conductor was of no help. *Uh-oh*, thought Cal, *this is going to be an interesting ride for her.* He handed her the tear gas pen he routinely carried for self-defense, in case she absolutely needed it.

Mimi took a seat on the train and one soldier leaned across the aisle, offering her the seat next to him.

"How is that a better offer than any of the other soldiers?" asked Mimi.

"Well, I can protect you from them," he said. And he did just that, staying awake for the full trip until they reached Colorado Springs, and Mimi never had to use the tear gas pen.

Mimi, too, had grown up with grandparents next door, and with a jungle to explore, at the Lolwa mission station in the Ituri Forest among the pygmies. Mimi's grandparents had first arrived in Africa with their teen-aged children in 1929. Years later, as newly-weds Mimi's parents, Ella and Bill Spees, returned to Africa to establish the Lolwa mission station. Mimi's father was a missionary builder. He built their house, the neighboring house for her grandparents, the hospital in which Mimi's mother worked, and various schools, churches, and other projects such as a leprosarium. Her mother delivered babies, taught school, and was part of the team which translated the Bible into Swahili and two Pygmy languages. One week per month her family lived with the Pygmies in one of their nomadic camps, teaching them about God and how to read the few books available in their language. Her parents talked about it as though it was the biggest treasure to get to sleep in a Pygmy hut, so Mimi always looked forward to it.

Mimi was considered an easygoing child. "I was from Africa—I was African," quips Mimi. She and her younger brother, Alan, played with anything around them, including bugs and ants. They were particularly fond of disturbing the orderly march of the army ants and watching the monkeys playing overhead. For most of her childhood, Mimi was a sickly child. She couldn't seem to break recurrent cycles of malaria, and spent days and days in bed. Like Cal, Mimi too had committed her life to follow Jesus at an early age, and had continued to grow spiritually as she began to understand more of the Bible she heard taught almost daily. She developed a close relationship with her Father God that was able to sustain her through many of the difficult periods of her life.

Her older sister, Nancy, went to live in Kansas City with a church family for high school, and so Mimi saw her only on furloughs to the US. Beginning at age seven, Mimi and Alan attended a mission boarding school several hours' drive from home for three months at a time, with one month breaks at home. Mimi sobbed whenever she had to leave for school. At school she doesn't necessarily remember the grade levels of her companions, but she does remember whether her friends got along with each other. And Mimi did. She was the one others wanted to sit next to.

At the Lolwa station, Mimi was close to her little granny who lived next door, who preferred to be called Grandmother because she was a real lady. With nothing for her to entertain children, Grandmother recited stories and poems from her own childhood. Both Mimi's mother and grandmother were wonderful story tellers, and Mimi grew up loving to tell stories. They had few books out in the jungle, so they did with what they had. Life was hard, but her parents and grandparents did it, and they did it well.

Mimi often heard her little granny singing a hymn at the top of her lungs when she trekked to the outhouse in the middle of the night, and finally asked, "Why are you doing that?" Grandmother replied, "I think it would take a madman to hurt somebody singing a hymn." Of course, the hymn was in English and nobody else spoke English there, but that was Grandmother's reasoning.

Mimi's godly grandfather set the scene for her family. She can still hear him praying with his Scottish accent. When she later left that environment for boarding school in the US, she remained deeply impressed with the reality that God is alive and loves to hear our prayers.

The road that passed their home was at that time basically the only African transcontinental road. It was dirt, and very sketchy in many places. But because of their location a steady stream of adventurers passed their house on the road. Their mission station, Lolwa, was at one point mentioned in the

Michelin Guide for Africa as a very welcoming and appropriate place to stop for an overnight or for a meal. However, the Guide warned, "Be prepared to receive some Christian literature, but they'll be very hospitable."

Mimi watched her mother welcome guests day after day, without any stores around other than tiny shops that might sell rice. Her mother always insisted, "Aren't we blessed to have a home here? Aren't we blessed to be able to open up our home?" Mimi heard this over and over and it left its mark on her. She learned to love the variety and uncertainties of African life. One morning Mimi woke up in the bathtub.

"Mama," she called out, "I'm in the bathtub!"

"Well," her mother explained, "we had guests during the night, and someone needed your bed." Her mother continued, "Just think, Heidi (from the Swiss story) slept in the attic, above her grandfather."

Put that way, Mimi felt privileged instead of offended.

At age 13, Mimi traveled to the US for high school, a Christian boarding school in Florida that catered to higher class, wealthier students but also accepted missionary students on scholarship. It was a very lonely time for her, and Mimi had to learn to cope with not having the resources that were required to fit in at the school. However, she learned to love the school, not only because of the deep and challenging daily Bible classes, but also because in her loneliness and separation from her parents she came to experience her Heavenly Father as a Daddy who deeply loved and cared for her. She talked freely with Him, told Him her jokes and problems, and watched in amazement as her Heavenly Father miraculously and generously provided the special clothing and resources needed for school life. Those were hard years because she was alone. Christmases, summers. And yet the Lord provided in each of these places.

Her one joy was her grandmother, who moved to Florida near the school following her husband's death; however even this joy was short-lived as she died during Mimi's second year at the school.

At the boarding school, Mimi learned etiquette: how to set a table, what meals go with what. She also learned to date. A boy had to invite a girl on a date every Sunday night, which she enjoyed because the boys were very polite, and they had some great talks. But when Mimi left the school for college she didn't even know where to begin with dating, because everything had been so structured at the private, specialized high school.

Mimi first attended Geneva College in Pennsylvania for a year, but then transferred to a nursing school in Colorado Springs, primarily because she really did not like the long winters in Pennsylvania and assumed Colorado Springs was similar to Palm Springs in California (since both were "Springs"; she really didn't know US geography). Shortly thereafter, Mrs. Brown arranged the first disastrous meeting for Mimi with Cal Wilson. And now, Mimi and Cal reconnected at the missions conference in Chicago.

At the time, Mimi was dating somebody else whom she had

met the year earlier, and she had time to think this through on her train trip back to Colorado Springs. Which one would she continue with? She had, in fact, just spent Christmas with the other young man.

Mimi had to admit that Cal looked pretty good to her this time. And he had two strong things going for him: everyone who knew him spoke of his strong character, and they both were very interested in international mission work. Mimi was pretty convinced she would switch over to Cal.

Back at college after the mission conference, Cal realized he had to follow up, so he invited Mimi out for a date. Not just any date, it had to be special! He took her to a nice restaurant and then to a movie, not knowing that as a missionary kid Mimi had never been in a cinema before. The movie was "Dr. Zhivago," which while a bit risqué in parts for a first exposure, was very romantic. It was a good choice!

Soon they were spending almost every free moment together, talking the entire time, often on long drives, all over Colorado on various occasions. Cal loved the Colorado mountains, and the drives were an excuse to be together and to talk. At least initially, Cal remembers talking about Mimi's other boyfriend. He envisioned himself as the wise counselor involved in helping Mimi understand more about (at least what Cal perceived of) this fellow, and he gallantly tried to help Mimi work through her dilemma.

They grew close very quickly, as close as they possibly could without being married. In addition, Mimi longed for a mother in her life, and Cal's mother stepped into that role without hesitation. Even though they were both young and still in college—Mimi had one more year of nursing school and Cal still had two years of undergraduate work at Colorado College—they knew it was the right time for them to get married. Cal was 19 and Mimi was 21.

Cal's parents had married quite young as well, so the actual age was not a problem for them. "Aunt" Dorothy Brown, of course, was very pleased. In fact, she suddenly switched into high gear and became the wedding planner. She handled all the details graciously and generously, preparing for 300 guests at the wedding.

They were married in Aunt Dorothy's church in Colorado Springs on July 13, 1968. Mimi's mother, Ella, flew from Africa to attend, as it was financially impossible for both parents to come. Interestingly enough, the Spees had some years earlier been guests in Cal's parents' home, because the Wilsons attended one of the churches that supported the Spees family. Little did either family know what the future would hold for their children.

Mimi's brother Alan, with whom Mimi was very close, was flying in from Pennsylvania to give her away in the place of their father. However, there was a little incident just a few days before the wedding. Alan was doing an experiment in the chemistry laboratory at the university, working with a very unstable compound. He briefly took off his safety glasses, and at that moment the material he was working with exploded and threw shards of glass in all directions, including in his face. Mimi's mom was in the air traveling at that time. When she landed in the US she called Alan and received the news. Then she called Mimi, and her first words to Mimi were, "This is your mother. Your brother's been in an accident, and I think he's blind!"

As it turned out, the glass had missed Alan's eyeball, but had lacerated his lid and a good part of his face. He was not blind, in fact he had no vision problems at all from it. So, he came to the wedding with a face that looked like it had been in an explosion and walked Mimi down the aisle.

Cal's parents insisted that Cal have a new suit for the wedding. Don Wilson, Cal's father, had most of his suits made in Hong Kong by a visiting tailor who would come through the city, take measurements, and then return to Hong Kong to have the suits sewn. Don set up Cal with this tailor in a downtown hotel. The tailor took the measurements, and Cal picked out a fabric that looked modern, a kind of shiny fabric. The suit was made, the suit arrived, and Cal thought, *well, good, it's here*. He figured it was either going to fit or it wasn't. He couldn't fix it, so he didn't even try it on.

The day of the wedding Cal put on the suit and suddenly remembered that the current mode of suit for young men in Hong Kong was skin-tight pants! The waist fit, but he had to tug to get his feet in the pant legs. He didn't really care—he was getting married, and Cal had never really cared that much about his appearance. But when they were taking the wedding pictures the photographer kept saying to him, "Cal, put your feet together. I can see between your legs. Put your legs together." Cal put his legs together, but you could still see between his legs. His Hong Kong pants looked like shiny, silk tights.

Cal and Mimi were just glad when the wedding was over. It was fun while it lasted, but they wanted to get to their honeymoon! They spent the first night in the old Antlers Hotel in Colorado Springs.

When they checked in, Mimi kept saying, "Shouldn't we show them our marriage license to allow us to be in the same room?"

"No, no," said Cal, "I don't think it's all that critical."

They walked up to the desk and the clerk gave them a knowing smile and said, "Congratulations on your wedding."

Cal looked at Mimi; they were wearing street clothes. "How did you know that we're married?" Cal asked.

"Because there's rice in your hair," responded the clerk.

The couple's goal was to drive to Mexico City. However, they really enjoyed being together and the truth was they didn't usually roll out of bed in their motel until about 10:00 or 11:00 in the morning. They'd drive for a few hours and decide, "Ah, this is getting old, let's check in again." So they'd check into a nearby hotel. After their first night in Colorado Springs, they made it all the way to Pueblo (about 45 miles). The third night they made it to … they can't remember. They do remember finally deciding to really push it, so they made it all the way to El Paso in one more day and crossed the border.

It took about three days getting through northern Mexico

with the same idea, just taking it easy. Their route took them through the northern part of Mexico toward the Gulf Coast, and they ended up one night in the little town of Tampico on the coast. They'd been driving for seven days by that point, and Mexico City suddenly seemed a long way away.

After looking at a couple of cockroach-ridden hotels in Tampico, they ended up finding a five-star hotel, which quickly felt very nice. They lounged for several days in this hotel, then turned around and drove home. They made it back to Colorado Springs in a leisurely four days, desperately in love.

CHAPTER 2

Making a Home

B ack in school in Colorado Springs, the young couple gathered their early living funds from surprising sources. Coming from a relatively well-to-do family, Cal had never held a job other than working for the family company. While contemplating marriage to Mimi, he realized it was time for him to get a job. His second year in college, knowing that he wanted to go into medicine, he visited three local hospitals looking for any kind of work. The St. Francis Hospital needed someone to do odd jobs in the laboratory, so he accepted the offer. In addition to the various odd jobs, he quickly began learning laboratory procedures under the supervision of the established technicians.

For the first time in his life, Cal was now earning a salary, although not enough to begin married life. To make matters worse, he was fired shortly before the wedding, which was a truly humiliating experience. However, after the wedding, during his third year at Colorado College, Cal found a job as a night on-call laboratory technician at a local osteopathic hospital, which allowed him to study during the day. Later, he found this to be a strong advantage during his first two years in medical school, as he was already familiar with medical testing, and able to use these skills to continue providing some income.

As they continued discussing what they would live on, Mimi suddenly told Cal, "Well, I've got money." She had never talked to him about this before.

"What do you mean, you've got money?" he asked, and she explained. While attending Geneva College in Pennsylvania, she had been invited to speak at a variety of conferences and service clubs, such as Lions, Rotary, and Kiwanis. Her only criteria was that she wouldn't accept more than three speaking engagements per day. Often her hosts paid more than the agreed stipend, so she made quite a large sum of money.

After every weekend, she deposited her earnings in the bank because she didn't know what else to do with it; her parents had just told her to save it. So, she kept putting it in without adding it up, with no idea of the total sum. After some searching, Mimi found her bank book and, to their delight, they were able to buy a 10 ft. by 50 ft. mobile home already on a rented lot outside of Colorado Springs, as well as a second car for Mimi to get back and forth to school. So, when people implied to Mimi that she married Cal for his family's money, she retorted, "No, he married me for mine!"

Cal was accepted into medical school at the University of Colorado in Denver, who waived his final year of premedical training because he had already completed all of the medical school admission requirements at Colorado College. He had received a four-year Boettcher Scholarship to attend Colorado College, but was uncertain how the Boettcher Foundation would respond to completing only three years. Would he lose that generous assistance? When Cal explained to the Boettcher Foundation that he had been accepted to medical school after just three years of college, they said, "Well, it's a four-year scholarship," so they applied it to his first year of medical school. They were very generous and even tripled Cal's book allowance, knowing how much medical books cost. This was most unusual and saved them a whole year of school expenses. The young couple saw this as clear evidence of God's provision for their needs, and confirmation of this next step of their journey of faith.

After all the lonely years living far from her family, Mimi Wilson now had a home! So what if it was a trailer? She made it the "coziest, coziest ever, ever!" In fact, everybody who came just loved it. The lady who bought it years later sketched every detail so she could duplicate Mimi's homey touches. Mimi said, "I just loved it because it was the beginning of my hospitality, and Cal made it very easy," as he loved getting to know new friends and offering hospitality as much as Mimi. She kept thinking, *I have a home, I have a home* after all those years of living in a dormitory.

The front part of the trailer was a dining room with a little round table that could be removed to allow a Murphy bed to be folded out of the front wall, then the kitchen, a living area, a tiny but complete bathroom, and bedroom that was big enough for a ¾-sized bed. The newlyweds appreciated that they had to squeeze together in the small bed. They wanted to be close, so they didn't feel constrained in it at all. Their only housing expenses—especially nice for college students—were the monthly lot rental, which at that time was $28 a month, a small electric bill, and a monthly supply of propane for the heater and stove.

Mimi invited over anybody she could think of, including children from the trailer park. Soon after they returned from their honeymoon, Cal's parents came for dinner to see them and their new home. Mimi thought she would make chicken soup, so she went to the store and bought the cheapest chicken she could find, a whole chicken. She put it in a large, wedding-gift kettle with four cherry tomatoes and a handful of rice and boiled it thoroughly. When Mimi served it, they all chewed and chewed, without much success. She suddenly realized that the chicken was so cheap because it was most likely an old rooster, as tough as rubber. But Cal's dad was so gracious; he pushed back his chair and he said, "Christine, we just must get this recipe!" Mimi gave it to him with delight, and her cooking career was launched.

Cal, however, found it necessary to adjust his expectations.

He realized very quickly that, to his surprise, Mimi had never learned how to cook, primarily because most of her life had been spent in boarding schools. Of course, he had never learned how to cook either, assuming that every woman back in that day would know how to cook.

Mimi's relationship with her mother-in-law was a great benefit at that point. Mimi learned much from Chris, especially cooking skills, and spent a lot of time with her. Mimi adored Chris, and they did everything they could together. It was a marvelous relationship.

When Cal started medical school, they moved the mobile home up to Denver and parked it on a lot in the Flying Saucer Trailer Park on West Hampden Avenue, which is still operating to this day. Cal worked as a laboratory technician at Porter Hospital during the first two years of medical school. His 16-hour shift on Saturdays did not interfere with his weekly classes. Mimi also took a job as a newly registered nurse at Porter Hospital, and was placed on the pediatric ward, which she absolutely loved.

Following Cal's first year in medical school, their first child, Kurt, was born. Mimi had been on birth control pills to allow time to settle into their marriage and medical school for at least a few years. But the birth control pills in those days had such high doses of hormones, especially estrogen, that they produced all kinds of side effects. The pills triggered serious migraine headaches in Mimi, including transient loss of vision or speech.

The gynecologist Mimi was seeing advised, "Well, the doses of hormone are high in this pill, so why don't you just stop it for a month and let your system readjust and then go ahead and start them up again."

"What do we do about preventing pregnancy during that month?" Mimi asked.

"Listen," he said, "the doses of hormones are so high that I have never seen anybody get pregnant just being off the pill for a month. It takes two to four months for your system to be able to get pregnant again."

They took him at his professional word, and Kurt was conceived that month. Cal performed the pregnancy test at the hospital. He had to do it twice to deal with the shock. Kurt was born right at the end of Cal's first year of medical school, which required some adjustment to their little mobile home. Cal removed the Murphy bed in the little dining area, and in its place built in a small crib, covered with hinged louvers, with additional drawers and storage space. When they had guests, they'd put Kurt down for bed, and guests would ask, "Where's the baby?" Cal would point to the louvers and say, "He's in that little closet there."

Mimi continued working as a nurse after Kurt was born. He was a very undemanding baby, and Mimi was thrilled. She had always wanted to have a family, and now she had it! But there were challenges, such as Kurt refusing to drink from a bottle, but only the breast. He would wait the eight hours for her to come home, and both Mimi and he were desperate by that point. This aspect was so difficult that Mimi finally said, "We cannot go on like this; I've got to devote my time to him." So she quit work at Porter Hospital when Kurt was only nine months old.

CHAPTER 3

Medical School

*T*here was no doubt that medical school was right where Cal was meant to be, given the rarity of being accepted to medical school before completion of his premedical studies, as well as the extension of his undergraduate scholarship to the first year of medical school. Although Cal was able to work Saturdays in a hospital laboratory that first year, he realized during the second year that the demands of school were becoming so great that he would not be able to continue his outside job. Knowing that the third year was totally consuming, he decided to borrow some money to pay the tuition and cover some living costs.

The fourth year of medical school was still financially problematic. However, Cal discovered that the US Public Health Service (PHS) had just started a program called the Early Commissioning Program. The program offered an officer's commission for the fourth year of medical school, with full salary and tuition, in exchange for two years of service in the Public Health Service following the internship year. This also fulfilled the military service requirement imposed at that time by the active war in Vietnam and would allow the family to stay together while still serving their country. Cal and Mimi recognized this opportunity as yet another wonderful confirmation of God's provision for their needs, and a generous provision at that!

Even before starting medical school, and especially once he began, Cal began to refine his motivations and objectives in becoming a physician. His primary objective was to be able to deal with people in need in a holistic approach that integrated medical, psychological, social, and spiritual aspects. In addition, he wanted to be able to help the needy in the more underserved or remote parts of the world.

To fulfill these objectives, he began looking at the various specialties, trying to decide which would give him the greatest degree of contact with people who were open to a holistic approach to their life. Some of the available specialties, such as surgery or radiology, offered only limited contact with actual patients. In addition, he began to realize during his training that he loved all aspects of medicine, such as dealing with children, adults, the elderly, and pregnant women, and found it hard to see himself confined to a specific organ system or stage of life. He wanted to deal with entire families and communities.

At that time Family Medicine was in its infancy, having

only been declared a specialty a few years before Cal started medical school. There were only a very few Family Medicine training programs in the country. But Cal saw Family Medicine as exactly what was going to help meet his objectives, and he began to follow this path. He identified multiple medical issues that were commonly managed by family physicians and took additional classes during the summer in skills such as obstetrics and gynecology and ear, nose, and throat issues.

On the home front during medical school, time at home for Cal was severely limited, and space was getting tight. During the last two years of medical school and the year of internship, the call schedule required staying at the hospital every third night and then working the entire next day, meaning that out of a three-day period Cal only had one night in which he could come home after only eight hours of work.

During this time Mimi planned a desperately needed weekend away for the two of them that she thought would provide some valuable time together; she couldn't wait! When Cal came home that night, after a 36-hour shift at the hospital, Mimi delightedly began explaining the get-away and all her preparations. Unfortunately, in the middle of her description, Cal fell sound asleep with his head on his empty dinner plate on the dining room table. Sadly, Mimi realized that her great anticipation was not going to be soon realized, so she called it off. Mimi calculated it was five years before she and Cal had a full weekend together.

As Kurt turned into an active one year old, they realized he needed more space to roam. They bought a small home in southwest Denver, which was impressively inexpensive, primarily because of its location. Its backyard bordered a four-lane freeway and its side yard bordered a large shopping center parking lot. Although they couldn't use the backyard much because of the highway noise and engine exhaust, the house itself was wonderful. It had five bedrooms and three bathrooms. It was their home and they were delighted with the space and the opportunity to invite over even more friends.

Although Mimi had decided to forgo the income of full-time work, she again demonstrated her creative ingenuity as she began making decorative centerpieces and selling them to large department stores for their displays. She took inexpensive plastic fruit, dipped it in glossy paint, and arranged it in large clusters on a Styrofoam base. She walked from store to store, with Kurt in the stroller and fruit arrangements piled over and around him. She only dealt with the upper management of the larger stores, and unashamedly charged top dollar for them. Mimi's practice of going to the top to offer her wares would stand her in good stead in many ventures to come.

In these years as a young family, Mimi was learning to cook under the mentoring of Cal's mom, and she loved it. She could afford only the most inexpensive groceries, so it was a wonderful surprise to find that since Cal was a commissioned PHS officer during his fourth year of medical school, she was eligible to shop at the military commissary at Ft. Logan airbase in Denver. Mimi used it to the maximum and they all enjoyed it immensely.

Cal's graduation from medical school brought several wonderful joys. Cal had earlier made the choice to not try to graduate with honors, because at that time it required completion and presentation of a full research thesis, which would have required significantly more time away from his family. He was content with this decision, but as the graduation awards were announced, Cal was unexpectedly called to the stage to receive the award for Outstanding Achievement in Medicine. Mimi and Cal's parents were shocked, as Cal had previously warned them he would not be graduating with any honors. In addition, Cal had only days before been informed that he would also be awarded the bachelor's degree that he had forgone by leaving his premedical studies a year before completion. Mimi fully felt that she was graduating as well, having labored day and night to support Cal during these difficult years.

Following the joyful graduation, Cal, Mimi, and a happy, three-year-old Kurt enjoyed a full two weeks of blissful vacation prior to beginning Cal's internship year. Cal had applied to several Family Medicine residencies and decided to stay in Denver at the University of Colorado program, which had been active only three to four years at that time. One primary reason for staying in Denver was that Mimi was anticipating the birth of their second child.

On the day Mimi went into labor, Cal was on-call at the VA hospital, only a few months into his internship year. Cal's dad had to drive Mimi to the delivery ward at the hospital across the street from the VA hospital. Cal got permission to leave his hospital for a few hours to be with Mimi for the birth of Kyndra, and then went straight back across the street for the rest of the night. Mimi came home with a healthy baby girl on the day Cal was only working eight hours, so their little family of four had a wonderful first evening together.

Cal and Mimi were involved with the Littleton Bible Chapel (the church in which Cal grew up), which offered great support to both of them, but this was still a lonely time for Mimi. Medical school and internship went relatively smoothly in retrospect, but required total dedication and concentration, which strained their relationship. They had started their relationship spending most of their time together, but now Cal often was not mentally, emotionally, or physically available. It was a difficult time for them both, but at the same time Cal thrived in mastering the volume of knowledge and judgment required of a physician, while Mimi was able to devote herself as mother to Kurt and Kyndra. They each realized they must put their heads down and keep going, with the assurance that this would not last forever.

One day the doorbell rang, and there stood an African-American man selling Fuller brushes, and he was blind. He was very friendly, but Mimi had to tell him, "I'm sorry, but my husband is in medical school, and we don't have an extra dime." She asked if he would like to use the restroom ("Oh no, I can't because of the law," he said) and offered him something to eat, but she was not able to buy any of his brushes.

With that, the fellow reached into his pocket and gave

Mimi a dollar. She was so touched by his generosity that she said, "If I see you when my husband has graduated, I'll buy one of everything you have!"

Years later, when they had moved to another part of town, Mimi opened the door one day to find the same gentleman, selling his brushes. By then Cal was in private practice. Of course, he didn't recognize Mimi because he was blind, but she recognized him and said, "You gave us a dollar several years ago because we were so poor!"

He said, "Ma'am, I did that a lot." He couldn't remember giving the dollar to Mimi, but she did, and of course she bought one of everything he had. It was a reminder of kindness that Mimi will never forget.

Shiprock, New Mexico

1974-76

MIMI AND CHILDREN AT CANYONLANDS NEAR SHIPROCK

MONUMENT VALLEY NEAR SHIPROCK

CAL AND KYNDRA WITH MIMI'S BROTHER, ALAN,
NEAR SHIPROCK, 1975

CAL AND MIMI, KURT AND KYNDRA
NEAR SHIPROCK, NM, 1975

MIMI & KYNDRA HIKING IN SHIPROCK AREA

KURT & KYNDRA
ON LONG DESERT TRIP NEAR SHIPROCK

CHAPTER 4

The Community

The year after completion of medical school Cal and Mimi stayed in Denver so that Cal could complete the first year of a Family Medicine residency. Although he petitioned the US Public Health Service to allow him to complete his residency over the full three years, the Early Commissioning Program at that time required that he begin his active duty service after the first year of internship, with no exceptions. So, they were off to active duty with the Public Health Service. Cal had previously requested the Indian Health Service branch for his active duty, mainly because he knew that eventually he wanted to work with poor, isolated communities in a cross-cultural context, and he thought this might be good preparation for him. Although this could be on any of the many Indian reservations across the US, Cal requested a Navajo reservation post at Shiprock, New Mexico, and was accepted.

The Public Health Service provided a moving company for their household items, so after the van left, the family drove their mid-sized Plymouth 8 hours south to Shiprock, which is in the Four Corners area of northwestern New Mexico.

Their first impression of the reservation was that of a vast emptiness. Although it was a high plateau desert it was not barren, but scattered with trees and shrubs, cactus, and huge volcanic and red-rock formations. There was a wild beauty about it.

Shiprock was a little town near the edge of the reservation, population at the time of about 4,000, with one industrial factory, two trading posts, two churches, and a post office. The small hospital in Shiprock held 80 beds, but it served a huge geographic area of many square miles and was relatively well-staffed. The tiny market in Shiprock was more like a trading post than a market, so Cal and Mimi ended up doing most of their shopping in Farmington, New Mexico, about 30 miles away.

Without much available housing around, the Indian Health Service provided housing for the Wilsons in a compound right next to the hospital. They were all three-bedroom, sub-urban-type houses with some grass in a front yard, which was unusual because it took a significant amount of water to keep that grass going in the desert. All the doctors and some of the auxiliary health personnel such as pharmacists and nurses were billeted to those homes.

What a treat to meet their neighbors! There were ten general medical officers (GMO in military terms), who functioned as general practitioners, all of them at exactly the same stage of life as the Wilsons, from all over the country and all kinds of backgrounds. Only one of them had finished a Family Medicine residency. There was one pediatrician, one surgeon, one obstetrician, one internist, and a visiting radiologist. Most of them were married, and some had small children about the same age as Kurt and Kyndra. Two or three of the new doctors were committed followers of Jesus who sincerely tried to live out their Christianity. They became an instant community.

When they all got their first paychecks, they asked around, "What did you buy with your check?" The first major items were a big water pitcher and a washing machine, as most of the new staff had exhausted their savings. With the arrival of the second paycheck most put down payments on a four-wheel drive vehicle, to better explore the reservation and all its wonders. It quickly became a close-knit group, bound by the relative isolation, the common tasks of family life, a love of the high desert, and their work among the Navajo of that area.

CHAPTER 5

Practicing Medicine

$\mathcal{T}$he Navajo medical team proved to be an ideal general practice. Although young and full of medical knowledge but lacking experience, Cal and his colleagues attended to everything from very serious illnesses to many less serious problems. The four specialists at the hospital were of great value, because they patiently worked alongside and were constantly guiding the generalists. All the generalists were straight out of their internships, and there was a lot to learn about patient care and management. Cal saw this as another evidence of God's patient guidance and direction in the development of his medical skills.

The two years in Shiprock were structured so that each of the generalists could spend six months on each of the four major specialty services: obstetrics, surgery, medicine, and pediatrics. Combined with the ongoing teaching and discussions about managing difficult patients, they all learned incredibly. Cal found that it was the same scope and depth of training that was offered in more structured Family Medicine residencies. In addition, they were allowed more freedom to work with the patients than would have been possible in an academic setting.

The one thing Cal missed was community outreach, specifically the community service and public health aspects of the Indian Health Service. The Shiprock Hospital had a strong outreach program that used well-trained community health workers, but the tribal elders insisted they be native Navajo.

The Navajo in that region received most of their medical care from the Indian Health Service and from the Shiprock hospital. From the perspective of the Navajo patients cared for at the hospital, these PHS doctors were constantly rotating faces. They seemed to trust the care that the doctors provided, but it was difficult for the doctors to develop a relationship with the Navajos, because they knew the doctors would be gone in two years. The doctors tried to develop an understanding of their ancient culture, including their concepts of traditional herbal remedies and the value of their healing ceremonies, which they called "sings" because of the extended chanting. The medical team would often negotiate a combination of indicated Western medicine such as surgery following a traditional five- to seven-day sing.

One memorable patient was a young boy who presented with obvious appendicitis with at least a prior four-day history of excruciating pain and vomiting. The appendix was already ruptured, and his recuperation was relatively prolonged. One of the doctors, trying to understand the delay in coming for treatment, asked the patient's father about this. The father replied, "Well, of course we took him to the medicine man first. He looked at him and told us that because he was very ill, instead of the usual five- to six-day sing, he would shorten it to three days. At the end of the three days, he told us that our son was now back in harmony with nature, but added … he also has appendicitis—you should take him to the hospital immediately!"

The doctors did develop some good relationships with Navajo employees in the hospital, most of whom were very skilled, who worked in areas like physical therapy, respiratory therapy, the laboratory, or the pharmacy; and some of these relationships endured for many years after the doctors left.

On a typical day, Cal arrived at the hospital at 7:30 a.m. and made his rounds on all the hospitalized patients currently on his assigned service, with the Navajo staff and specialist on that service. Mid-morning Cal went to the outpatient department and attended to a steady stream of patients with a variety of complaints and chronic health problems.

Well over half of the patients they saw required a Navajo interpreter, as many of the adult patients were limited in English. This has changed over time and now almost 90 percent of the Navajo people are skilled in English.

One of the more common problems seen in the outpatient department was ingrown toenails in the young men, an average of two to three each day. Most young Navajo males fancied themselves as cowboys, and they all wore cowboy boots with very pointed toes. These compressed the toes and forefoot while they walked for miles herding their sheep up and down the hills, which led to the ingrown nails. Very few had horses, but they loved their boots.

CHAPTER 6

Life on the Reservation

*F*or a while Mimi worked at the hospital too, training the hospital ambulance drivers in emergency service techniques. However, Mimi felt she could ask only a few of her friends to take on the full-time task of watching two-year-old toddler Kyndra, so she chose to stay home. Kyndra had to be watched every minute, or her creative mind and spirit would invariably lead her into difficulty.

For example, one day Mimi answered the door to find Kyndra being held by one of the neighbors, who said, "I just wanted to let you know that I was driving out of the compound and spotted Kyndra on her way out of the compound and almost to the highway."

When Mimi asked Kyndra what she was doing, she said, "I wanted to go to Farmington," which was 30 miles away. Kyndra had prepared for the walk, hugging a diaper under each arm.

Kurt had reached kindergarten age, so Cal and Mimi enrolled him in the local Navajo school. After a couple of weeks with no apparent difficulty, Mimi noticed that Kurt stooped to pick up rocks from the driveway and stuff them in his pocket on his way to school. She asked him about it when he came home that evening.

"A lot of the Navajo boys make fun of me. They push me and try to hurt me," Kurt said, "so I throw rocks at them to make them stop." Cal and Mimi talked about that together, and definitely prayed about it.

A few days later Kurt came home whistling and happy. He said, "Hey, Mom, guess what? I made some friends in class."

"How did you do that?" Mimi asked.

"Well, I discovered that if I tell a joke or if I say something funny, they start laughing and now we're friends." So that's how he began his career in intercultural relationships, by making them laugh.

In their amazing instant community, Mimi had lots of opportunity to practice hospitality. One Sunday she and Cal had invited all the doctors who were available to come to their house for Sunday dinner. An emergency at the hospital, a common event, pulled the doctors away just before the meal, leaving Mimi looking forlornly at a table set for 12. Outside a group of Navajo children were playing with Kurt. Why not invite them in for dinner?

As the children sat down, a little boy named Joseph asked Mimi, "Can I invite my sister to come?"

"Joseph, you would have to go down to the village to get her, and I'm ready for us to eat right now," Mimi said.

"Well, she's just right close."

"Where is she?" Mimi asked.

"I have her in the bush outside," Joseph replied.

Mimi went outside and found the cutest little darling girl you ever saw waiting for an invitation to come in. Mimi has thought often about how the little girl would have spent the entire afternoon in a bush if she had not been invited.

After another dinner party, Mimi and Cal had gone to bed without putting the silverware and serving pieces away. The night was hot and they slept with the windows open. Halfway through the night Mimi awoke to feel someone's hands sliding beneath her—not from Cal's side of the bed. Mimi gasped, and Cal let out a yell like a trumpeting elephant. Cal saw a shadow jump up and literally bounce off the door frame as he raced out of the room, crashing through the length of the house toward the utility room window where he'd cut the screen to gain entry. The window was high up and small, so they could hear him scrambling to crawl through it before they heard him running into the night.

When they relayed this incident the next morning, Cal and Mimi learned that many Navajo women were accustomed to sleeping with their stash of silver jewelry underneath them. It appeared that the man was reaching underneath Mimi to try to get at her stash of silver, not knowing it was laid out to dry in the dining room! During the farewell ceremonies two years later, Cal and Mimi were presented with a rather large box as a parting gift from the Navajo staff labeled "Navajo burglar alarm." When opened they found a small brown puppy! He became a part of the family as Cal started the next phase of life in private practice.

The pace of living on the reservation was a welcome relief from that of medical school, and Cal began to relax. The family had more evenings together and time together on the weekends to explore new areas with one or more of their medical friends. It was an ideal lifestyle for them.

Given the amount of time together, both in the hospital and the housing community, the medical families quickly learned the best and worst of each other. All their backyards were fenced in typical suburban style, but the Wilson's yard had a large patch where the grass refused to grow. Mimi had Kurt, with some of his neighbor friends, scoop out a hole, then Mimi soaked it with water to make a mud pit. (Mimi believed that most small children were part piglet.) This became one of the childhood attractions of the entire neighborhood.

One neighbor had a beautiful 4-year-old girl who was often impeccably dressed in frilly white, and Mimi noted her longingly watching through the fence while other neighbor children frolicked in the mud. One day, the neighbor asked Mimi to watch her daughter for an hour while she attended an appointment at the hospital. Mimi decided to give this little girl the fun of playing in the mud. She stripped off her frilly dress, put on some of the designated "mud clothes," set the alarm clock for 30 minutes, and watched as she delightedly splashed in the mud, intending to wash her down and get her redressed in her white dress before the mother returned. Her heart sank when the mother reappeared after only a few minutes, stunned to find her beautiful daughter covered in mud. Mimi apologized profusely and put her daughter back together again; they are still very close friends, fortunately.

The Wilsons grew to love the desert. The Southwest desert is beautiful and varied, with deep canyons, mountains, rock formations, and an endless sky. They were captivated by its beauty. It wasn't just piles of sand and a few bushes; it was dry, but also beautiful. They grew to love the Navajo people and their culture; they were gentle and almost never conflictive, except perhaps when they were drinking. The medical staff saw and treated a lot of injuries, but many of the incidents were associated with alcohol.

CHAPTER 7

Immanuel Mission

*A*fter visiting churches near the compound and as far away as Farmington without finding one in which they felt comfortable, Cal and Mimi decided to investigate one at a Christian mission boarding school for Navajo young people in the middle of the reservation. The drive took over an hour from Shiprock, the last 14 miles on a dusty, winding dirt road. They had no idea what time the service started and found upon arrival that it had already begun. As they walked into the chapel building, the congregation was singing the old hymn *"In Immanuel's Land,"* which was one of Cal's favorite hymns even from childhood. *Oh, wow,* he thought, *this sounds like home!* They started attending every Sunday and had great pleasure in getting to know the staff at the mission.

Immanuel Mission had been established in the 1920s. There were a few other mission-sponsored Christian boarding schools around the reservation, but this one was right in the center, and Cal and Mimi fell in love with the workers there: the teachers, the principal and his family, and the mainte-nance workers. Most had been on staff for 15 or 20 years. The principal of the school had raised his family at the mission. His children left the reservation for university, but one came back with his bride and remained for another 30 years. These were Greg and Kathy Staley, who were about Cal and Mimi's age, and to this day are among the Wilsons' closest friends.

The Navajo live in isolated family groups, usually several miles from each other. The pasture on the reservation is very dry and sparse, and since most families own sheep and goats, a sizable amount of land is needed to adequately feed their flocks. Although a few of the children who live within a mile or so could walk to school, most children rode the Mission buses that were sent out each morning in all directions.

The Mission tried to be as comprehensive in their ministry to entire families as they could, initially, of course, through the children as their point of contact. For example, they had drilled a well deep enough for a plentiful supply of water, and placed a water tap just outside the school for families to fill their 55-gallon water barrels for home use.

This was not a school that sought to replace Navajo culture, as had occurred in an earlier era through federally funded schools that mistakenly thought the indigenous peoples needed to be "Westernized." Immanuel Mission strongly encouraged the Navajo culture and worked with the surrounding families to facilitate the varied expressions of their culture.

Every Sunday the Wilsons drove out to the church at the Mission, and then, because it was so far from home, they were usually invited to join one of the missionaries for dinner. When they were invited to the Staley's home, almost invariably they got in their 4-wheel drive vehicles to explore remote parts of the reservation, often involving deep canyons, quicksand to get stuck in, and ruins never before explored. It was pure adventure, with no one else around except perhaps for a distant *hogan* (a traditional Navajo hut of logs and earth) or a flock of sheep.

Cal and Mimi bonded closely with Greg and Kathy Staley for a variety of reasons, such as similarities in their age and that of their three children, but most certainly because Greg and Kathy were unique individuals. They were both passionately devoted to following God and lived out their lives in intensely practical service to the Navajo people and their colleagues at the mission. They both had incredibly agile and curious minds and read more widely than most of the academics with whom Cal had studied. For example, Greg took an interest in astronomy and the universe, and decided to make his own reflective telescope, hand-grinding his own mirror and using a PVC tube he found on a scrap pile to complete the telescope. Along the way, he had to create an instrument to control the micro-millimeters of depth to which his mirror should be ground. He delighted in taking the boarding school students out at night to discuss the various galaxies and constellations in the desert sky unpolluted with ambient light. With limited finances, he made all of the repairs on his Jeep and those of the mission staff, always drawing in two to three young Navajo men to work with him so they could learn the basics of auto repair. Kathy became the school counselor, guiding young Navajo students to consider their future careers and how to prepare for them. The conversations between the two couples were varied and invariably deep, and always resulted in mutual learning.

At Immanuel Mission they learned what faithful, dedicated mission work over decades of commitment can accomplish. It was more than just a school, but an oasis of loving care reinforced by constant learning and communication with the Navajo of that area, regular advocacy with outside agencies, and creative acts of service. The church functioned under the joint leadership of selected mission staff and established Navajo elders, many of whom had come to follow Jesus through the consistent lives of the mission staff and loving care of their children over many decades.

CHAPTER 8

So Long, But Not Goodbye

As the two-year commitment in Shiprock drew to a close, Cal was already anticipating partnership in a medical practice. While he was completing his internship, he had been approached by a group of Family Medicine doctors in Lakewood, Colorado, to work with them when he finished his Public Health Service commitment. They had constructed a new building and completed a suite of exam rooms and an office for Cal while he was on the reservation. Cal accepted the formal offer to join their practice when he returned. It was a wonderful security to be able to anticipate joining an established practice over two years in advance! Interestingly, two of his three new partners had also served with the Indian Health Service for two years on the Navajo reservation prior to entering private practice, and had benefitted from this work as much as Cal.

But Cal and Mimi would leave some of their hearts in the desert. "I could not look at pictures of deserts without crying," said Cal, "I missed it so much." They were much stronger as a family when they left Shiprock than they had been in medical school. And they had new close friendships with their medical colleagues at the Shiprock hospital and with staff members of Immanuel Mission such as the Staleys.

"We had never been in a situation where we were so loved and we loved back," said Mimi of the families on the compound. "We just loved those people, and to this day we're crazy about them."

As Cal and Mimi left the reservation, they received, almost like a seal of approval, another nearly unbelievable example of God's provision. About six months before they were due to leave, concerns about inadequate staffing of federal health facilities in the US, especially such as the Indian Health Service, had led the government to pass significant legislation to try to incentivize doctors to work in those facilities. Legislation was passed that provided for repayment of up to 80% of university loans in exchange for a commitment of two years of service in a clinically underserved area of the US. Incredibly, Cal was notified that because of his nearly-completed two years of service on the medically underserved Navajo reservation, he was retrospectively eligible to receive repayment for 80% of the medical school loans he had taken to cover his second and third years. With this, he was able to begin private practice with minimal outstanding debt.

Lakewood, Colorado, and Nyankunde, Zaire (DRC)

1976-86

CAL, MIMI, KEVIN, KYNDRA, AND KURT ON WAY TO ZAIRE, 1980

KURT WITH PYGMIES IN ZAIRE, 1980

MIMI AND PYGMY BABY, 1980

KYNDRA IN AFRICA, 1980

KYNDRA, KURT AND KEVIN, 1980

KYNDRA, KEVIN, AND KURT, 1982

MEDICAL PRACTICE PARTNERS: JIM SHANE, CAL,
BOB WILLIAMS, DUANE CLAASSEN
(NOT PICTURED: DAVID MILLER)

CHAPTER 9

Settling in Lakewood

When they returned to begin life in private practice in Lakewood, a suburb of Denver, the Wilsons purchased a home near the clinic, a very nice ranch-style home with a full walkout basement. It was in a mature neighborhood—maybe a little too mature. When they were looking at the home, one of the neighbors came over and said, "Oh good, a young family with children … finally." The neighborhood elementary school was within walking distance.

The property was zoned for horses, and the large backyard had a horse barn, a corral, and a fort. The nice thing about the corral was that it was basically dirt overgrown with weeds, which was a wonderful confirmation of Cal and Mimi's conviction that every family with young children needed to have a bit of raw dirt for children to play in. The previous owner had erected a fort about ten feet off the ground that required a ladder to get into. The children spent a lot of time in the dirt and in the fort.

Mimi found the home easy to decorate. It had many amenities such as a covered back porch, two bedrooms and a bathroom in the basement, and was just the right size for their family. They continued extending hospitality in this new place. In fact, Mimi said, "When we didn't have company, we questioned what was wrong with us." It helped that since Cal was now part of a medical group they had instant new friends, and they loved it.

Cal had met the three doctors in the Lakewood Family Medical Clinic while he was in medical school. Two of the doctors were leaders in the Christian Medical Society group in Denver at that time, and they made a point of reaching out to interested medical students. Cal attended several chapter meetings and developed a good relationship with the other doctors, including spending time at their homes. They were all family physicians. The senior partner was Dr. Jim Shane, with Dr. David Miller, Dr. Bob Williams, and sometime later they added a fifth partner, Dr. Dwayne Claassen.

The American Board of Family Medicine had been established just a few years earlier, and Cal's new partners had each achieved board certification and practiced in a similar manner. All four of the doctors were committed believers, active in their respective churches, and each one had an interest in mission work. After some discussion, they agreed that each doctor could take a three-month sabbatical every four years for mission work of his choice, with ongoing salary support from the rest of the group. Over the years, almost every needy region of the world was visited by one of the group.

Cal and Mimi's third child, Kevin, was born on Christmas Eve their first year back in Lakewood in 1976, in the hospital where the group was on the medical staff. Since Cal was on-call that weekend, he was the doctor who performed Kevin's initial checkups, and was happy to proclaim him healthy.

Kurt, the eldest and most serious, came to Cal and Mimi soon after his brother's birth and asked, "What would happen to us if something happened to you and Dad?" They sat him down and explained that in their will it was arranged that all three of them would be taken care of by their Uncle Craig for as long as necessary. A couple of days later Kurt came to Mimi, again concerned. "Do you think Uncle Craig would give me a ride to his house? I don't think I can take the two children in the wagon to his house by myself!" As the responsible one, Kurt pictured himself walking along the side of the road hauling the two children in his Red Flyer wagon, all the way to Uncle Craig's home in Sedalia, at least 25 miles to the south. Mimi solemnly assured him she was sure Uncle Craig would give them a ride.

Time went by at home and Kevin, at five years of age, was now walking with Kyndra to the elementary school for kindergarten. One day Kyndra came bouncing into the house in her usual happy manner, followed soon after by a woman looking ashen and upset. She stammered, "You know, I almost hit your daughter with my car!" She had been driving in front of their house when suddenly Kyndra jumped off the sidewalk and ran right in front of her. She slammed on the brakes and barely avoided hitting her, then watched to see which house she belonged to.

Kyndra, of course, was totally unaware that anything bad had happened.

Mimi asked her after the woman had gone, "Did you watch for cars? Did you look both ways for cars before you crossed the street?"

Kyndra responded indignantly, "Oh no, I don't have to do that now; I did that last year."

Mimi visualized Kyndra sitting on the sidewalk for a half hour watching all the cars passing in both directions, assuming she had completed her duty. Mimi's creative solution was to make little brother Kevin, the more responsible kindergartener, in charge of the street crossing. Kyndra was not allowed to cross the street until Kevin gave the go-ahead.

Through a friend, Dottie Davis, who had served with her husband as a missionary in Laos for many years and knew the language, Mimi was introduced to a group of Hmong refugees who had come to Denver from refugee camps in Laos during the Vietnam War, and began helping them sell their exquisite, quilted handwork. Most of the people had been rice farmers and found it difficult to find decent jobs in the US, so they were struggling financially. Mimi was able to take the handwork these women produced and sell it not just as handwork, but rebranded as pieces of art, which they truly were.

Mimi found great joy in changing the public perception of these Hmong women from refugees to artists. The handwork was exquisite, with each tiny stitch perfectly placed. Many of the women creating this art were elderly and needed glasses, so Mimi and Dottie provided them with glasses, which made it much easier to sew the intricate embroidery, cross-stitch, and reverse applique traditional patterns.

Although Mimi enjoyed meeting with the women and watching them work, she was able to do much of the marketing work from her home. She was creative in identifying organizations that might be interested, such as a bank looking for decorations for their foyer, or various local community centers. The response was extremely positive, so she knew she was onto something. She had the artwork insured, so that if it was stolen, lost, or destroyed the women would not lose their incredible investment of time. For months Mimi kept handwork in the trunk of her car and sold it to interested parties as she had opportunity. With Dottie as interpreter, she would periodically distribute the money gained directly back to these women, who used it for the support of their families as well as those family members still in refugee camps. Years later when Mimi left for Ecuador two of her close friends took over the marketing and sales of the handwork under the auspices of the United Way of Denver.

After several years the handwork became so valued that, with Don, her father-in-law's help, Mimi began collecting some unique pieces that showed individual styles, such as a quilt made in a refugee camp with backing from a discarded US Air Force parachute. She procured work that demonstrated the evolution of the pieces from those made in the camps to those made after several years in the US. The collection developed into a full exhibit of Hmong artwork that was displayed initially in Denver, and then in various art museums around the US. Even the Smithsonian institution in Washington, D.C. expressed an interest in the collection.

During these days with a young family, Mimi decided she needed time to study the Bible and to be alone with God, and she chose Monday mornings. She got the children playing or gave them a special set of paints or a special toy so they would be entertained. Then she came into the presence of God. The first couple of times she cried because she did not know enough about God to spend an hour, so she spent time getting her soul ready.

At first, she developed the habit of listening to Handel's *Messiah* in its entirety, doing nothing else. The words are phenomenal because it consists entirely of phrases from the Old and New Testament of the Bible. Then after an hour she would make sure the children were all right, turn over her bread, throw the laundry into the dryer, or whatever, and go back in. She became increasingly skilled in exploring deep spiritual topics.

She needed this discipline because her mind wandered. She immediately felt the urgency to clean out the dust underneath the sofa. It was a big thing to choose the time, and then choose a place. She had a place in her bedroom with a prayer chair, a chair made in Spain with short legs for women to kneel while in Church. That was where she prayed. As the children grew older she could tell what kind of day they had had at school by whether they went directly to the prayer chair and prayed themselves. So, the prayer chair became a special place where they prayed and worshipped as a family.

CHAPTER 10

Sabbatical in Africa

*C*al settled into the Lakewood Family Medical Clinic with little difficulty. The practice had become quite busy, and so many of the new patients were assigned to Cal. He took advantage of the initially light schedule by spending additional time getting to know the patient and their family. He took great pains to take every complaint seriously and be alert for less common problems or the early signs of a true emergency.

For example, on one occasion he completed the examination of an older woman with a minor problem, who then asked him about her accompanying husband, who had recently been diagnosed in an emergency room with a "slight stroke." As Cal examined the husband, he found that the symptoms he noted on the right side were actually not weakness, but a stiffness and lack of coordination not typical of a stroke. He asked permission to send him for a CT scan of his head, which showed no evidence of a stroke, but a large brain tumor. This was subsequently removed without difficulty, and the function was completely restored to his right side.

On another occasion, he saw a large man complaining of a respiratory infection, but with the initial handshake, Cal knew something else was going on—his hand was so huge that Cal's hand just disappeared into it! He began asking the patient some unusual questions unrelated to his respiratory complaints, like whether or not his shoe size or hat size was changing, and with some surprise the man responded in the affirmative. Cal asked permission to take an immediate single X-ray of his head with the equipment in his office and found what he had suspected: an enlarged and eroded sella turcica, the bony structure that surrounds the pituitary gland, indicating a probable tumor of the pituitary gland. The diagnosis was *acromegaly*, the ailment suffered by the famous wrestler and actor Andre the Giant. This pituitary tumor produces abnormally high levels of growth hormone, causing sustained growth of the entire adult body, and usually leads to major complications. Although the patient was expecting treatment for his cold, he left the office with something far more extensive, but potentially life-prolonging.

The doctors in the partnership joked among themselves that their patients might suddenly switch to a different partner and stick with that one. It was hard for Cal when he first lost a patient to another partner, but Jim Shane, the senior partner, simply laughed and said, "Look, this happens all the time. The patients just happen to prefer one personality type over another. Just watch, within a short period of time you're going to be seeing patients that I've seen for years," which turned out to be true.

The relationships between Cal and his partners were not only professional, but also personal. The partners regularly consulted with each other on difficult or interesting medical cases, encouraged each other, prayed for each other, and loved to get together socially. This was greatly facilitated by a similarly close relationship between the partners' wives, who met together for encouragement and prayer twice each month. When considering a new partner, one of the criteria had to be the compatibility of the potential partner's spouse with the other spouses, as some had observed a partnership dissolve simply because of fighting between the wives. The partners and their wives had dinner together at a nice restaurant most months, where the conversation became so animated and the laughter so uproarious that a private room was usually requested. The practice also financed a weekend retreat at the Lost Valley guest ranch each year for all four families, which typically included significant strategic planning episodes between horseback trips into the forest.

After four years with Lakewood Family Medical Clinic, it was Cal's turn to take a mission sabbatical the summer of 1980. To Mimi's delight they chose to visit her parents, still at the mission station in Lolwa, Zaire (now the Democratic Republic of the Congo or DRC), and to assist with the medical work at Nyankunde Mission Hospital. Mimi's parents were overjoyed at this incredible opportunity for a reunion on their turf. They met the tiny plane that brought the five Wilsons from Nairobi and took them straight to the house that Mimi had lived in for many years. Mimi was coming home.

Mimi was eager to smell a certain aroma again, a distinct fragrance reminiscent of her childhood. Upon their arrival, Mimi noticed her mother went from room to room opening the screens and airing the house. "Mom, what are you doing?"

Her mother replied, "I've got to get this mildew smell out of here."

The cozy smell Mimi remembered from her childhood was actually mildew! But it was a treat beyond imagining just to be back home.

They spent two weeks with Mimi's parents, enjoying all that had been accomplished there. It was impressive what the Spees had carved out of the jungle over the past 40 years, with intermittently one to four other missionaries working with them. They had built their own home and two guesthouses, an airstrip so that Mission Aviation Fellowship (MAF) planes could fly in, a small hospital, a bookstore, a public school, a leprosarium to provide long-term treatment and rehabilitation, and a large chapel—all located along a major (but dirt) highway through the dense Ituri forest.

There were scores of Christian believers from multiple tribes, from nomadic jungle Pygmies to ones who lived along the road, filling the Lolwa chapel with 400-500 people every Sunday.

Although the road running past the Spees' house was one of the primary trans-Africa roads, with steady traffic day and night, visitors were often late because there was a place in the road near the Lolwa station that was essentially a deep hole. The Spees' were convinced the villagers filled the hole with water so that most everyone would get stuck, giving the villagers the opportunity to pull them out, and of course get paid for it. There was even a designated place for spectators to sit and watch as the cars entered the hole hoping to make it to the other side. But that was the jungle.

One day to their surprise a couple arrived at Lolwa mission earlier than anticipated. How was this possible? The couple related that because night was approaching, they had decided to try to get across the hole, not wanting to spend the night camping on the hillside or down in the hole. They started across the hole and jiggled and juggled, and unbelievably arrived on the other side. This just did not occur! They stopped to look back, and discovered they had gone right over the top of another vehicle deep in the hole.

The Wilson children, three-year-old Kevin, six-year-old Kyndra, and nine-year-old Kurt, were adventuresome, and each took on Africa in their own way. Kevin especially made friends easily. Mimi found him one day sitting in a mud hole with two little Pygmy boys. The three boys were obviously communicating in spite of speaking different languages. The Pygmy boys had dug up some peanuts and without washing them were breaking the shells open and feeding the peanuts to Kevin. Mimi found Kevin with mud around his mouth, chewing on the peanuts, and immediately visualized his death within the next three days. With obvious anguish she asked, "Kevin, what are you doing eating those muddy peanuts?" Kevin simply looked up and said, "Mom, they're just being kind to me."

Mimi, of course, carried the grim specter of her malaria-ridden childhood. Before the trip they had all begun taking prophylactic medication for malaria, which at that time was chloroquine, one of the bitterest of all pills. They had to cut the tablet twice in order to give a quarter of a tablet to Kevin. The family all ceremoniously took their first tablet and Kevin swallowed his, washed it down with a big glass of water, and ran off.

A short time later Mimi found him totally dissolved in tears, crying his heart out. "What are you crying about?" she asked. "Did the medicine bother you?"

He sobbed, "I'm crying because I can't go to Africa with you."

"You can't go to Africa with us; you just took the pill. Of course you're coming to Africa with us!" Mimi replied.

He said again, "No. I can't go. I can never take that pill again!" It really was that bad. Just the worst!

After a two-week visit with Mimi's parents at Lolwa, the Wilsons were driven three hours into the open land to the hospital in Nyankunde where Cal would assist as a volunteer physician for the remainder of the summer. Mimi was to serve as his Swahili translator, so that a staff person would not have to leave his or her duties to do that. Mimi was anxious at first because many years had passed since she had heard or spoken Swahili. The first night in Nyankunde she lay awake, but phrase after phrase washed over her. Her fluency in Swahili came back, and she was able to do it.

Cal was assigned to the diarrhea and the pediatric wards, as well as the afternoon outpatient clinic in the hospital, where he was basically the third level of attention for the visiting outpatients. The first and second levels were African-trained medical professionals, and if those two levels couldn't resolve a problem, the patient was sent to this special clinic where a missionary doctor would see them. That was Cal.

After a few days in the clinic, Cal discovered that well over half of the patients fit into a pattern. Most were women ages 35 to 45 with the same complaint. All of them described with great intensity and distress a generalized pain that would start in various parts of their body but then migrate to other parts, all the way from their stomach up to their head, down to their feet, occasionally migrating out their arms or even their hair. Often these symptoms had been going on for a year or two, and as hard as he tried, Cal could not make it fit any known pattern of which he was aware.

He asked a more experienced doctor, an obstetrician-gynecologist at the hospital, about this pattern. She smiled and said, "Really? Let me help you here. The next time you encounter a patient with the same complaint, ask this one key question: 'When was the last time you delivered a baby?'" So, he did.

When he asked the patient this question, she immediately burst into tears.

"Oh, it's been four years and my husband is about to take another wife because I can't produce him another son." Every single woman with these vague complaints had the same tale. The obstetrician explained that in this culture a woman was valued only as long as she could produce children. If she stopped producing children, the husband would invariably take another wife, usually a younger one, whom he spent more time with, and the older wife was relegated to the sidelines. The most common reason for this secondary infertility was that most of the women had contracted a gonococcal infection in her pelvis that had totally scarred her fallopian tubes and had rendered her unable to conceive, most probably contracted from her husband, who had been fooling around. The pain was real, but truly psychosomatic: the emotional anguish of being potentially sidelined for a new wife.

One night while Cal was on call, the nurse in charge of the Obstetrics floor summoned him to please come because a woman had been laboring for hours and could not push out the baby. This was a fresh memory for Mimi, having delivered Kevin not that long ago. She and Cal threw on some clothes and walked rapidly to the hospital, where they could hear the woman struggling as she lay on the delivery table. The midwife was also there, and behind her another nurse holding a lantern, because the lights were out throughout the mission. Cal was in charge.

He asked Mimi to take care of the mom while he dealt with the baby. Mimi stood behind the mother, holding her in her arms as she watched this drama unfold. Using forceps, Cal pulled out a beautifully-formed baby boy. However, the baby had not begun to breathe and the heartbeat was not palpable. He put the baby on the table, stretched a little piece of gauze over the baby's mouth, and started breathing into the child while compressing the tiny chest. Mimi could see the effect of the air going back and forth into the baby, but she was heartsick because the baby was not responding. She prayed to the Lord, "My husband breathes air into this child, but what the child needs is life. Could you not give us another touch of Yourself?" As she prayed, she could suddenly see this tiny chest responding, and pink color coming into the pale face. Mimi could only think, *We need to take off our shoes; this is holy ground!* The realization swept over Mimi that all we can offer in circumstances like this is support for what God has already accomplished. God had already given this child life, and they had merely supported helping it breathe.

Cal gave strict instructions to the attending nurse that this was an extremely high-risk baby. He required oxygen, warmth, and careful observation. However, when Cal and Mimi came to see the baby about five hours later, they couldn't find him in the incubator. The mom and baby were out in the waiting room where she was showing off a healthy, contented baby to friends and family.

The chapel at Nyankunde now seated over 2,000 people,

and when the congregation sang, it was glorious, especially with the accompaniment of six trumpets and trombones, two pianos, an assortment of stringed instruments, and several sets of African drums. In fact, one of the children leaned over to Cal and Mimi and yelled, "How come we don't sing like this at our church?"

On this particular Sunday the African elders of the church had invited Cal to speak. Another doctor served as translator. Mimi watched spell-bound, because not only was Cal trying to relate to this huge group of Africans, but the translator was truly capturing the essence of the message. Using contemporary illustrations that Cal had picked up during his time there, he encouraged the believers to follow God with their whole heart, regardless of where that might lead. The translator was known among the Africans for his godly life, which added greatly to the impact of the message.

After the elders saw the impact that Cal's message had made on the congregation, they invited the Wilsons to join the 12 distinguished African elders sitting around a large table for an afternoon meal. The impressive setting was solemn; there is nothing quite so dignified as a group of African elders, regal in their bearing, and very measured and deliberate in the way they addressed each other and talked with Cal and Mimi.

As they approached this auspicious gathering, Mimi instructed the children, "Now you're going to find food that you have never seen before, but I don't want you to say or even think 'Yuck.' I want you to be gracious about it because they're all going to look at you, not at us. They know we will eat their food, but they will wonder about you." The children behaved like royalty, showing their enjoyment of the food.

Each of the Wilsons had been assigned a person behind them to be sure they had enough to eat and drink. During the meal an enormous beetle flew into Kyndra's long blonde hair. Kyndra held very still as the lady behind her gently took the large beetle out of her hair and threw it out the open window with disdain, saying, "Don't you dare return and disturb our guests again!"

The reason for this august gathering—with all 12 elders of the church and just the Wilson family—was that they wanted to formally invite the Wilsons to return and work long-term at Nyankunde. Cal and Mimi were stunned, because the invitation didn't come from the missionary community, but from the African elders of the church.

They seriously considered it, but regretfully concluded they didn't feel they were yet ready for long-term mission work. It was a hard decision to make because this was something they had always considered as a possibility. It was enticing to serve in a setting that was so well-established and equipped, but they decided that at that point Cal needed more medical experience, and especially that they needed to spend more time with their developing children. It was almost certain their children would have had to go to the same boarding school Mimi attended, with all of the painful memories that surfaced in Mimi's mind. So, they respectfully and reluctantly declined.

CHAPTER II

A Life-Changing Headache

O n a spring day in the early 1980s, Cal went skiing alone in the Colorado Rockies and had a glorious time. He fell a few times, but nothing out of the ordinary. The next morning, he rose early to make rounds at the hospital, but when he got out of bed he had a bit of a headache, which was highly unusual for him. He dressed and went to the hospital, but the headache became more intense as he was making his rounds. Fortunately, he was able to finish his rounds, but by the time he got into the car to go see his clinic patients, the headache was so severe he started to lose his vision. On the way home he had to stop the car two or three times to throw up. He finally got home, crawled across the doorstep, asked Mimi to call the office to say he couldn't see patients today, and collapsed in bed. Within a few minutes of hitting the bed, the headache disappeared. That was strange, but wonderful.

After lying there a few more minutes, Cal decided, *well, the headache's gone, I guess I might as well go to work.* But the minute he sat up the headache hit him again. Boom! Just like a hammer, it knocked him flat, but again disappeared within a minute of lying down. Obviously, this was a positional kind of headache, because as long as he was lying flat he had no pain whatsoever, but the minute he sat up he had a severe, throbbing headache. Cal knew of only one medical situation that was similar to this, and that was a spinal headache after a spinal tap. Occasionally some individuals continue leaking spinal fluid from the needle puncture, which decreases the spinal fluid pressure, and produces an identical positional headache. Although this was a reasonable diagnosis, the problem was that Cal had never had any kind of spinal puncture.

Within a few hours, because he hadn't shown up at work, Cal's partners called him wondering what was going on. The senior partner, Jim Shane, immediately came to a different possible diagnosis, that of an intracerebral bleed, a broken blood vessel in the brain, and insisted Cal go to the hospital. In fact, he picked up Cal and drove him to the same hospital in which Cal had just seen his own patients a few hours before.

After a week in the hospital undergoing a variety of tests and sophisticated X-rays and scans, Cal was diagnosed with an apparent leakage of spinal fluid, as a spinal tap had discovered that he essentially had no spinal fluid in his brain, barely enough to obtain even a small sample. This led to a round of neurology and neurosurgery consultations, with no real identified cause for the low spinal fluid pressure. Interestingly, among the incidental findings was evidence of an old neck fracture that Cal had sustained as a child. The childhood injury had nearly damaged his spinal cord but appeared unrelated to his current malady. The final conclusion determined no specific treatment for his condition other than bedrest and time. The few reported cases of this situation—and it was very rare—had usually recovered spontaneously, however the average time required was three to six months. So, Cal went home and the family settled into a daily routine with Cal confined to his bed, without even a pillow, lying absolutely flat.

This was a time for reconsideration of life priorities and brought the Wilsons much closer as a family. At that point in their development the family had evolved an incredibly tight schedule, figuring out how to make the most out of every day and all their activities. The rigid structure was productive, but not good for family relationships. Changes were required on the spur of the moment. For Cal it became a reflective time for reconsidering his ambitions and priorities, especially facing an uncertain future. Among many other adjustments, Mimi made sure all of their meals were eaten around the bed, with Cal eating lying on his side with his head flat on the bed. The children ate their meals on cookie trays, and each meal was truly a fun family time.

"He was a different man," recalls Mimi. "He was more relaxed, not with his usual hyper gotta-go attitude. It was a joy for us to be together, especially because we knew it was a gift that he was with us at all. It was a marvel to see him relaxed and so resigned to being in bed 24/7. We had a constant stream of guests, which increased that level of joy and helped Cal pass the time and consider others. We had never experienced time for that level of hospitality, but we definitely made time for it now, and it was glorious. Some of his partners came every single day, and some came to eat because they knew what times we would eat. It was just the most marvelous time!"

Humor always helped. One good friend (Alex, the husband of Mary Beth Lagerborg) visited almost every day with cheerful banter and a few jokes to try to cheer him up. One day he appeared with a small can of liquid he had picked up at the hardware store, saying, "Here, I think this is what you need." It was a can of Wynn's Stop Leak, a solution normally put in your radiator to plug up any holes. Cal had no idea how that was going to get into his spinal fluid, but he appreciated the gesture.

Slowly, Cal started to improve. Within about a month he could sit up for two or three hours before the headache got severe enough that he had to lie down again. Consequently, the family tried to make the most of the time when he could sit up. The medical consultants still had no idea of the source of the spinal fluid leak.

On one of these "up" occasions, Cal's father took him out for a ride in his new car, spinning around the corners. When he got back Cal noticed he had completely lost hearing in one ear. He reported this to the neurosurgeon whom he was seeing at the time, who sent Cal for a specialized x-ray that revealed an open skull fracture that had gone into his middle ear through the thickest part of the skull. Spinal fluid was leaking through this fracture into his middle ear and then he was swallowing it. Since it flowed through his Eustachian tube into the back of his throat, he was not conscious of it. His hearing had suddenly disappeared because the centrifugal force of going around a corner had forced a volume of spinal fluid into his middle ear. Before the skull fracture was discovered, Cal had faced the possibility that the prior neck fracture could somehow be related to the spinal fluid loss.

Putting probable pieces together, Cal remembered that when he was eleven or twelve years old he had gone skiing in a car packed with family and friends. With his mother driving, the car slipped on ice and went down an embankment about 50 feet with the car rolling twice. There were nine children in the car as well as Cal's mother, and none were wearing seat belts. Cal had suffered a concussion, with memory loss for several weeks and hospitalization until the concussion improved. Few studies were available at that time to further define his injuries. In retrospect, he theorized that he had fractured his neck (confirmed by the recent X-ray) *and* sustained the skull fracture at the same time, an injury that went undiagnosed until now.

According to the neurosurgeon, this type of skull fracture (technically called a basilar skull fracture) often heals with fibrous scar tissue rather than bone, and a sudden force can break open that scar tissue and allow spinal fluid leakage through the fracture. One long hospital night, Cal reviewed the whole medical scenario in his mind, anticipating surgery on his upper neck and the operation going badly, leaving him a quadriplegic the rest of his life.

Understandably, Cal felt the immense weight of this scenario. But at the same time, he sensed the presence of God Himself. He could sense God saying, "Look, I'm going to be with you and bless you regardless of what happens; you can trust Me and my love for you!" Being forced to deal with the possibility of a severe, permanent disability and its effect on his family caused a major shift in his view of life as a gift, and his priorities.

The neurosurgeon was an old school surgeon who had seen everything and drew from a deep well of experience. He decided to try a high dose of corticosteroids, and when Cal questioned the rationale behind it, his only response was, "I have seen this help in a few cases." The prescribed dose was over ten times higher than the average dose used for other conditions, and it nearly drove Cal crazy. Such a high dose is well known to produce psychosis, ulcers, and a total disruption of the normal circadian rhythm. Cal couldn't sleep at all, day or night. The side effects were miserable, but within a few days the headaches disappeared even with prolonged sitting or standing, and the symptoms have never recurred.

Cal was able to resume seeing patients about two months after the headache started. It took a month of self-imposed rehabilitation to be able to get through a day after being supine for so long. But the whole episode helped reorder his priorities. It is hard for a doctor to have to cope with an illness that's totally unknown and undefined, that the best of medical science could not diagnose or treat. He had previously assumed that careful investigation and modern medicine could resolve most any problem, but now he was going to have to practice medicine with a different perspective. Medical science was indeed wonderful for most problems, but some illnesses simply required time, patience, and a lot of support from those who love the sufferer.

As Cal resumed practice, the patients who presented complaining of headaches received a far different level of attention, compassion, and treatment from him than they would have received before his illness. He literally oozed with empathy for them. Now understanding their suffering, he began to read everything he could find and take every course he could attend on the management of various types of headache, and quickly became the headache expert for the clinic.

In the several years that Cal was in private practice, the Wilsons had slipped into a suburban lifestyle of comfort and financial security, and they were finding it difficult to give up any of the comforts that they had come to enjoy. Cal never felt that he was near death, but he had confronted the possibility of a permanent disability. Like most people who come close to a serious situation, he came to appreciate that there were more important priorities than financial security and a comfortable lifestyle. God had challenged his fundamental assumptions and expectations of life, his ambitions and priorities, and his fear of uncertainty—and began remolding his perspectives and dreams.

CHAPTER 12

Cooking Once for the Month

*I*n the early 1980s, Mimi unwittingly launched a venture, as an outgrowth of her love of extending hospitality, for which she would become widely known. It began with a call to her friend Mary Beth Lagerborg, with whom she had written a couple of magazine articles. "I've just assembled 30 dinner entrees and I'm freezing them," Mimi said. "Why don't you call the *Denver Post* and see if they'd like an article on how to do it."

Mary Beth lacked Mimi's talent for "talking to the top," and suggested that Mimi make the call. Mimi did, and the *Post* sent a writer and photographer to Mimi's home within a week to produce a food feature on what Mimi and Mary Beth would henceforth call "the method."

As a result of the *Denver Post* article, Mimi's phone rang constantly with people wanting to know how to do it (since the phone number was published in the article). She had devised the method to save time, to save money, and to have meals always on hand, and she did not want to spend her days on the phone. So, in response, she and Mary Beth created a book, *Freeze and Save*, with a typewriter and a comb binding machine, and they were off! They agreed not to do anything unless it was fun, because they basically didn't know what they were doing in the publishing world. Over the next few years, they sold over 10,000 copies of this homemade version of the book through the mail and local bookstores.

After a couple of revisions, name changes, and a video production with Mimi cooking (in July heat, no air conditioning) and Mary Beth holding cue cards, they submitted the expanded book to St. Martin's Press, who published it as *Once-a-Month Cooking* in 1986.

They learned a lot and had many adventures. For instance, at one point they went to a local bank to take out a line of credit to finish production of the pre-St. Martin's Press *Dinner's Ready* book and video. What could they offer as collateral, the banker asked? Mimi and Mary Beth looked at each other. "Six children," they said. "And a dog," Mimi added. For some reason, the banker was not amused!

A highlight came with the invitation to tape a broadcast on Focus on the Family Radio with Dr. James Dobson which originally aired in 1992. After recording the interview they were invited to join Dr. Dobson in his office. "Ladies," he said, "we would like to publish your book." He left the room to summon the head of publishing and the two women erupted on the sofa. "What?!" "What does that mean?" "We already have a publisher (St. Martin's Press). How is that even possible?"

When he entered the room with Dr. Dobson, the women could see that the director of publishing was taken aback. Dr. Dobson explained that the publishing department didn't believe a cookbook could make it in their market, but he believed it would.

It was possible for Focus on the Family to license a "Christian edition" from St. Martin's Press, and it became a bestseller on the Christian book list, leading to many speaking engagements for Mimi over several years. Cooking tastes and practices have since changed, but at that point it was the right thing at the right time, especially for busy young moms on a budget. Still today, Mimi rarely goes into a place around the world where someone doesn't say, "Did you write a cookbook? I still have that cookbook. I can't remember where I put it, but I know I've got it." The method and cookbook, now published as *Once-a-Month Cooking* is still actively selling to this day through Macmillan Press.

Wycliffe Yarinacocha Mission Station, Peru

JUNE–AUGUST 1984

MISSION HOUSE OFFERED TO WILSON FAMILY
IN YARINACOCHA, PERU

FIRST VIEW OF SICK YORAS IN JUNGLE

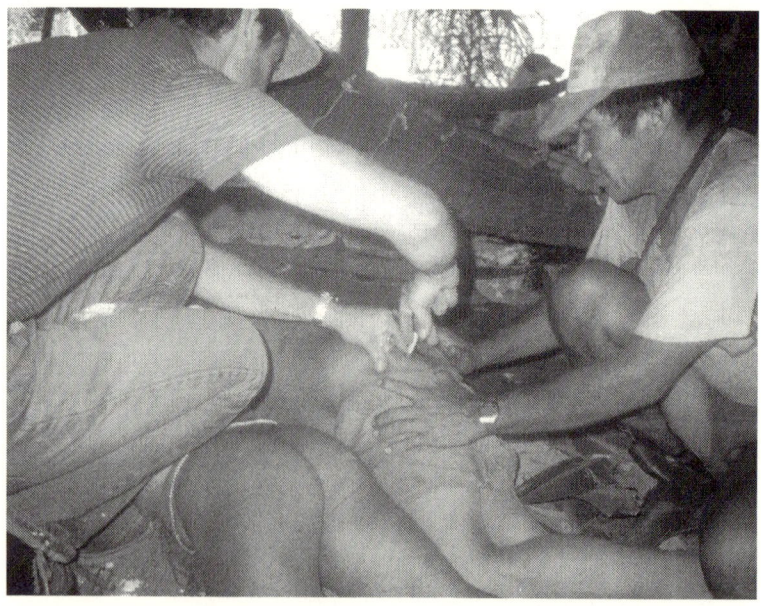

CAL GIVING AN INJECTION TO ILL YORA GUIDE

CAL EXAMINING SICK YORA,
AMAZON BASIN PERU

CAL BACK WITH FAMILY
AFTER YORA TRIP

CHAPTER 13

In Search of a Place to Pioneer

A year or so after Cal's spinal fluid leak had healed, and with the practice thriving at Lakewood Family Medical Clinic, Cal and Mimi's opportunity to take a full three months off for a mission trip came again.

Although Cal and Mimi still sensed the Lord was calling them into mission work, they were uncertain regarding when or what form this would take. One factor that solidified in Cal's mind after their sabbatical in Africa was that he felt most comfortable in pioneer work: exploring fresh opportunities, dealing with people groups that had no reliable medical resources, and presenting the good news of Jesus Christ to those who had never clearly understood it. Medical mission work in Africa was so well established in many areas that Cal knew he would be a small contributing part of a big operation, and his longing was to try to reach totally isolated people or to work in areas where no other mission work had been done before.

Cal had always been intrigued and fascinated by stories of jungle doctors who worked deep in the jungle in a pioneer fashion, such as Dr. David Livingston or Dr. Carl Becker. Previous trips to South America had been primarily as a tourist, and he had never been in the Amazon jungle. He did not fully understand the challenges or opportunities of jungle work, and so this was an opportunity he welcomed.

After much investigation, Cal and Mimi received an invitation to work for the summer with the organization Wycliffe Bible Translators, which had a large support mission station called Yarinacocha next to the town of Pucallpa in the upper Amazon basin of Peru. This station had been in operation for at least 40 years, and served to support the language translation, literacy, and Bible teaching outreach to Indian tribes scattered across the Peruvian Amazon basin. The translators and mission workers would travel out to the various jungle tribes by walking if they were close enough, by canoe in some cases, or by float plane. The mission base had been built on the edge of the large Lake Yarinacocha, and was equipped with two float planes that would take off from the lake and land at airstrips or on rivers throughout the jungle.

The Yarinacocha mission station attended to the needs of close to 80 Wycliffe workers and families stationed there, and also to the surrounding Indian population. Besides a few spacious, comfortable houses for the long-term missionary families, the station included a school for the children living there, a library, housing for the singles and short-term workers, and a medical clinic. The clinic doctor was scheduled to be gone for the summer, and Cal was invited to replace him. There was no overlap; he was already gone when they arrived, so Cal hit the ground running.

On the station, the Wilsons lived in the home of another missionary who was also on furlough. It was a basic but relatively large and comfortable jungle home, with only screens in the large windows and a tin roof, but with stable electricity and running water, a stove and refrigerator, and an indoor toilet.

Their children adapted to jungle life quickly and easily. At the time Kurt was 14, Kyndra 11, and Kevin 7 years old. There were lots of children to play with, and the big daily event was swimming in the lake. From a large climbing tree they would swing on a vine rope out over the water. However, the lake was full of piranhas, who would bite indiscriminately. They were especially fond of biting off a mole, which if it bled much would draw the rest of the piranhas racing to the blood. Mimi didn't do much swimming because she has lots of moles. But it was fun to watch the children in pure jungle play.

The children also enjoyed fishing for piranhas. They'd take a fishhook and a line, put a little meat on it, and toss it out into the water. Within thirty seconds they could count on a piranha nibbling the meat. When they pulled in the piranha, even if they had stunned the fish, they had to use extreme caution in releasing the hook from its mouth. More than one of the local children had reached in to try to untangle the hook, and the piranha had clamped down its jaws and taken off part of a finger.

The town of Pucallpa was not far away, and Mimi and the children would cross the lake by canoe to visit tiny shops and see what food they could find to cook. With a refrigerator/ freezer in their jungle home, Mimi honed her skills in cooking one time for the entire month.

Mimi said, "Our time in Peru was pure fun. We'd all climb under our sheets in the evenings and read the books I had brought. It was just cozy, so different from the American rat race."

The medical work was also very different from Cal's clinic in Lakewood. He reported to work every morning to find a number of Peruvians from various areas gathered around the clinic. Cal asked a nurse who had been there for many years, and who was the continuity point for the medical work, what prompted the gathering.

"Well," she said, "You may have heard that there is an epidemic of rabies around here. The local government estimates that over half of the dogs that aren't attached as pets to individual families are infected with rabies. Every one of these people has been bitten and is here to continue their series of 14 consecutive rabies shots." So the morning began with checking on these patients to ensure none of them were progressing with rabies. Already in the Pucallpa area several children had died of it.

At the Yarinacocha mission station, Cal got his first taste of what mission medicine could be like—dealing with serious problems with few resources. For example, one man came to the clinic with his hand severely infected, as big as a balloon and swollen with pus, from a thorn in the palm of his hand. He couldn't bend his fingers at all, and the infection had progressed to the point that antibiotics alone were not going to be effective. It had to be open and drained.

In medical training Cal had been taught that only specialists should dare to venture surgically into the palm of the hand. There are so many nerves and tendons crossing that area that one ran a serious risk of injuring one of the main nerves or tendons to the fingers, rendering the hand useless. Cal told the nurse, "You know, he needs to have this drained, but I don't think I'm the one to do it." To this the nurse informed him there was nobody, even in Pucallpa, who could manage any better. She looked at him almost severely and said, "Doctor, out here we trust our Lord to produce the results. Cut!" So he cut and was grateful that within a few days, as the man came for dressing changes, the swelling had gone down and he was beginning to move his fingers. There were no nerves injured, and he ultimately regained the full use of his hand.

CHAPTER 14

Give Me a Shot Too

*D*uring the Wilson family's first month at Yarinacocha, they caught bits of conversations about a tribe of Indians deep in the jungle whose existence was known primarily because of their extreme hostility to anyone who tried to approach them. Whenever Peruvian loggers or hunters wandered into their part of the jungle, they'd be met with arrows and spears, and several of them had been killed. So most everyone avoided that part of the jungle. These Indians were known at that time as the Choshonahuas, or Nahuas for short. Later, it was discovered they called themselves the Yora.

About that time, word came from a missionary who was working in a small town on one of the rivers. He relayed that four young men from the Yora tribe had suddenly shown up in town—for the first time in anyone's memory. The Yora had always avoided contact with any of the other tribes or any other villages, staying strictly remote and to themselves. But the young men had appeared looking for hard goods like metal machetes or axes to replace their homemade hardwood machetes and stone axes.

During the few days the Yora visitors were in town, the missionary was able to communicate with them to some extent. Among other things, the young men admitted they were tired of the isolation. As the new generation of the Yora tribe, they desired more contact with the outside world. The missionary arranged to meet them a few days later, near the river a little closer to their area and the four men kept that meeting, plus a few others from the tribe.

They talked, and both sides were excited about what this meeting might represent. A young Yora couple attended this gathering, presumably married in some way. The missionaries called them George and Betty because they couldn't communicate fully in their language. The missionaries invited George and Betty back to the station at Yarinacocha, with the idea that this young couple could provide the beginnings of understanding their tribe. Hopefully some missionaries at the station could begin to learn their language and open more communication with them.

Shortly after arrival at the mission, however, George and Betty became sick with a severe cough and bronchitis. It hung on so badly that they were not able to do much for a week or more. They finally improved a bit, but the severe coughing continued. Ominously, the news filtered out from the jungle—via a jungle grapevine that truly exists!—that their entire tribe had become sick and several had died. Most probably one of the four men who had first shown up in the small village had acquired the illness and had carried it back to the tribe, including infecting George and Betty.

Given their generations of isolation, this group of people had no immunity to any of the common diseases that North Americans grew up with. Even a simple respiratory infection, such as bronchitis, could easily overwhelm their immune system. This tragedy is a well-known historical fact. For instance, in Ecuador, the country to the north, when the Aucas were first contacted in the early 1950s and missionaries like Elizabeth Elliott started living and working with them, a whole series of epidemics swept through the Auca (now called the Waorani) tribe, killing many of them.

The director of the mission discussed this grave problem with Cal. "The entire tribe could be wiped out. Would you be willing to travel in to assess what's going on and see what could be done to help them? But I must warn you that nobody that we know of has ever gone into the tribe and come out alive." The director hoped to assemble a small team to leave the next morning.

Cal had a difficult conversation with Mimi and the children that evening. She had just returned from "town," (Pucallpa), but it couldn't wait. He told her he'd been asked to visit and assess what could be done for this tribe far into the jungle. Not much was known about them, other than the fact that they were historically aggressive. Adding to that stress, the Shining Path guerrillas were hiding out in the jungle around Yarinacocha, and had already threatened the mission group during two or three episodes. Everybody at the mission stayed on alert to be ready to evacuate if necessary, including laying out their clothes at night so they could dress quickly.

But no matter how frightening this sounded, Mimi knew that Cal's dream had always been to be the first person from the outside to visit an isolated tribe, and there were not many tribes like that around. This was the chance of a lifetime for him, and Mimi thought, *I'm not going to stop him.*

She told him, "You go and may the Lord be with you."

The children cried, "Mom, don't let him go!"

But Mimi insisted, "No, I cannot stop a dream like this!"

That night Cal and Mimi held each other closely, as he read to the family from Psalm 91, where God promises, "***He who dwells in the shelter of the Most High will rest in the shadow of the Almighty***. *I will say of the LORD, "He is my refuge and my fortress, my God, in whom I trust. Surely he will save you from the fowler's snare and from the deadly pestilence. He will cover you with his feathers, and under his wings you will find refuge; his faithfulness will be your shield and rampart.* ***You will not fear the terror of night, nor the arrow that flies by day, nor the pestilence that stalks in the darkness, nor the plague that destroys at midday.*** *A thousand may fall at your side, ten thousand at your right hand, but it will not come near you.*"

There was no other quotation from the Bible that more clearly and specifically addressed what Cal and the family were facing, and these promises served as strong confirmation that they could all trust and rest in the sheltering hand of the Most High God.

The next morning Mimi and the children walked Cal down to the tiny airport on the water. The generous workers at Yarinacocha loaned Cal the camping equipment he needed and supplied the team with canned food. The medical team consisted of Cal, two Peruvian guides familiar with the jungle, a nurse, and an experienced translator from Yarinacocha who had worked briefly with George and Betty. She found that the language she had learned from another tribe was similar enough that she could serve as a translator.

When the plane disappeared into the sky, Mimi thought, *Oh Lord, what am I going to do? Three children … we're out in the jungle! Will he come back?*

Mom and the children comforted each other. Seven-year-old Kevin said, "Mom, don't worry, I'm going to hold you just like Dad holds you at night." So that night Kevin held Mimi, and the jungle was so hot that she was pouring sweat and he was too. He finally said, "Mom, would you be just as comforted if I just laid here?" Mimi agreed, "I will still be very comforted."

George and Betty had begun to recuperate and were homesick, so the mission group arranged to fly them back to their part of the jungle with the medical team. Upon landing on a river that appeared to be close to the location of the Yora tribal grounds, Cal was shown to a tiny hut built up off the ground with a little roof over it in case it rained, which provided sleeping space for one person. He unfolded a sheet and settled down for sleep, a mixture of emotions surging through him—excitement and delight at being able to be part of this adventure, major uncertainty, but also a deep peace from the conviction that God Himself was opening the way ahead and was protecting him.

Cal woke before dawn, mainly because he heard a blood-curdling sound in the jungle, like a strong wind or an approaching hurricane, but coming from two or three directions at once. It turned out they were howler monkeys that, just like roosters, greeted the dawn with their piercing howls that reverberated through the jungle.

After the howling stopped, Cal heard George and Betty coughing in a little structure next to him. This was part of their illness, of course. But suddenly off in the jungle he heard another cough. Then one of the couple would cough, and from another part of the jungle came an answering cough. This went on ping ponging with answering coughs in four or five places through the jungle. Cal's adrenaline level shot sky high, imagining that George and Betty were communicating by coughs with their armed companions who were surrounding and working their way toward them. But then Cal heard one of the coughs out of the jungle end a bit differently, more like an extended bird call! With this, Cal realized parrots in the jungle canopy were mimicking the Indians' coughing, and his adrenaline level subsided.

The two guides, Jose and Gustavo, had brought a small dugout canoe, a single hollowed out log with a homemade outboard motor. They loaded their supplies of food, medicines, living supplies, camping supplies, and shortwave radio into the canoe. The nurse, the translator, Cal, Jose, and Gustavo got in with the supplies and motored upstream. George and Betty, in a different canoe, took a different route.

Cal had learned that the Yora lived in a small village right at the headwaters of many of the streams coming out of the Amazon, up on a mountain ridge, so the team motored upstream for a day and a half. At night they made camp on a sandbar and the next day they set off again. The stream became smaller and smaller, and finally turned too shallow and small for the canoe to navigate.

The team members loaded as much as they could carry on their backs and set off on foot, leaving behind almost all the food, which was primarily heavy canned goods. Cal only had a small daypack that he stuffed full of what he thought would be essentials for survival and dealing with the illness, especially various medications, but there was still much that was left behind. They walked in the water, continuing upstream, primarily because the surrounding jungle was so thick that the streams became the only trails. The stream became a trickle, and at that point they camped for the night. The next morning Jose was getting anxious to move along. He felt they weren't making very good time, so he suggested that he and Cal go on ahead as fast as they could, while Gustavo stay with the two ladies and follow a bit later at their own pace.

Cal and Jose left the trickle of a stream and climbed over a ridge, down into another river drainage, and again started hiking upstream. They finally reached a village that Jose identified as the main village of the Yora, a series of large thatch-roofed huts with no sides. The village sat in eerie silence; not a person could be found in any of the buildings. In the largest building, which seemed to be a communal hut, the two men noticed a large store of dried corn and two freshly dug graves in the floor.

Jose and Cal sat down, wondering what to make of this, until finally Jose concluded, "You know, these people are children of the jungle. Whenever something threatens them the only security they know is in the jungle. With the threat of this infection, they have probably scattered into the jungle, and we have to go find them."

There were several trails leading out from the village in a spoke-like fashion. They arbitrarily chose one of these trails and started walking down it. Invariably each one of these trails led down to a little stream and they would spend the rest of the time walking in the stream, usually upriver. At times the jungle encroached so closely on the stream that bushes grew over the stream, unfortunately often with prickly thorns, forcing the hikers to crawl on hands and knees through the water. Jose cautioned that snakes loved the cool of this overgrowth, and so they became even more vigilant.

As they walked, Jose made a loud call every so often. It sounded like a bird, like a loud "woo!" He'd call, stop and listen, and then they'd go farther; then he'd call out again. Within an hour or two they heard an answering call off in the jungle. The intensity of the calling increased and got closer until they were met in the streambed by two men, an older man resting on what looked like a staff but turned out to be his bow, and a younger man, both very muscular and dressed only with a string around their waist. The two men led Cal and Jose up an embankment to a tiny clearing in the jungle. Nearly 30 people of all ages lay in hammocks, looking very sick and miserable. The two guides also collapsed into their hammocks.

Small smoky fires underneath some of the hammocks looked like an attempt to keep them warm and presumably repel some of the insects. Jose identified the older man who met them as the chief of the tribe, remarking how fortuitous to find this particular group with the chief first. Cal took a quick look around to assess the security of the situation, looking for weapons. He saw only one bow and arrow tied up for travel and leaning up against a tree. The bow wasn't strung, obviously not ready for battle. Cal's first impression was that the scene looked like an old illustration from *Dante's Inferno*, with all the hazy smoke filtering through this scene of sheer misery and dejection.

Cal relaxed a bit and Jose suggested he start with the chief, so he did. Without the translator, Cal and the patient couldn't communicate other than nonverbally. Jose translated as closely as he could into Spanish for Cal, bridging languages somewhat.

The old chief felt feverish, coughed constantly, and appeared to have difficulty breathing. He looked as though he hadn't been eating and had been confined to his hammock like the rest of his tribe. Cal examined the chief with as careful a physical exam as he could, which the old man permitted. When Cal listened to his lungs, he discovered the chief had consolidated pneumonia, as opposed to a more scattered pneumonia such as seen in many viral infections. When the chief communicated that both he and some of the others in his group occasionally spit up what looked like blood, Cal realized the pneumonia was most likely caused by the bacteria *Streptococcus pneumoniae*, or pneumococcus, which historically is one of the more common causes of severe pneumonia and is often fatal if untreated.

In trying to decide what medicines to bring, Cal had gone through the various possibilities, realizing that a respiratory infection of some sort was probably the more likely, mainly because George and Betty had started with intense coughing and lung problems. He couldn't exclude the possibility of some bowel or even a more exotic type of infection, and so had brought some medication for these as well, but he suspected respiratory problems would be the most likely. Since he had heard that people had already died from the infection and had observed the fresh graves in the communal house, he knew he had to act fast, even if there was no way of confirming the specific identity of the bacteria.

Cal had brought some penicillin, both in tablets and injectable. One known aspect of the pneumococcus, at least in that time, was that it was universally sensitive to penicillin. (Unfortunately, there are now penicillin-resistant strains of pneumococcus that have developed around the world, especially in those areas where antibiotics are frequently used.) Cal realized that the pneumonia was going to require injected penicillin rather than pills because a high dose was needed to treat severe pneumonia with most probably accompanying sepsis.

Cal told Jose, trying to choose concepts that the chief would understand, "You're going to have to tell the chief that I need to stab him with an arrow. I don't know how you're going to tell him that, but if you could somehow convey that my stabbing him with an arrow is going to help him recover, that's what I'd like you to do."

Jose and the old chief bantered back and forth, and finally the chief nodded in agreement. At Cal's request he rolled over without hesitation in his hammock, stuck his rear end in the air, and Cal gave him an injection of penicillin. He grunted a quick "Uh" and then rolled over again.

Cal looked around at the rest of the group, all of them in their hammocks. Everyone was sitting up as much as they possibly could, watching this drama. As soon as the old chief rolled over after having received the injection, Cal was suddenly the man of the hour. They all started motioning to him to "come over here, come over here, do that to me too, do it to me." Cal approached the next hammock to find an older man even sicker than the chief. In fact, he was gray and barely breathing. Cal examined him and realized that he was on his way out; the elderly man died within a half hour of their arrival in the tribe, right in front of him.

After examining three or four others, Cal found they had similar symptoms—fever, weakness, cough and sometimes bloody sputum—all evidence of consolidated pneumonia, many of them in both lungs. Since everyone probably had the same thing, Cal started to abbreviate his physical exam. He didn't make a point of examining the neck as carefully or palpating the joints or testing the reflexes, and his patients began to show signs of concern. If he skipped a point in his physical examination, they would take his hand and put it where it should have been, essentially insisting that he go through the exact same pattern of physical exam as he did with the old chief. He realized that in their mind this wasn't an examination, this was the therapy. His touching them had something to do with something good, and so he had to repeat each exam in exactly the same pattern as in his examination of the chief.

At the end of each exam the patients looked at Cal with plaintive, sorrowful eyes and said something to him that he couldn't understand, but it was obviously about how miserable they were. They would take his hand and put it on their chest and begin to make massaging motions. They wanted Cal to massage their chest, which intrigued him. Because of all the coughing, their chest wall was undoubtedly sore and achy, and a massage most probably felt good. This was something they may have earlier done to each other, but now since all were so sick, none of them were able to help each other. Cal thought it was interesting that they had developed techniques that could in a small way help them feel a bit better.

Cal gave a shot to everyone who was ill, and the only ones who objected were the smaller children, who had the same level of pneumonia and were just as sick as the adults. Of the whole group of 30 there was only one boy, a young teenager, who had a normal exam and showed no signs of illness.

Meanwhile, Jose had been talking to some of the men in this group who said they knew of at least one other group of their tribe a little downstream. So Cal and Jose went downstream to treat the sick people there as well. By then it was getting late, so they returned to the main village and set up camp. Meanwhile, the two women had arrived with Gustavo and had already set up their mosquito nets.

Now they wondered what to do about food, since they hadn't been able to bring much other than some granola bars. That night they ate granola bars for dinner along with some bananas and papaya the Yora had fortunately planted. This was their diet over the next two to three days.

The next morning Jose and Cal began a pattern of work. They would take off down one of the trails leading out of the camp that would invariably lead into a streambed. They walked up the stream, calling all the way until they found another group. There were pockets of groups of 20 to 30 people scattered all over the jungle. Cal developed an elementary system of medical record keeping by consecutively numbering each Yora, and drawing this number on their bare chest with an indelible felt-tipped pen. This number was then entered into a small notebook with the date and time seen, findings and medication given, and any other pertinent information about this particular patient. Every one of them had this pneumonia. The farther away from the main village they were, the sicker they were. For the first couple of days, in addition to finding new groups, they visited the previous groups to give them another injection, trying to maintain a high level of penicillin in their system by administering it every 12 hours.

On the third day they came into a group two or three hours away from the main village. This group was sicker than any of the others, much weaker and dehydrated. They told Jose that the night before three had died. Cal examined them as usual, this time a bit more briefly, just to confirm they had the same pneumonia, then gave them their injections. Jose encouraged them to begin working their way toward the main village because a single injection was not going to be enough, and it was needed twice daily.

As they were leaving this group, Jose whispered to Cal, "Doctor, do you have any matches? Their fire has gone out." When he heard that, Cal nearly broke down. Their fire was one of their few comforts. They used it to boil water, to cook their bananas, their jungle greens, their bits of food, and they used it to warm themselves during the chilly night as well as ward off the incessant mosquitos. But beyond this, their fire was something that they preserved through the generations. They would carry embers of a fire from camp to camp and use those embers to start a new fire. If the fire went out, they could use something like a fire drill to start a fire again, but when they were so weak this was impossible. To lose their fire was to lose the only thing that might give them a bit of comfort. And in a sense Cal saw it as symbolic that the whole Yora tribe knew they were in the process of dying, and the fire of their existence, of their history, was going out.

Fortunately, Cal had brought matches and was able to start a small fire. He was certain they would keep that fire going for several more generations. It was one of the more emotional moments of Cal's time in the Amazon jungles of Peru.

CHAPTER 15

We Need Food

*A*t great physical expense, the team had dragged a short-wave radio with them along the trails and the streams. The radio required a long wire antenna to function and was battery-powered with a solar charger for the battery. They set up the radio the first day in the village and began calling on an assigned frequency, not knowing if the mission station would hear or if the radio was even going to work. They kept at it, calling and calling, until finally a voice answered on the other side. They had established contact.

Back in Yarinacocha, Mimi was called to the radio office. It was raining and she looked back to see her children playing under the porch roof. *What do I say to the children if Cal doesn't come back?* She suddenly realized she was reliving the experience of the wives of the five missionaries who had been killed by Auca Indians, now known as the Waorani, in Ecuador. These five women had gathered for hours around the shortwave radio waiting for news of their husbands' first contact with the Waorani. One of those killed, the pilot Nate Saint, was the father of Mimi's boarding school roommate, and so this was all too real in her memory. Mimi knew that the tribe Cal now visited was as isolated and hostile in reputation as the Waorani had been, except that the initial communication with the Waorani had been more extended than the current communication they'd had with the Yora. To the five missionaries, the Waorani had appeared willing to accept them because the tribe had accepted the gifts airdropped to them. Based upon this, the doomed missionaries decided to take the chance to meet with the Waorani in person. Had this happened to Cal? *What would she say to the children?*

Mimi got to the radio and tremulously said, "Hello."

She was greeted by Cal's upbeat voice. "Mimi, we are here and safe, and I'm having a ball!" But they needed food, indicating, "We don't want to take the tribe's stored food because they're going to need to eat when they get better." He asked Mimi to find food that would survive a drop from the airplane.

Fortunately, Mimi was prepared, having cooked and stored in the freezer enough entrees for several weeks. She grabbed several frozen meals, divided them into newspaper-wrapped bundles, and packed them in boxes. One bundle was wrapped in fewer layers of paper, with a notation that this should be eaten first. The other two were wrapped more thickly for greater insulation to be eaten later. She took a quick look around, wondering, *What could I give to Cal that would help relax him?* He liked reading *Time* magazine, so she stuck in a new one. She picked fresh grapefruit from the tree in front of their house and packed them in the box with some hard-boiled eggs.

Mimi brought her bundles to a waiting plane at the mission airstrip, a total of 10 boxes of food. The plane, called a Helio-Courier, was specifically designed for mission work and could take off and land in very short distances. But it also had huge flaps and could slow down and stay in the air at a low speed compared to most other aircraft.

The pilot spotted the camp and flew over with the door open, dumping the boxes with no parachute. He tried to fly as low as he could, and the team on the ground warned people to stay clear. The boxes all hit the ground, some farther away than others.

One of the boxes landed off in the jungle, so Jose sent one of the young men to get it. When he came back empty-handed, Jose asked him, "Did you have trouble finding the box?"

He responded, "No, I found it."

"Well, why didn't you bring it back?" asked Jose.

"Well, it was wedged up against a tree with a large bushmaster snake wrapped around it. That box is going to stay there!"

Unfortunately, that box turned out to be the one with fresh grapefruit. However, Mimi's technique of wrapping the food thickly worked to keep some of the food frozen, even in the jungle heat.

The team stayed in touch with the mission station daily by radio, and they relayed messages of the team's progress to Mimi. On the second day at the village, the first group they treated had already made their way back to the village with the chief. They set up their hammocks in one of the buildings and that made it easier for Cal to give them their every-12-hour doses of medicine. Every group they encountered had been encouraged to make their way toward the village as soon as they felt stronger. If they couldn't, the team would go out and give them their injections.

Not only did the contacted groups come, but also other groups that they hadn't encountered, because word spread that help had come. With all of that, Cal began running out of medicine, because he had only brought a limited amount of injectable penicillin in his small daypack. As people started improving, he tried switching them to penicillin tablets, but the Yora complained that the pills were bitter, and the concept of swallowing the pills without chewing them was a hard skill to teach in a different language. A few of them mastered it, but in general most required every-12-hour injections for at least 5 days.

On one of the radio calls Cal talked to the clinic pharmacist. Cal needed a specific formulation of penicillin (procaine penicillin) that gave a high blood level but needed to be repeated every 12 hours. The pharmacist stocked another form of penicillin (benzathine penicillin) that's commonly used for strep throat, but it provides a lower concentration of the antibiotic and is not as effective in acute infections of this kind. However, the pharmacist indicated that he would send what he could find. The next morning the airplane dropped out a few boxes, one of which held almost 200 vials of the procaine penicillin that Cal needed, along with boxes of sterile syringes.

On radio contact Cal asked the pharmacist how he had found such a treasure. The pharmacist explained, "About two years ago I put in an order for benzathine injectable penicillin, but somehow the order got mixed up and I received all these vials of procaine penicillin, which we don't use often. I stuck it away in the warehouse, unsure what to do with it, but not able to send it back. After you talked to me, I realized that all of this was available." Cal immediately saw this as yet more evidence of God's amazing hand in this situation—stockpiling just the medication needed, a full two years in advance, in addition to the resources necessary to get the medication out into the deep jungle with a simple radio message.

It became quite a task to give well over 100 shots in the morning and then again in the late afternoon. But to Cal's surprise, as the recovering Yora began to feel better, they would hear Cal coming in the morning and knew it was time for the shots. Of their own accord, all of them in a hut, at least the men, would get out of their hammocks and walk outside, cut down a banana leaf and lie on it with their rear ends up, all in a row just like cordwood. So, all Cal had to do was go down the row sticking needles into rear ends. The fact that the Yora wore little clothing made them much easier to treat.

The most common piece of clothing for the men was nothing more than a string around their waist. The women generally wore a short skirt woven out of jungle fabric and a series of beads strung over their breasts.

Following several days of intense activity, a pregnant woman and three children came walking into the camp. All including the baby had pneumonia, except that the oldest child, a boy perhaps in his early teens, seemed to be quite well. As they settled into a hut and had been treated, the translator asked the mother where her husband was. She sorrowfully shook her head and said, "I don't know where he is. He was too sick to come, but I felt I had to come because of the children, so I left him in the jungle." Then she said, "My son knows where he is. Would you go with my son and try to find him?" She seemed to indicate that he was within a short walking distance.

So, Cal put a couple of syringes of penicillin in his pocket and set off with the boy, who was happily swinging a machete to open the trail for him. They went up one of the little creeks for a time, then stepped out of the creek into the jungle following no trail but walking through the underbrush and stepping over downed trees. They climbed up a ridge, where the boy looked around and give the now-familiar jungle call. No answer. They went a little farther and the boy called again. Still no answer.

After several attempts, the boy began to look desperate. Obviously either his father had moved, or he didn't know exactly where he was, or he had died. But then Cal could almost see the boy square his shoulders and say to himself, *We're going to do this,* so he turned around and they kept going. They eventually found the father in a hammock strung between two trees. Cal saw immediately that he was gray in color and barely breathing.

Cal examined him and found pneumonia filling both lungs. He was so weak he couldn't sit up without help, and when he tried to stand up to greet Cal, he fell and they had to help him back into the hammock. The son went to get some water, as he was dehydrated and had had little to eat or drink for some time.

After giving him an injection, Cal sat down with the son and looked at him with sorrow, thinking the dad didn't have long to live. The boy was studying Cal's face, and suddenly burst into tears, as if he were reading Cal's mind. Looking at his watch, Cal realized they were only about an hour from sunset, and he motioned to the boy that it was time to return to the village area. But as he suspected, the boy motioned, "Nope, I'm staying here with my dad!"

That left Cal with the choice of either spending the night there with absolutely nothing, not even matches, or trying to make it back to the village on his own. He was concerned because there were a lot of people back at the village who needed their injections. So Cal started off on his own, committing the whole situation to the Lord, because they hadn't followed any trail, but had taken a circuitous route to get to where they were. Cal had tried to memorize landmarks along the way just in case something like this happened, and he noted that it was as if the Lord opened up a map in his mind. He could see the landmarks one after the other in reverse and, praying the entire time, he made his way back to the village just as the sun was setting. Upon his arrival in the camp, the entire team gave thanks for yet another sign of God's tender protection.

Two days later Cal looked across the camp to see the boy coming up the trail. When he saw Cal, he waved his machete with a big grin on his face as if he was happy to be back, and Cal's first thought was *My, he's awfully cheerful for having just lost his dad.* And then Cal saw the reason for his joy; his dad followed right behind him, barely able to walk, but walking. This man had been only a few hours from death with bilateral pneumonia that had totally consumed his lungs, yet the strength of one injection had suppressed the infection enough to enable him in a couple of days to get up and walk all the way back to camp. It was extremely gratifying for Cal to watch how the Yora responded so quickly to the penicillin and recovered so quickly from a truly life-threatening infection.

One evening near the end of Cal's stay among the Yora, one of the men they were treating became tearful, coughing miserably, but crying out and very agitated. Jose went to talk to him and then came to see Cal, saying, "Doctor, the man who's making all this noise is afraid. He says he's being surrounded by evil spirits that are trying to take him." Lucy, the linguist, got up in the middle of the night, sat by his hammock, and talked to the frightened man about God and His love and care for him. He finally settled down. The next morning the man announced that he had made Jesus his owner, the wording they used for accepting Jesus Christ as one's Savior and Lord. It implied a total commitment to following Jesus, as little as they knew of him at first. Before Cal left, three or four others had done the same.

Cal was nearing the end of the time he could spend with the Yora tribe, which was about eight days. The original plan was for this to be a survey trip, but given all that had happened, with the Yora begging them not to leave, and knowing there were perhaps many others even deeper in the jungle who were sick, both Cal and the mission decided it was important to maintain a presence there.

It was decided that Cal would leave because of his previous commitments, including a plane reservation to get back to Denver. But the two women–the translator and the nurse– would stay, and at the same time Cal was leaving, two men were making their way up the river to replace him. One of the men was a missionary who had previously committed himself to work with this tribe if it ever opened up. He and his wife both had made quick arrangements to come to Peru to be ready for this moment. Since the situation was still a bit fluid, it was decided he would come with another man rather than his wife the first time.

A couple of Indian men from another tribe and Cal left about dark, planning to travel all night. First they had to climb up and over the ridge and down to the river drainage that they had traveled up, and this took many hours. But they arrived at the river in the early morning hours where a canoe was waiting. The river was just a little creek at this point.

As they glided down the river in the early morning hours in total darkness, Cal tried to sleep but was awakened frequently because of the cold, which in certain seasons can drop to the 60s, which with the high humidity feels quite chilly.

Cal kept hearing splashes and every so often felt something brush up against him as he was lying in the canoe. One of the boatmen explained they were flying fish. The canoe was disturbing them, and they would leap into the air and jump over the canoe and into the water on the other side.

Eventually their river merged with a much larger one, and they traveled farther downstream than where they had begun days earlier, ending up in a small village with an airstrip on the side of the river. The mission group had one airplane that could land on a solid strip rather than a river, and this plane was there to meet them.

Mimi and Kurt had been invited by the pilot to come along, and they were a wonderful sight to Cal! The thought of seeing Cal was overwhelming to Mimi. The whole trip felt so dreamlike, surreal, that she was amazed she and Kurt could actually witness it. They were beside themselves with joy. Although Cal had lost about 15 pounds and looked quite thin, he was very happy. It was marvelous to be together again.

Before takeoff, a radio message indicated that someone in a village on their way back to Yarinacocha was very ill and needed to be flown to the Wycliffe base. But the plane was now full. Could this person take Kurt's seat, leaving Kurt in the village overnight, and a pilot would return to get him in the morning? Here was another instance of trust! Kurt was willing, even though he would be alone and did not speak the local language or know the people. At age 14 he knew it was going to be an adventure, and that was enough for him. A local school master let Kurt stay in his house, and the Wycliffe plane returned as promised to bring him back to the mission station. He had all kinds of exciting tales to tell of what he had eaten and how kind they had been to him. It was a great experience for Kurt.

The day after Cal returned to Yarinacocha, the entire mission group gathered to hear Cal tell of the events that had just transpired. They insisted on specific detail, and so Cal ended up talking for over three hours, with periodic questions from the group and no evidence that he was going on too long. Many of them had also dreamed for years of being able to participate in something like this, and so they were personally engrossed in every little event.

Back at the main base the mission kept close track of what was happening to the tribe. Cal had treated well over 100 people in the eight days he was there, and after he left, well over another 100 people came into the central village with the same illness. The people who had come in to replace Cal were able to treat them, and the couple who had committed to work with this tribe ultimately stayed with them for at least four years.

The Peruvian government recognized the vulnerability of the Yora and so set up a cordon around that area of the jungle, prohibiting anybody, especially local logging companies or other adventurers, from entering it. The only people allowed in were the missionary couple and a Peruvian-appointed anthropologist to document their situation and make recommendations as to what the next steps would be.

The attention of the Peruvian government was significant. Because of the illness, the tribe lost an entire season of planting, and faced severe hunger requiring supplemental food assistance for at least a year until another crop could be harvested. The government office for indigenous peoples decided it would be best if they left that part of the jungle and moved onto the main river that Cal had come down, where they would be more accessible for aid. The chief agreed and most of the people relocated there, making access easier. At the same time, the missionary couple began working very closely with the Peruvian government to introduce the Yora to their new world.

Over the years, news of the Yora tribe indicated they had become more and more sparse. They eventually began to disperse from their new location in the jungle. Some migrated farther downriver and became more integrated into Peruvian village life. Others returned to the jungle, convinced the old ways were still the best ways, and that's where they are to this day.

Decades after the Wilsons finished their mission trip to the upper Amazon basin of Peru, Cal noticed a short clip in a news magazine about a small group of jungle Indians who had shown up in Brazil. The news story stated Peruvian loggers chased the Indians out of their jungle area so they could take the wood. The jungle Indians crossed the border into Brazil to escape violence by these loggers. Cal recognized from the picture and description that the refugees were nearly identical to the Yora tribe he had treated.

CHAPTER 16

No Holding Back

*C*al began to understand what had kept him from committing to long-term international medical mission work. Treating critically ill patients deep in the jungle opened his eyes to what he had been resisting—he preferred to deal with life's uncertainties by being fully prepared to deal with any scenario that might arise. In other words, he wanted to be in control of the vagaries of life.

However, in the Peruvian jungle pneumonia crisis, immersed in total uncertainty, preparation had been virtually impossible. Cal didn't even have suitable camping equipment or any of the supplies he had diligently accumulated at home in Colorado and left with the canoe. Much of what the medical team did take had to be left behind when they discovered there was no one to help carry the supplies. So, the always-prepared doctor entered a situation he had never experienced before with an absolute minimum of equipment: for instance, he had only one water bottle for hydration that broke when he slipped in mud and had to be duct-taped to slow the leaks.

What impressed Cal was how God had provided for them every step of the way. When they had gone for two or three days without much food while walking into the affected area, there was food at the village. Then the mission very kindly air dropped them food (which Mimi had on hand!) and replacement medications. When he was getting sore from sleeping on the ground, he mentioned it over the radio and hesitantly asked if an extra foam mat was available, and if so to please slip it in with the next airdrop. The next day the plane flew all the way from Yarinacocha to drop only one item, something Cal had never seen before—an original Therm-A-Rest air mattress, one of the first ever made, that one of the dear Wycliffe workers had donated. Cal felt like he was sleeping on a cloud for the rest of the trip.

He was in awe of the way the Lord allowed them to be successful in eliminating the infection and preventing death. Not one person died whom they had treated. The only ones who died were so deep in the jungle they couldn't be reached in time or couldn't get to the village. At least 60 died before any of the team could get to them. All told, the missionary couple who worked with the Yora tribe later estimated the entire tribe numbered about 300, so Cal's medical team had ended up treating at least two-thirds of the Yora.

Cal returned to Lakewood fully aware that regardless of the

uncertainty of any situation, the Lord Who put him in the situation was present, and He would provide not only security, but the resources necessary to accomplish God's purpose there. This was a primary turning point for Cal, and he began to look seriously at international mission work.

As Cal returned to his comfortable suburban medical practice, he noted that dealing with the everyday complaints of ear infections and backaches seemed almost superficial, even though he still empathized with his patients' suffering, when people whom he could now visualize were literally dying of easily treated medical problems.

He didn't want to put any pressure on the rest of the family because of what had happened in him, so he decided to say nothing to Mimi or the children about the fact that he was thinking seriously about full-time mission work. This essentially would mean leaving his thriving and supportive private practice, leaving their home in Lakewood and all their life-long friends, and striking out into the uncertain wild again. He thought Mimi sensed all of this, but neither could talk about something so weighty right away. All he could do was pray.

Interestingly, several months after returning home, Mimi slowly began to realize her attitudes were changing as well, especially in those areas where she felt she was holding back. For example, Mimi felt she had sacrificed enough in all the mission work she had grown up with, so she did not feel any current obligation to do more. She had suffered greatly from long months of separation from her parents in an African boarding school, and even more when she did not see her parents for the four years of high school. Whenever she thought of the possibility of placing her own children in an international boarding school, she literally froze at the thought. But God gently began to show her His love and compassion for her, regardless of her struggle.

During that time, Mimi appreciated the fact that Cal did not push: they both wanted any decision to be clearly guided by God. She noted a progressively stronger sense that she was going to miss out on the best of her life if she could not trust God for every area, including her children. After much discussion, it came to a climax when Cal suggested, "Why don't we just go as a family to Ecuador and together see what the needs are, and see if we fit?" adding at the same time, "There's no pressure. There's no pressure at all," for which Mimi was grateful.

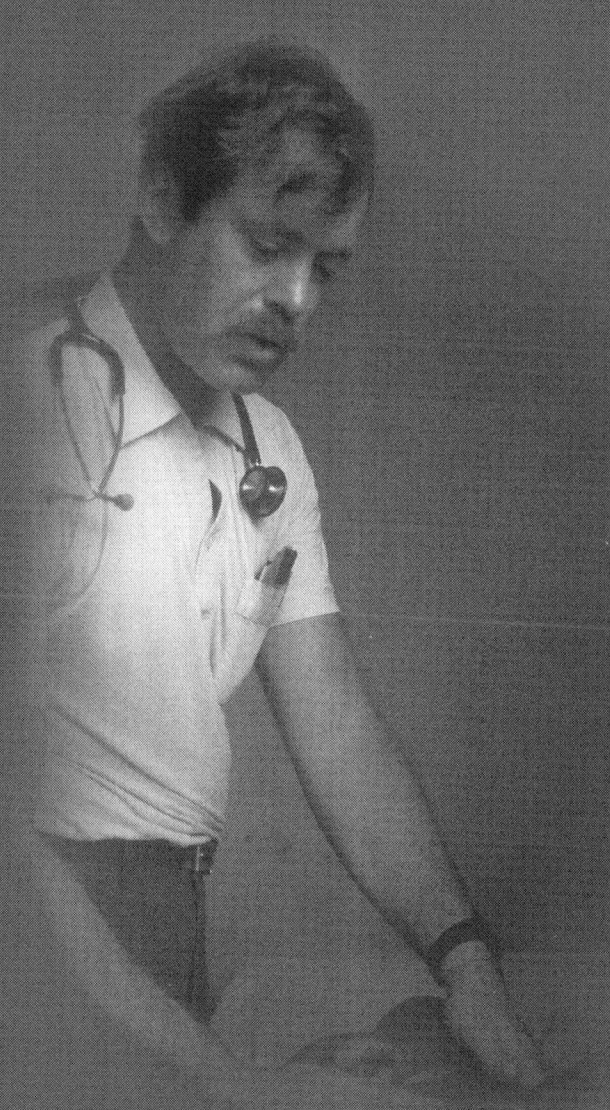

Quito, Ecuador

1986-95

CAL EXAMINING A PATIENT AT THE CLINIC
OF SANTO DOMINGO DEL ONZOLE

EARLY BIBLE STUDY GROUP QUITO, 1988

NESTOR AND
REMBERTO, 2013

ROSA AMUGUIMBA,
COWORKER
IN ECUADOR

CLINIC BUILDING IN SANTO DOMINGO DEL ONZOLE

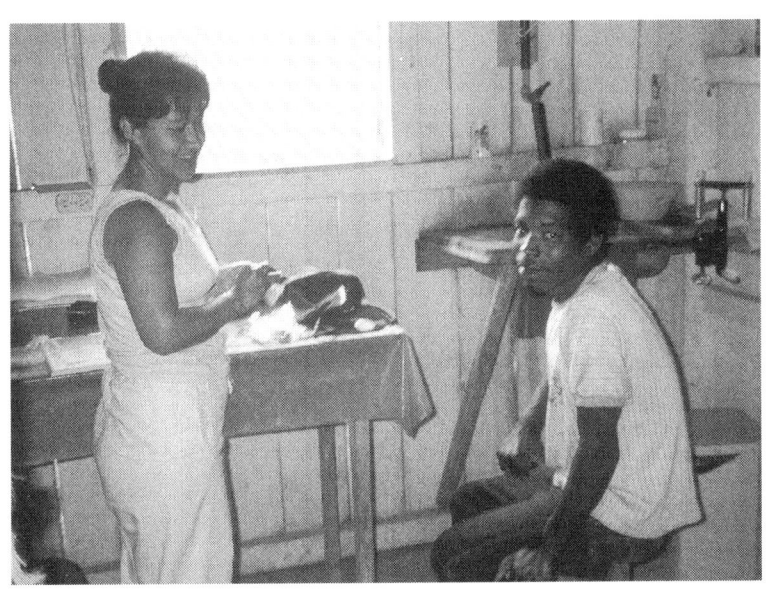

NURSE PATRICIA WITH PATIENT IN
SANTO DOMINGO CLINIC

MIMI HOSTING A GROUP IN QUITO, ECUADOR

GLEN AND SHELLY VOLKHARDT AND
SON, CARL – FIRST FRIENDS IN ECUADOR

WILSON FAMILY PRAYER CARD, 1986

MOUNT COTOPAXI, AN ACTIVE VOLCANO
IN ECUADOR, 19,347 FEET

CHAPTER 17

To the Mission Field

*T*wo years after the adventure in Peru, Mimi was willing to
at least *look* at the *possibility* of mission work, although
she was still hesitant about it. Together, Cal and Mimi investigated a wide variety of missions on various continents, with
serious possibilities in Papua, New Guinea and in several areas
in Africa. Cal wasn't interested in simply replacing personnel
for a mission, but in an initial, pioneer work. Africa fell off
their list because, at that time, remote pioneer mission work
in Africa required their children attend boarding schools,
often two or three countries away. Given Mimi's unfavorable
childhood experience in boarding schools, she was not willing
to do that, which Cal understood, as he really did not want
that either.

During this time of expectant waiting, Lloyd Rogers, a
missionary who had been working in the jungle of Ecuador

for at least 20 years, including with the Waorani tribe, passed through Denver and hosted a couple of meetings that Cal and Mimi attended. In private, long conversations after the meetings, Lloyd encouraged the Wilsons. He said, "There are many situations you could work into, and a lot of medical mission work that still needs to be done all over the country." Cal and Mimi began to focus on the jungle in Ecuador.

Their only two criteria in selecting an area of mission work were that it be an area where medical and spiritual needs had not yet been met, and that there would be a good school for their children that could adequately prepare them to integrate back into the US with a minimum of difficulty. The two had seemed almost mutually incompatible, but in Ecuador both existed. Mimi was willing to go and check out the situation, but certainly not willing to commit. They planned an exploratory trip to Ecuador.

It was now time to talk to the children. Cal felt strongly that all five of the family had to be in agreement before they would engage in fulltime mission work. Each child had to cope with this idea at their own level. Were they willing to uproot themselves from what was a comfortable, wonderful existence?

Several years prior to this they had moved from their home near the clinic to live on the family farm where Cal grew up. Their house was situated between Cal's grandfather's house and his parent's house. It was a wonderfully comfortable place for them all. Still, with no pressure, one by one each of the children came to Cal and Mimi and said in their own words,

"Yeah, I think this is going to be good for me, and for us as a family." For example, while Kurt was attending a camp for high schoolers where Mimi was the speaker, he came to her after a couple days at camp and said, "Mom, I don't know if you've ever heard of this man, but his name is Jim Elliott. I just finished a book about him, *Through Gates of Splendor*, and he was working in Ecuador, and if it is like he described, I'd like to go." Jim Elliott was one of the five missionaries who were killed in January 1956 by a group of Waorani tribesmen, including the father of Mimi's high school roommate. Following her own decision-making process, Kyndra took a long walk on the farm, and upon returning said, "I will do what you all decide." The youngest, Kevin, who was about eight at the time, came to Cal and Mimi and said, "You know, I've thought a long time about this, and realized that I just don't know enough about any of it. I'm too young to make that kind of decision, so I'll just go wherever you go."

A few days before they left for Ecuador, Mimi was speaking to a group of women in a Bible study when it dawned on her that although she was teaching about trusting a faithful God, her attitude did not match that sentiment. The truth was that she wanted to raise her own children; she could not trust anyone else to do it for her—including her Father God! In the middle of her message, standing in front of these women, she realized that if she couldn't trust God to raise her children, she had no right to speak about trusting Him at all. If God couldn't be God, she had no right to speak of Him to others.

Mimi decided she was not going to speak again until God could be truly God, and she could be transparent to others in her thinking. She abruptly ended the talk in mid-message, certain that some of the women would question why it only lasted 30 minutes instead of the usual 45. She dragged herself home, in mental agony over the question of how much she really could trust her Father God with the future of her children in such uncertain circumstances as the Ecuadorian jungle.

She walked into the house that day and greeted her visiting parents. They had just arrived a few days earlier because of worsening illnesses of both parents, including an acute exacerbation of chronic leukemia in her father, who was about to enter the hospital for tests and treatment. Mimi's mother, who was affected by Alzheimer's dementia, handed Mimi a list, saying, "These are the 12 people who called while you were gone." But pointing to one, she added, "This one is unique. You should call her first." That aroused Mimi's curiosity, wondering how her mother was able to pick up on that. She called that number and suddenly, the life of her extended family was forever changed.

Years before, when Mimi's older sister Nancy was 18, one of the elders of their church in California had offered to take in Nancy to live with his family for a year while she attended college. During that year this man seduced Nancy and she ended up pregnant. She hid it as long as she could, but eventually had to tell her parents the sad truth. They returned home to California on their scheduled leave about that time, with Nancy well along in her pregnancy. Mimi was 13 years old at the time.

Nancy delivered in a hospital in California, and the baby was immediately put up for a private adoption. Because this was 1959, an event such as this was incredibly shameful, especially within the Christian community, so the adoption was quietly arranged by the nurse who attended the delivery. She knew of a family looking for a child and took confidential responsibility for the arrangements. The nurse was the only one who knew the adoptive parents and location of the child, ostensibly to protect everyone. Nancy was not even told the gender of her child, and she stayed with her family until her folks returned to Africa. She then transferred to Wheaton College in Illinois where she finished her degree, while Mimi started in a residential high school in Florida. Nancy eventually fell in love with a young seminary student, David Pavey, from England, and married, with his full knowledge of this event. The event was now behind them. It was never again discussed, and the family tried to put it out of their memory.

So, with her heart already bruised from the crushing insight about her lack of trust in God a few hours earlier, Mimi called the number that her mother said was "unique." The voice at the other end said, "I am the nurse who made the adoption of your sister's child. She (the child) has some questions for you, but you need to hold this in confidence."

Mimi agreed and was told that her sister's child would call soon. She thought the questions might be about a genetic problem or family health history. Very shortly, the phone rang, and a young woman softly gave her name and said, "I would like to meet my mother; do you think she would be willing to meet with me?"

Nancy already had plans to fly into Denver that Sunday to take care of her folks when the Wilsons left for Ecuador. The young woman asked if she could meet Nancy's plane.

"Where do you live?" Mimi asked.

"I live close to Denver", she replied

With shaking hands, Mimi called her sister. "Nan," Mimi said, "I just talked to your little girl."

"My little girl?" Nancy had two sons. There was a pause. "You mean my baby?!"

With that, 25 years of pent-up emotion flowed. In tears, Nancy agreed, "I will meet with her at the airport tomorrow."

Mimi suggested Nancy's husband Dave accompany her, so she would have support on the plane ride to Denver, and not such a big shock when she arrived.

After the long-awaited reunion at the airport of mother and daughter, along with their husbands, they all came to Cal and Mimi's house. Here was a gracious young woman who was meeting her birth mother for the first time, and everyone had burning questions. They learned that shortly after the adoption the girl's adoptive family had settled in Colorado. Nancy's little girl was now a nurse and had married a young doctor about four years prior, who accompanied her on this visit. It was as if a Hallmark movie was unfolding, it was so unreal and beautiful.

That night Mimi lay in bed amazed at how God had bonded them all together. A crushing event 25 years earlier had come to fruition the day before she was to leave for an uncertain future. Her Father God whispered to her wondering mind, "You didn't even know where this child was, or my plan for her, for you, and for Nancy these past decades. Yet I raised her to honor me, and have sustained you and Nancy through these years. Now can you trust me with your children?"

That was the key for Mimi, as she worshipped her Father, *"Oh my God, you have orchestrated all this joy at this point in time, to simply prove to me that You are faithful and worthy of my unquestioning trust. I will go to Ecuador, but You must walk with me—and my children—every step of the way."*

CHAPTER 18

What They Thought They Would Do

*I*n early 1986, the Wilson family set out for two weeks to explore mission possibilities in Ecuador. Their goals were clear: to find a place where there were real medical and spiritual needs that had not been filled, and where there was appropriate schooling for their children that would adequately prepare them for university and life in the States.

Upon arrival in Quito, Lloyd Rogers, who had earlier encouraged them to consider Ecuador, picked them up at the airport and spent the next several days showing them the country. They traveled into the jungle near where he lived, and he let them see various areas where there were still real medical and spiritual needs. They sensed they could enjoy relationships with the people they met.

They also spent a fair amount of time examining a Christian Missionary Alliance School in Quito. This international school was the obvious choice for schooling for Kurt, Kyndra, and Kevin. They not only used an American-style curriculum, they also deliberately pushed the curriculum forward so that when a child moved from that school to a school in the US, they were at least four to six months ahead of the average US cycle. This was to allow for a family's travel time and getting settled. It was a boarding school, but impressive.

They returned home satisfied that Ecuador was a suitable place to begin this next phase of life. The schooling was appropriate for the children, there was an abundance of both medical and spiritual work that needed to be done, and they felt welcomed. Now there was much to be done, including selling a large family home in the middle of a family farm and leaving a stable medical practice with wonderful relationships. Full steam ahead!

Selling the house proved challenging. Because it was in the middle of a family compound on a farm, anyone who looked at it realized they would be moving into a unique situation, and not many people were interested. Cal and Mimi also realized they were not going to be able to move to Ecuador until the house sold, mainly for financial reasons. It carried a large mortgage, and the amount of money they would make as medical missionaries was not even a fraction of what was needed to pay the mortgage. So, the house sat for five or six months with no bites whatsoever.

At church one Sunday a friend asked Cal, "How are you doing with selling your house?" Cal said it was difficult. "How is this influencing your plans to go to Ecuador?" the man asked. Cal explained that they weren't able to even think about moving to Ecuador until the house sold because of the cost of the mortgage.

"I'll tell you what. I think you need to go. Why don't you just set a date for when you want to go to Ecuador, and I will pay the mortgage until the house sells."

"But that could be a long time. It could be a year or two," Cal replied, overcome.

"I will pay the mortgage until the house sells," the friend repeated.

With that they began packing, planning to arrive in Quito shortly before the school year began in August. And the man stood true to his word for the additional six months it took the house to sell.

Before they left for Ecuador, Cal and Mimi gave a power of attorney to handle the sale of the house to Cal's brother Kirk, who had by that time, even though he was the youngest brother, already bought and sold several houses and was well aware of the issues.

Kirk checked on the house periodically, as it stayed vacant with no buyer interest. Around Christmas that year Kirk called them in Ecuador and said, "You know, every time Dawn and I go over there we think, *Boy, this is a wonderful house. We would love it here!* I think I've come up with a way to buy it." And with that, God answered the prayer of many months in the most ideal way possible, both in providing for the needed mortgage payments and in keeping the house within the family on the farm.

The sale closed in late December 1986. This was significant because Congress had increased the rate at which capital gains were going to be taxed as of the beginning of 1987. They had accrued a large amount of capital gains, so this closing date enabled them to pay a much cheaper tax rate than they would have had to pay a few days later. This was yet another of the many confirmations God provided in support of this transition, the Lord's gift to them.

Leaving the Lakewood Family Medicine Clinic wasn't easy either. Cal had been in practice with this group for ten years and had become very close to his partners and his regular patients. They had established a tradition that the four doctors and their wives got together monthly to talk about the past month and get caught up on everybody's lives, which was hard to do in the office where their interactions were professional.

It was hard to leave that kind of relationship, but the partners took it well. They realized it was something the Lord had ordained, so they set about looking for somebody to replace Cal and found a well-qualified young doctor who stepped right into the practice and stayed for several years. Even Cal's patients took it well; on one trip back to the practice a couple of years later, some of his former patients commented, "We were very sorry to see you go, but your replacement thinks a lot like you, and we really like him too!"

Then there was the matter of what to take to Ecuador and what to do with everything else. How does one pack for a family of five for an indefinite period of time? They had no idea how long they were going to stay, or what Mimi was going to do there.

Mimi laid out her fine china on the ping pong table and looked at it longingly, wondering what she should do with all this beauty. Their current houseguest, Kathy Drowns, was Mimi's roommate whose father had been martyred in Ecuador, and Kathy had herself been on the mission field for years. As they surveyed Mimi's favorite pieces, Kathy asked "Do you use your china?"

"I use it every week," Mimi said.

"Then you'll use it there. Whatever you use here, you will use there."

Mimi packed it all up and ended up using it constantly. She also shared her beloved china with other missionaries who didn't have china and needed it. In fact, in Ecuador she stored all the china in what became a famous big basket. Someone would borrow it to use at one party, and from there someone would take it to another, and nothing ever broke. Upon leaving Ecuador Mimi began a tradition that she continued in other countries where they lived. She would pick out a woman who was extremely hospitable and who had perhaps borrowed the china several times, and upon leaving the country Mimi left the whole set with her. When they moved to a new country, Mimi bought a new set to use and eventually give in the same generous way.

Their plan upon leaving the US was to live temporarily in the capital of Quito for a few months to a year so they could get accustomed to the culture and the language, and the children to their school. The children could live with their parents while they acclimated to the excellent school run by the Christian Missionary Alliance. About 50 percent of the students were Ecuadorians, enabling cross-cultural interaction. Since it was K-12, all three of the children could go there.

Kurt had two years of high school remaining, stepping into his junior year in Quito. Kyndra started eighth grade and Kevin started the fourth. The plan was that once everyone was well-accustomed to their new situation, Cal and Mimi would migrate to the town of Shell, Ecuador, in the jungle. Shell was the headquarters for Missionary Aviation Fellowship (MAF) for Ecuador and home base for Lloyd Rogers. Cal would work at a mission hospital in Shell, and Kevin would transfer with them and attend the K-8 school in Shell. Kyndra and Kurt would remain in Quito, living in one of several boarding rooms or houses around the school. That was the plan, although Mimi still had serious reservations, knowing that it was going to be very emotionally difficult for her to leave two of her children in a boarding school. Kurt and Kyndra were happy with the idea; they saw it as part of the adventure!

CHAPTER 19

Settling in Quito

*J*ust getting to Ecuador was a trek with the three children and Cal's mother, Chris, who came along to help. An air freight shipment was scheduled to deliver most of their belongings, packed into several large boxes. They took with them items they needed immediately or that were essential for their work, including a heavy (also called "luggable") portable computer, which in the '80s used floppy drives. It weighed approximately 30 pounds, and since it was going to have to be checked as luggage, Cal made a padded wooden box for it which added another 20 pounds. They checked 22 pieces of luggage, obviously paying for additional bags, although the fees were much less than those charged now.

At the airport in Quito, they were met by Glen and Shelly Volkhardt, who were with a mission called HCJB: the call letters of their primary ministry of short-wave broadcasts.

Cal had offered to help as a physician in the associated HCJB mission hospital in Quito and HCJB had assigned this staff couple to pick them up. Amazingly, all 22 pieces arrived with them. And fortunately, they all fit in the Volkhardt's van.

Glen had identified a home for them to borrow from HCJB missionaries who were on furlough for at least six months. Glen drove them to the home, and they settled in for what would be their first two months. The comfortable house was fully furnished, with lots of space for all the luggage. Plus, it was close to the hospital, the children's school, and transportation.

Early the next morning Mimi awoke to the sound of banging around in the entry way to the house. Was someone breaking in? She quickly dressed and discovered a woman who looked as surprised as Mimi, although the woman also looked quite at home.

"Who are you?" Mimi asked.

"I'm your housekeeper, Rosa."

The homeowners had hired Rosa to come every day to clean and cook for the Wilsons. Mimi didn't know that would be part of the arrangement, but she quickly became grateful.

Rosa lived in a densely populated part of town and commuted by bus. She was married, had several children, and was the same age as Mimi. Rosa had been orphaned at an early age and had basically raised herself. So she was extremely self-sufficient and innovative, which was a great asset. But best of all, Rosa was a Christian believer, loved the Lord, and faithfully attended a little church in her community.

Mimi couldn't speak Spanish and Rosa couldn't speak much English, but somehow they never let that hinder their communication. Rosa had attended only a few grades of school, although she didn't tell that to Mimi. When Mimi needed vegetables from the market, she would give Rosa a list, written in the extent of Mimi's Spanish. Mimi didn't know it at the time, but Rosa couldn't read the list. Rosa would very carefully go down the list, pointing out one word and saying, "I'm not sure I can read your writing on this word." Mimi would read the list to her while (unbeknownst to her) Rosa memorized the whole thing and came back with everything on the list. It was years before Mimi learned that Rosa was illiterate, which came out when she excitedly announced she was taking special classes to learn to read.

The two women loved each other immediately, but since Mimi was so new in the country she anticipated it would take some time for her to learn how much she could trust Rosa to make her own judgments and handle responsibility. When Mimi taught Rosa to do once-a-month cooking, the housekeeper looked at Mimi as if she had just come out of the stars because it didn't make any sense. It was indeed difficult for Mimi to explain it in broken Spanish, but the two of them persisted in learning about each other.

The school year in Quito started within a week or two of their arrival, and the three children seemed to fit in quite well in their respective classes. They walked the few blocks to school together every day.

Cal's mom, Chris, stayed for two weeks to help them get settled. During that time, they found an English-speaking church to attend, also within walking distance from their home. Chris discovered a chapter of the Christian Women's Club in Quito, a group she had been very involved with in Denver. She planned to attend the next meeting in Quito, but overheard at church that the speaker had canceled and that they were looking for another. Chris offered boldly, "Well, you know, my daughter-in-law has done a lot of Bible teaching and speaking at conferences for women." Mimi was immediately lined up to speak.

She didn't have time to be nervous. She came up with a topic and made a point of meeting and getting to know the women. "It was fabulous," said Mimi, who loves to tell stories and to speak to women. Afterward she invited some of the ladies to her home, and they each came bringing flowers. Mimi enjoyed this custom of Ecuador, but she never dreamed she would have such a big handful of flowers that she couldn't even close the door by herself.

Soon after, Melinda Echeverria, one of the women Mimi met at the women's conference, invited Cal and Mimi for dinner to her home, which was located in one of the nicer parts of town. Leaving the children with new friends, Cal and Mimi hired a taxi, and were taken to a home behind a high metal fence with razor wire at the top and an imposing steel gate. The house was not at all visible, not uncommon in that part of town.

When they rang the bell, a porthole window opened in the gate, and the barrel of a machine gun extended through the hole, pointed at them. A voice behind the gun gruffly asked, "Who's there?" Cal hesitantly gave their names, and the guard said, "I'll check."

Shortly later, the guard opened the gate and was quite cordial. The rest of the evening was delightful. Melinda, an American from California, and Luis, from Chile, had met while Luis attended graduate school in San Francisco. Both husband and wife were firm Christian believers. They explained that the reason for such high security was that Luis was the current President of the Bank of America branch in Quito.

That dinner sparked a close relationship that has continued to this day. Luis was a man of vision and action, the kind of guy who likes to get things done and knows everyone. Melinda was an intellectual equal to Luis, and loved raising their three children and developing deep relationships with other women. Luis and Melinda began introducing Cal and Mimi to many of their friends and acquaintances, often over wonderful dinners filled with animated conversation in a variety of homes. As Cal and Mimi came to know these friends, most of whom were Ecuadorian and worked at the highest levels of government or business, they realized there were tremendous spiritual needs right there in Quito. Even after just one or two visits, many new friends would want to talk about difficult situations and ask for counsel. Some expressed frustration with their spiritual life, wanting to know how they could know God more deeply.

Within the first two to three months in Ecuador, it became obvious this population of people had been essentially isolated from anyone who truly cared about them as a person, much less their spiritual life.

In a poor country like Ecuador the elite are viewed as the humanitarians of the country. Consequently, they're continually on their guard because they are so often asked for money or for influence, and they become wary of others wanting to get to know them. Cal and Mimi realized this very early, and made it a point to assure them that they needed nothing from their new acquaintances; they would never ask anything of them. Truly, they were simply interested in the Ecuadorians as individuals whom God loved.

On this basis a variety of relationships blossomed, to their mutual great enjoyment. The Wilsons began meeting with some of their new Ecuadorian friends to review spiritual issues the friends were struggling with, and it became apparent the Lord was opening a door for them to serve this group of people. They began to see this was what the Lord had in store for them, and that continuing with these relationships would not happen if they moved to the jungle. They found themselves facing a major decision—should they stay in Quito and continue with these relationships, or should they stick with their plan to work among the various tribes of the Ecuadorian jungle?

The difficult part was that they had committed to the missionary group in the village of Shell that they would work with them in the jungle. Cal called Lloyd Rogers, the veteran missionary who had first introduced them to the country, and hesitantly outlined all that had happened and told him their thinking. Cal concluded by saying that if this was what the Lord was asking, it would be better if they stayed in Quito to work with this group of people who frankly had little other access to good Christian teaching, leadership, and discipling. Cal could hear Lloyd swallow hard, but he was very gracious. Lloyd said, "Well, if you feel that's where the Lord is leading you, then we can accept that, and we'll continue to do what we can to support you."

This opened the door for the Wilsons to make plans to stay long-term in Quito. They started looking for another house to rent and put the word out with people in the English-speaking church and their new Ecuadorian friends. In short order, an ideal rental house became available, located only a few blocks from where they were currently staying. It was a single-family home with a driveway that would hold two vehicles, built in a more traditional Ecuadorian style, mostly wood rather than cement, with nice wood accents on the sides. The house was built around a small courtyard and interior garden, with a short bridge over a small fountain leading to the entryway. The owner was a well-known lawyer, and he was asking a fair price. This became their home for the nine years they lived in Ecuador.

Perhaps the greatest blessing of those nine years for Mimi was Rosa, who followed the Wilsons to their new home. The two of them prepared for guests every day. "If we didn't have guests there was something wrong," said Mimi. Rosa prepared a buffet every day at noon for anyone who happened to stop by to talk and then go about their business. The three children would often come home for lunch as well because the house was so close to their school. All their friends who lived out of town knew they could come and count on a homecooked meal. Mimi now understood why it was important that she brought her china.

Rosa managed the noon meal, and sometimes when Mimi arrived at home, Rosa would say, "Well, they ate all your food," which meant there had been a lot of company that day. On occasion Rosa would use her famous saying, "No one dies from not eating three meals a day," and that was Mimi's clue that she mustn't ask for anything more because there wasn't any food left; guests had eaten it all. But it was such a joy for Mimi to have people come in and say, "I just came into Quito, and I know that your house is open. May I have dinner?" And they would always be served.

On days when there was extra food, Mimi would package it on a paper plate with plastic flatware, cover it with tin foil, and put it on the edge of the wall around the house. Mimi arranged it that way so that whoever took the food would not feel like a dog digging through their trash. In this way the many street people were served as well, understanding the food had been set aside just for them. The plates of food never remained on the edge of the wall longer than a few minutes.

CHAPTER 20

Partners in Hospitality

O ne early event demonstrated to Mimi how well Rosa fit into the purpose for which they had come to Ecuador. Rosa had faithfully laid out the day's buffet, but Mimi came home and noticed that one couple whom she had expected was missing from the table. When Mimi asked Rosa where they were, Rosa quietly took her to the garden at the back of the house where the couple sat eating a quiet private meal of *locro*, the famous Ecuadorian potato soup, universally recognized as a comfort food. The husband had just received word that he had cancer, and Rosa decided they needed some time alone. That so touched Mimi because Rosa understood the concept of having meals frozen and immediately available for unexpected needs and was already skillfully putting it to use. Mimi realized she could train Rosa in more complicated skills.

Mimi and Rosa began teaching interested women to cook

once for the month, women who lived in Quito from various places in the world. This was a trick as they never knew the women's background experience in cooking. Mimi would say, "I'm going to teach you once-a-month cooking," and would get only a blank stare with "What did you say?"

One time Mimi and Rosa were invited to a home near the country club to give a demonstration. They never knew what they would find for a kitchen setup since many of these wealthier women had maids. They arrived with their bags and boxes, all the food supplies they would need for the demonstration. "Could you show me to your mixing bowls?" Mimi asked the hostess, who waved her arms across the cabinets, indicating they were somewhere up there. Rosa and Mimi started looking, but every one of the cabinets was empty; the hostess and her family ate most of their meals outside of the home.

Mimi and Rosa looked at each other and in the corner of the kitchen they simultaneously noted the dog dish. Neither said a word, but when the demonstration began Rosa brought out the dog dish scrubbed clean, with a few chew marks on the rim. Ever afterward when preparing to demonstrate once-a-month cooking, one would say to the other, "Just get the dog dish."

One woman explained Mimi's presentation to her friends in her home, "You're going to learn to cook one day for the month and have all of the meals ready! One of the biggest advantages to this is all the money you're going to save because you don't have to go out as much and you can buy food in bulk. The only thing you will need to do is buy a freezer, a microwave, and probably a nice heavy-duty mixer. But think of the money you're going to save!"

Rosa became the partner who made it possible for Mimi to extend hospitality nearly daily during the years they lived in Quito. She was also Mimi's trusted colleague in working with the needy. It became a sweet relationship to the point of a sisterhood.

On the street outside the Wilson's house people were constantly walking by. It seemed that many of them, if they had a home at all, were living in dire circumstances. Mimi noted they would walk up and down the streets of the more affluent neighborhoods looking to see if they could find anything of benefit. Residents would put junk outside, and on the day of trash collection there were organized groups who would go through the trash pulling out recyclable materials or anything they might be able to salvage.

The residents of each block hired a night guard who walked up and down the street, as a deterrent to thieves roaming around looking for houses they could break into. The neighborhood committee had placed the guard shack immediately outside the Wilson's house. The guard shack was no larger than a phone booth, but a shelter from the elements. Some of the food from their evening dinners was regularly taken out to the guard on duty.

Because they lived in a middle-class neighborhood, a constant parade of poor people from the surrounding barrios, the extremely poor areas, would knock on their door asking for handouts, sometimes for money, sometimes for food, sometimes for their children's school supplies. Mimi had a hard time discerning who were professionals at this and who were legitimately needy, so she asked Rosa to answer the door and make that judgment. Mimi gave her a monthly stipend for her to buy rice, beans, and potatoes that were set aside for the needy. Rosa would talk with them for a bit and, because she also lived in a poor barrio, she cut right through to the need.

One day Rosa came to the gate to find a woman holding a child with very red cheeks. She handed Rosa a prescription and said, "I've just been to the doctor. He says I need to give my sick child this medicine. You can see how sick he is. I need money for the medicine." Rosa looked it over and keenly replied, "Let me tell you what I'm seeing. This prescription was dated six months ago. The baby doesn't have a fever. His cheeks are red because you've been pinching them. I have a good notion to call the police and to report you for child abuse. Don't ever do that again." Rosa was merciless to those trying to game the system, and a fair number tried. But for those who had a genuine need, she would empathetically help. Sometimes, upon her recommendation, Cal and Mimi helped in a special way; they trusted Rosa implicitly.

As delighted as Mimi was to have hospitality at the core of their home in Quito, and to have the children at home, it was also a difficult, rather isolating, time for her. Entry into the Ecuadorian culture was proving more difficult for Mimi than it was for Cal. Cal was able to speak Spanish and so was immediately able to get into the culture, while Mimi struggled with Spanish and finally admitted to herself that her dyslexia as a child was affecting her ability to learn it. Fortunately, she could understand almost everything from the very beginning, but that didn't help her in speaking with others.

Mimi was accustomed to being a vital part of a conversation, and suddenly she was not. This was hard! But to compensate, since she couldn't speak, she decided she had to learn to listen, and it turned out to be a great benefit to listen carefully to the conversations around her. Everybody would be talking and joking and Mimi would be listening. Then it would be quiet and Mimi would say to the person who had been the most vocal, "Oh, you were talking about your grandmother," and that would spark a whole renewal of the conversation. So she learned how to make the most of simple vocabulary.

Mimi longed to get to know her neighbors, but initially hadn't yet found an acceptable way. One night, when Cal was out in the jungle, she woke up to feel the whole house shaking. The neighborhood dogs were screaming—a sound she had never heard before. She could feel a rippling through their house.

Mimi had never been in an earthquake before. She got up quickly, checked the children, and had them get underneath their beds. Out in the hall the chandeliers were swinging from wall to wall. She was frightened with Cal out in the jungle, where unbeknownst to her, he was experiencing the same earthquake.

Then the phone calls began from children in the school whose parents were not home, so she told them to come over. She positioned the children under the massive dining room table and any place where they could get protection. They waited together for daylight that came ever so slowly that day.

To have gone through an earthquake without knowing her neighbors was the last straw for Mimi. She had to do something about this. She decided to host a luncheon for neighbor ladies to discuss their reaction to the earthquake, using a translator. She contacted the older lady named Maruja who lived next door to them. Maruja had lived in the area long enough to know most everyone in the community. Mimi shared her idea of a ladies' luncheon on a specific date and said that all the ladies were invited. Would Maruja pass the word? A twitter of excitement went through the neighborhood, and it was fun for Mimi to think she was creating something enjoyable for everyone.

Finally, the day arrived and Mimi answered the doorbell expecting about ten women. The carport was packed with people, and she asked Maruja how this happened. "I know you told me it was just for women, but all the men took off work as well," she replied. Altogether, around 30 people arrived for lunch.

Mimi prayed a word of thanks over the meal, then Rosa served the plates from the kitchen. Mimi made good use of one of her meal-stretching tricks that day; if there isn't enough food to go around, simply make some adjustments—like fill in with more bread. Serve the plates from the kitchen, so that you can manage the portion control. Besides, it looks so terribly formal!

After lunch she showed the neighbors where she hid her children and others for protection in an earthquake. She showed them the dining room table and the different places around the house where they could hide. Their apartments don't have that kind of comfort or space, so they walked around as if the house was a museum, thrilled to have an excuse to take it all in. That luncheon opened up new doors she had never dreamt of.

In Ecuadorian culture it was unusual for people to become involved in their neighbors' lives. The casual relationships are often more formalized, and true empathetic communication is uncommon. So, it was unusual for Mimi to invite people over to her home. But her hospitality broke the ice after a crisis like the earthquake, especially when everybody was anxious to talk and relive the experience but didn't know how to do it. She provided a gathering place, in the neutral zone of a foreigner's house. Mimi knew that she was breaking the cultural norm, but under those circumstances met a genuine need.

From that point on, Mimi's neighbors began to introduce her to others in the immediate neighborhood. She never went anyplace that she didn't see people she knew, and she felt comforted that if something were to happen to Cal, she would have ready support immediately around her. Wherever she went in the market and on the streets, she always found people to talk to, and that turned out to be a lovely thing. Even if she didn't speak very good Spanish, she communicated. Nobody cared as long as she shared a heartfelt smile and spoke with them, demonstrating her love for them regardless of their condition or status.

Following her strategic involvement in Mimi's plan, Maruja came over every day to visit. She lived with her ill husband who could not leave the house without difficulty, so she came alone. Mimi got so used to her being there that she didn't have to stop what she was doing, and Maruja simply entered into the life of the home. She didn't come to stay for dinner, but came to make sure it was going right, and that there was enough for all. She would sit in the corner of the kitchen as Rosa cooked and say, "No, no, no, not half enough lettuce." If there wasn't enough time to go to the market Marjua went to her own house, picked up food, and came back with what was lacking. Mimi used to say that Maruja would come over dressed in anything except her slip—but then one day she came over in her slip. "It was just so cute, so, so darling, so comfortable!" Mimi noted.

Christmas was fun because Marjua would bring over all her decorations that she wanted Mimi to use in her house. And Mimi told Marjua's son, who lived in Brazil, that she called her Tia (aunt) Maruja and that she didn't hold the title lightly. Maruja was Mimi's aunt, and if something were to happen to Marjua, Mimi would take care of her, and she did. Mimi gave her shots and took her to the hospital. She became an auntie, and it was a lovely experience. One time Mimi was in the car leaving to see a student having trouble with academics, and Marjua abruptly jumped into the passenger side. "Do you know where we're going?" Mimi asked.

"It doesn't matter," said Marjua. "I'm with you." So that's the kind of relationship they had. It was just sweet, sweet friendship.

CHAPTER 21

Medicine in the City

A lthough Cal had become acquainted with a few of the medical staff in Hospital Vozandes, the HCJB mission hospital in Quito, he was rusty on medical Spanish. With a desire to learn more of the Ecuadorian medical culture, he spoke with the director of medical education who invited Cal to attend the morning teaching rounds of the hospital.

A group of 10 or 12 interns met every morning with an experienced US doctor to discuss the cases they had admitted the previous 24 hours. The teaching rounds were conducted in a somewhat formalized but non-threatening manner, and Cal found it all fascinating. The discussions submerged him right into medical Spanish, gave him a clear idea of the medical and social problems they were dealing with, and enlightened him to the medical capabilities of the hospital and its philosophy of treatment. Cal benefited greatly from those early months of daily morning rounds.

The morning teaching rounds also gave him the opportunity to get to know many of the staff physicians as well as the interns. A small group of medical missionaries worked there, both in administration and the medical staff, but the majority of the doctors treating patients were conscientious, well-trained Ecuadorian doctors. The hospital had a strongly positive reputation in the country, allowing the hospital staff to pick from among the brightest of Ecuadorian physicians.

In discussing the various patients, Cal began to get a view of the underlying principles the Ecuador doctors applied in treating patients. In most respects their methods were similar to Cal's training. However, in some decisions the Ecuadorians applied a definite cultural distinction. Their choices dealt with some of their priorities, particularly family priorities. The Ecuadorian medical staff understood the critical importance of including family in decisions.

In the US, as an example, the patient is totally autonomous, and it is the patient and most commonly *only* the patient who can decide between the various options for medical treatment. However, in Ecuador, in many cases the patient seeks consensus within his family before deciding on treatment options, such as the choice between medical management or surgery. Medical decisions still prioritize the patient's desires, but the final decision often involves the entire extended family.

One day as Cal waited for an appointment, he sat in the waiting room close to a family who had come in from the high mountains of the country. The patient was the grandmother with a serious illness. The family had brought her for consultation at the hospital and surgery had been recommended—a surgery that would lead to an extended hospitalization and strain the family's resources. The grandmother listened quietly as the family discussed where they would get the money. One family member stated he was going to sell his flock of sheep, while another said he could sell some chickens.

Finally, the grandmother spoke up. "Enough! I am not going to have you jeopardize the future of my grandchildren by spending all this money. My hospitalization will put you into poverty. It is not worth it. Take me home." And they did. Cal began to appreciate that kind of interaction and extended family decision-making in Ecuador.

The medical education group that ran the internship planned to open a postgraduate residency program—a specialty training program—in the HCJB hospital. Of course, the various Ecuadorian specialists expressed interest. The surgeon preferred a surgical residency. The internist, who was very bright and a good teacher, wanted to open an internal medicine residency program. And some of the missionary physicians felt a Family Medicine program would be more appropriate for the needs of the country as a whole, even though Family Medicine as a specialty was unknown in Ecuador at that time.

After much deliberation, the medical education team chose Family Medicine as their first residency, a decision that excited Cal. As an outsider from another mission group and a guest by their invitation, Cal's role was primarily to listen. But as the team discussed how to put the program together, it became evident to Cal that the resources available were quite specialized, and that they were going to miss a big part of what Family Medicine was about.

Cal and Mimi had already decided to stay in Quito for an indefinite period rather than moving to the jungle, so Cal ventured to add, "You know, if you're going to have a Family Medicine residency you probably ought to include a family physician in addition to the specialists." The hospital administrative council agreed, and asked Cal to help write the initial curriculum. The training would focus on preparing doctors to work as high-quality generalists in both large and small Ecuadorian communities, rather than solely in a hospital. Many primary healthcare skills would need to be taught, skills unfamiliar to most of the specialists who spent most of their time working in the hospital environment.

This presented a problem. As a mission, HCJB applied an extensive preparation and vetting procedure before accepting a medical worker, or any other missionary, into their group, and the members primarily governed the group themselves. In other words, the entire membership voted on all major decisions. So here was Cal, a doctor who some of the staff at Vozandes Hospital felt could direct this new program, but he was not "one of them." Was he perhaps a rogue element they would not be able to control? One or two members started passing negative rumors about Cal. Fortunately, he didn't hear most of them.

Cal and Mimi had to completely trust the Lord for the outcome, having no idea how this was all going to end. Cal was certainly willing and able to help develop a Family Medicine residency program, but the final decision was out of his hands.

Missionaries go through interesting pressure sometimes. Very often the pressures they face come either from within their own mission or from other missionaries, rather than the local community. Cal quickly discovered they were no exception to that, but that the Lord in His mercy guided them through it. They did not push one way or the other, but simply waited to see what would happen. Eventually the HCJB mission resolved the problem for them.

As it turned out, the missionary in charge of personnel for the mission was a neighbor of theirs from New Zealand. He offered a solution to Cal. "I think there's only one way of resolving this. You need to become a member of this mission in addition to staying with your mission. We have a category for that. It's called an associate member. You wouldn't be a full member so you wouldn't have any voting privileges, but you would have every other privilege as a regular member. Let me see what can be done."

Within a relatively short period of time Cal was accepted as an associate member of this mission. Most of the rumors stopped. Cal heard later that some people complained about the fact that Cal had somehow "jumped the queue" and hadn't gone through all their rigorous procedures, which was true. But the responsible administrators justified Cal's associate membership since he had been there for almost a year and they knew him, so some of the vetting processes could be waived.

Cal's role involved developing, teaching, and directing the overall training program. He felt strongly that the major thrust of the teaching should be not merely talking about promoting good health and dealing with illness, and not just classroom teaching, but actually working with the residents as they saw patients. He wanted the interns to not only absorb the science of medicine, but also the holistic approach to the patient and their family within the context of their culture and society. To achieve this, Cal needed to see patients himself and ultimately see the patients together with residents in training. Family Medicine focuses on fostering a therapeutic relationship with the patient, going beyond the illness of a patient to offer care and counsel to the entire family.

The hospital directors were more than happy for Cal to see patients because they were always backlogged, so he was assigned a little exam room and two days a week to see patients. He learned a lot about examining Ecuadorian patients from the very beginning.

For example, one of his patients was a little lady in her 70s, very spry but with several medical problems. She came from up in the mountains, so most of her experience with the medical profession had been with the young rural doctors who were assigned to work in village clinics. These young doctors often struggled in dealing with patients because they had just graduated from medical school, were isolated and alone, and had few diagnostic resources.

Cal started with this elderly lady by introducing himself, asking about her complaints and how they affected her. She told him a little about her complaints, which were complex, so he asked her a series of questions to narrow down what the issues were—how long had it had been going on and what were the specific symptoms. After about the fourth or fifth question, Cal could tell she was getting agitated. She stopped his questioning and said, "Doctor, why are you asking so many questions?"

"Well, I feel I need a bit more information," Cal responded.

"You're the doctor," she said. "You're supposed to know all of this." Having observed a few doctors in rural clinics, Cal saw the usual pattern: the patient would come in, sit across the desk from the doctor, and give their primary complaint. The doctor would ask two or three questions, nod sagely, write out a prescription, and tell the patient to get it filled in the pharmacy. The whole interaction would take less than five minutes, and the patient would dutifully trot off with their medicine.

To both rural patients and doctors, the main act of medical care was writing a prescription. If the doctor tried to give some advice—you need to change your diet in this way, you need to begin exercising in this way, and so on—the patient would feel totally defrauded. To them the doctor existed to hand out prescriptions. And if the patient came away with more than one prescription, even though they had no idea what the problem was or what the medicine was supposed to do, they came away happy. That was the expectation.

This poor woman had come to Cal from that setting. He wanted to identify as clearly as possible her medical problem so he could tailor the treatment for her. He sensed her frustration and apologized. "I'm so sorry. You are absolutely right. I'm asking a lot of questions, and I know you're not used to this. The truth is I'm a foreigner, an outsider, and there are some aspects of your medical care that I'm still working to understand. And I wonder if you could help teach me. If you are willing to answer my questions, I'm going to be able to help you, I think, much more accurately, much better than some of the doctors you've seen before."

She thought about it for a minute and said, "Well, all right." So Cal asked a few more questions and got a better sense of what was going on. He wrote two prescriptions and asked her to come back a week later so he could see how she was doing. She returned a week later and this time she was all smiles as she settled in. "Doctor, just ask me anything you want."

This taught Cal that although many of the poorer patients (not only in Ecuador but almost any country in development) often have to deal with a medical system that doesn't fully meet their needs and isn't particularly interested in them as individuals, both patients and doctors can be retrained. A bit of understanding and explanation would go a long way toward giving the patient permission to participate more in their own care, to be a bit more assertive, perhaps even correcting the doctor if he or she were misunderstanding something. Up to this point, the poor or disadvantaged patients did not feel empowered to consider doing this. Cal saw this woman many times afterwards, and they developed a wonderful relationship.

CHAPTER 22

Raising Children in Quito

The three Wilson children were now teenagers. Their parents didn't want them roaming the streets of Quito, but what could they offer them? Mimi came up with the idea of "Friday Night." The premise was that the week was over, the weekend was beginning, we're all tired, so let's be tired and relax together on Friday night. The children could invite their friends, and Cal and Mimi invited their friends. Typically, 12 to 15 people showed up, wearing whatever was comfortable, the younger children in footie pajamas. The agenda for the evening was very simple—a light comfort-food type of meal, during which one or more topics of discussion were introduced. Topics varied widely but often included current events in Ecuador or other parts of the world, cultural issues, or dilemmas the children were dealing with. The only rule of discussion was that all comments, regardless of the age of the speaker, were taken seriously, and no one could feel put down. It was always fun to see how everyone, even the youngest in footie pajamas, would participate in the conversation. On some nights they might read to each other short stories they had heard that week. Later in the evening, the group often gathered around the TV for a family-appropriate DVD movie. The kids brought all the blankets and pillows from the house to the living room and made it into a huge bed where they'd watch the movie. The younger children often fell asleep on the floor or their parents' laps. It became a fun ritual, and a core group came every Friday night. All they had to say was, "We're going to have a Friday Night" and people were on board.

"We had tons of guests in our home," said Mimi. "With special guests, we tried to identify their skill or passion, such as their medical specialty or what they enjoyed, such as golfing or whatever. As they were invited, they were warned that the dinner was in their honor and our children had some questions for them. One of the children was assigned to start the discussion, so the child had to do a little bit of research and identify what they wanted to know and how they could ask it."

The children also had some unique adventures in Ecuadorian life. One night Kevin came into the house and told Mimi, "I just had a slug cross my face." They had nightmares about slugs. They were reported to sometimes go up people's nostrils. The children couldn't think of anything so gross.

"We eat those slugs," Rosa had told Mimi jokingly.

"We don't," Mimi said. That night, Mimi and Kevin went

around the garden and scooped up all the slugs they could find, probably 100 in their bucket. They gave the bucket to Rosa to dispose of, but *not to eat!*

Cal and Mimi tried to keep a pulse on how their children were doing. They realized that when the children graduated from high school in Quito they were almost certainly going to a university in the US. Cal and Mimi had heard many stories and had seen plenty of missionary children coming back to the States who felt totally out of context, struggling to adapt to US culture and norms. They didn't want that to be an issue with their children, either academically or socially. It helped that half of their classmates were missionary children, and the other half were Ecuadorian citizens. This provided a rich cross-cultural experience, but also provided many friends from America and the English-speaking world.

One thing the children lacked was familiarity with the television shows their peers in the US watched. Later, at college someone would tell a joke or refer to "Seinfeld" or "South Park" and they suddenly felt clueless. But a plus was that they were all fluent in Spanish, and had many Spanish-speaking friends.

There were things about growing up in Ecuador that would have been difficult to institute in the US, such as much greater freedom of movement. At that time the society was quite secure. Cal and Mimi didn't worry about the children being kidnapped or harmed because they were foreigners. If they went on a long walk and got lost, it was understood they could ask any Ecuadorian on the street where they were or how to get home, and this Ecuadorian would almost certainly go out of their way to help.

One Christmas Cal and Mimi gave the three children (two of them adolescents) a night alone together at one of the old haciendas in the countryside. The children caught the bus and while halfway to their destination a policeman stopped the bus and questioned what the gringo children were doing on the bus, because they were so obviously different. The other passengers on the bus in unison began reproving the police officer, shouting, "You leave them alone! They are our guests," making such a fuss that the policeman quickly said "Fine, fine," and backed away.

The entire family felt very protected. They were comforted by the acceptance and the general nature of the Ecuadorian society at that time. However, this has changed dramatically in the past decade; it is now more violent there, as it also is in the US.

CHAPTER 23

Bible Studies

*A*t the beginning of their second year in Ecuador, an American businessman named Mack Sasser, who was working with one of the oil companies in Ecuador, had started attending their English-speaking church. He invited Cal and Mimi for dinner, and as they were getting acquainted, he said, "I've got a Bible study that I've just started, and I would love it if you could come."

In that group of mostly men Cal met a young Colombian named Nestor, who supplied some of the materials needed for oil drilling in the Amazon basin. Cal could tell Nestor was uncertain about being there, in part because he wasn't sure he wanted his life to change. Nestor indicated he would be willing to continue studying the Bible, but it would be easier to do so in Spanish, and did Cal know anybody who could do it in Spanish? Cal offered to help with that.

The two men hit it off famously. Nestor had many questions and concerns, so they started opening the Scriptures to deal with some of Nestor's questions. They began meeting every week, sometimes with Nestor's wife Susana too, who had questions of her own.

Nestor had a huge network of acquaintances and friends all over Ecuador, especially, but not limited to, the Colombian community. A large number of Colombians had migrated to Ecuador in the mid-'80s, when an active civil war was going on in Colombia. Several rebel groups targeted the professional class for kidnapping or extortion, and many professionals fled for their lives to neighboring Ecuador.

Among his acquaintances Nestor found others who were interested in studying the Scriptures, so he started inviting some of his other friends, such as Remberto and Marta, Alfonso and Ines, to the weekly Bible study. Before long they had a group of eight or ten people, mostly couples, meeting on a regular basis to study Scripture. They started with the Gospels, studying each book of the Bible verse by verse, trying to understand what it said, its context, and how it related to other passages of the Scripture. They eventually progressed to studying major portions of the Old Testament, as well as the letters of the early apostles in the New Testament.

Mimi attended the Bible study too. Although she had some difficulty speaking Spanish, she could understand everything spoken in Spanish, so Mimi would simply listen, but not participate. Cal knew she had insights to offer, so he would ask her to speak in English and then translate for her. Most of the couples in this study were at a high enough professional level that they were fairly fluent in English as well, so they could understand Mimi when she spoke. This became the beginning of an incredibly close relationship with an expanding group of Latin American friends. Some Ecuadorians joined as well.

The study grew in interesting ways. For instance, one day during a trip downtown in early morning rush hour on a busy four-lane freeway, Cal suddenly ran out of gas. It was most embarrassing because he had always prided himself on being prepared enough so that didn't happen. But this day he ran out of gas, in a big American Buick.

He got out and attempted to push the car to the side of the freeway to get it out of traffic. As he struggled to get it to the side, a little car zipped around and stopped right in front of him. The driver popped out and asked in Spanish if he could help. Cal replied, "Thank you so much, you can." The man helped Cal push the car off to the side and asked what happened.

"I think I'm out of gas."

"Oh, I can take you to get some gas."

"Are you sure? You're not on your way to work?"

"No, I've got the time."

Cal hopped in his car and they drove to Cal's house where he had a container of gas. They returned to the Buick and filled it up. On their trips back and forth they quickly got to know each other. Juan was an Ecuadorian businessman who had just moved up from Cuenca, a city in the south, and was trying to get established in Quito. Detailing their difficulties, Juan mentioned, "One of the hardest things is that we had just started in a study of the Bible in Cuenca, and I was really enjoying it. I just can't find anything like that here."

"You know," Cal said, "we're part of a Bible study meeting in homes. Would you like to come and see what it's like?" Juan happily agreed and showed up at the next study with his wife, Beatrice, and they remained part of the study ever after. Cal never ran out of gas again in Ecuador but had to admit that small error was totally ordained by his heavenly Father so that he could meet Juan and Beatrice.

Over time, the study group came to include many others, primarily by invitation of those already in the group. This evolved into an eclectic group of closely knit friends who not only met to study the Bible and how its truths and principles could be applied to their individual lives, but to support each other and celebrate life's events together. Everyone's birthday was celebrated, and group outings to a beach or retreat center were common.

Even more important, spiritual growth was very evident in many of the members, and they in turn encouraged others with their stories of what God was doing in their lives and attitudes. Some of the group began to grasp the depth of Jesus' invitation to follow Him wholeheartedly, and wanting to demonstrate their commitment openly, asked to be re-baptized as believers in Jesus Christ. All had been baptized as infants by the Catholic

Church, but this group, such as Nestor, Remberto (with one of his sons), Patricia, and Alfonso, felt that they needed to declare their allegiance to Jesus as their Lord by being baptized as consenting adults. These were performed by Cal over several occasions, often during group celebrations, in local swimming pools and even a freezing cold, unused hot tub.

Over the following years, the group not only continued, but began adding other activities as well. For example, looking for an opportunity to worship together, the group added a Sunday morning gathering in addition to the mid-week gathering, with the goal of focusing on worship and praise of God. A neighboring missionary couple offered to take the children for a Sunday School class, which everyone appreciated. Some of the group members organized a semi-regular distribution of food to homeless families gathered in the central square. In addition, Cal began considering the need for long-term leadership of this group, and so offered a third gathering opportunity for those interested in studying biblical principles of spiritual leadership, primarily focusing on the characteristics and role of elders within the Church. Almost all of those who had requested adult baptism were also interested in this, and so some of the group members were meeting three times each week. Although Cal repeatedly surveyed them regarding the intensity of these activities, none were willing to do any less.

CHAPTER 24

Medicine in the Jungle

Cal had a fascination with the jungle, and especially the combination of jungle medical and mission work. He loved the lure of the unknown, the primitive aspect of it, the potential dangers, and the authentic medical and spiritual needs of isolated tribal groups. All of it appealed to him. That was one of the reasons why when they first arrived in Ecuador their original plan was to move to the eastern Amazon basin. He wanted to contribute to the medical and the spiritual needs of the jungle community in some way.

His friend, Luis Echeverria, the Chilean banker and head of Bank of America in Quito, asked Cal why he was ultimately planning to move to the eastern jungle, and Cal explained his desire to reach out to the most isolated and needy of the country. Luis provided a needed reality check for Cal. "I'm familiar with the eastern jungle. I'm not sure that area fulfills the criteria you just said you're looking for, in terms of medical and spiritual need. Missionaries have been active in that part of the jungle since the 1950s. They have a vigorous airline service run by the Missionary Aviation Fellowship, carrying people in and out with runways built all over the jungle. They have schools and established churches in many of the jungle villages. There's a mission hospital at Shell that attends to the serious medical needs. Those in need can be evacuated very shortly because of the effective radio network across the jungle. If you're really looking for something that's more pioneer work, you probably won't find it there."

Luis went on to say that he had just made a loan to a group of Ecuadorian investors who were interested in harvesting some of the heart of palm in northern Ecuador. He said most of this was harvested from a densely forested jungle area on the northern coast. "It's an extremely poor and very isolated area," Luis said. "The only access to the entire region is by means of three rivers that course through the jungle out of the Andes. I've been up one of those rivers with this investment group and have seen very few services available in that part of the country. Let me show it to you, and you can form your own opinion."

A few weeks later Luis, Cal, and Mimi drove to the coast and met with some of the investors Luis was funding. The group took a boat up one of the rivers (known as the Cayapas river) to the one evangelical mission station in the entire area, where they spent the night. They talked with the missionary, some of the indigenous Chachi people, and a few people in the small town that served as gateway to the jungle, called Bourbon. Luis was absolutely right: this area tremendously needed various services. The whole province was not often visited or considered by the central government. At least 85 percent of the entire province were black; the remainder included an indigenous tribe known as the Chachi Indians.

The story of how black people arrived in this area dates back to the days of slave trade in the 1600-1800's. Slaving ships from Africa went through the Magellan Strait at the tip of South America, then up the west coast of South America to land in Colombia or Central America, where they would sell their cargo of slaves.

Off the northern coast of Ecuador, a point of rock and shallow water juts out into the ocean. Over time, several slave ships were shipwrecked at that point, throwing their cargo of African slaves into the ocean. Survivors who made it safely to land found the jungle similar to their homes in Africa, so they escaped into the jungle and set up their own civilization.

This interesting group of people was very African. They spoke Spanish, although it had evolved into a dialect of Spanish with its own intonation and words. Many elements of their culture were very African. They coexisted but rarely mingled with the indigenous Chachi population, and Cal noted no evidence of intermarriage. The Chachi were very strict about that.

Sometime later, when Mimi was in this part of the jungle with Cal, a few moments took her back to her childhood in

Africa. Cal was changing the gas tank in their canoe so it was quiet, and Mimi heard someone singing an African tune. Where was it coming from? Around the river bend came a black mother with her baby in a tiny canoe. She was singing to the baby in Spanish, but the tune was African, a melody Mimi recalled from her childhood.

Three rivers, the Santiago, the Cayapas, and the Onzole, coalesced near the coast in this area near the gateway town of Bourbon (pronounced "Bor-bone"), but a distinct population lived on each of these three rivers. Cal found that two of the rivers already had some ongoing development work and services. On the Santiago River, a series of Catholic missions were helping the people with their development, education, and spiritual instruction. On the Cayapas River, an evangelical mission had become very involved over the previous 20+ years with the indigenous Chachi.

The Onzole River was the third river, and as far as Cal could tell it had almost no government services or Christian witness available. Over the next several months Cal traveled regularly to that area, passing through Bourbon, which was like a town right out of the Wild West. All the buildings were rough-sawn lumber; the people were rough and loud, and hardworking. There were thriving open houses of prostitution and gunfights in the streets. Almost every night one could hear gunshots for one reason or another.

A rough, deeply rutted road led to the town, ending at the river. Cal would park the 4-wheel drive vehicle, walk to the waterfront, and hire a canoe and a motorist. "Just take me as far as you can go on the Onzole River so we can get back today," he would say. They stopped at most of the small villages on the river so he could get to know some of the people and discover what resources were there. He found a few elementary schools, but they were irregularly spaced, and nothing beyond elementary school. Villages had a hard time holding onto teachers who would come for a few months and then leave. The only medical facility was in a larger village halfway up the river. The government doctor assigned there was only present half the time and did not appear very interested in helping the community. There was a government clinic and a couple of doctors in Bourbon, but the only way to get to them was by a long canoe ride. There were no roads at all cut through this jungle; everything moved via the rivers.

On Cal's third visit he took a backpack full of medications and spent a week visiting four villages at the upper end of the Onzole River. He decided to focus as far upriver as he could get. These villages were so isolated that the trip to Bourbon and the medical facility could take up to three days of paddling a canoe if no outboard motor was available. At each of the four villages, he would walk into the village and say, "I'm a doctor. Is anybody sick here?" Within a short period of time there would be a long line of people with various complaints.

Cal spent time in the villages trying to get a feel for who they were, what their life was like, and what their culture was like. People in the villages dressed simply. This was a tropical jungle, so they didn't need much clothing. Almost everyone had a supply of work clothes, and the women worked hard at keeping the clothes clean by washing them on stones in the river. Between the mold from the jungle and being washed on stones, clothing developed holes pretty quickly. However, most villagers also had a set of good clothes for a village ceremony or going to town and could look very fine when they wanted.

They all had a roof over their heads built of jungle materials. Most of the houses were built on stilts because of occasional river flooding, which could rise up to 20 feet and sweep right into the village. They cut the trees themselves and hand-sawed them into lumber. It was incredibly hard work. The only things they had to purchase to build a house were nails and sheet-metal roofing, which could be an overly-expensive cost for them. Each family had a plot of ground that had belonged to their family over hundreds of years. They grew corn, cacao, and plantains. The plots were not large fields, but simply small areas of cleared jungle.

The villagers ate well. Cal spent the first year of his visits to this river doing a health survey to determine the state of their health, and part of that included their diet. He selected a group that he asked to record everything that passed into their mouth over a three-day period, including the quantity, then he entered their logs into a computerized nutrition program. Adult males were getting an average of 1,800 calories a day, extremely balanced between protein, carbohydrates, and fat, including an adequate amount of protein. They supplemented the protein in their diet with eggs and chicken, together with occasional bush meat. It was an extremely balanced, healthy diet.

The birth rate was very high and the infant mortality rate was low, even though the babies were delivered by what appeared to be the oldest women in the village. Cal asked one acknowledged midwife how many babies she had delivered in her lifetime. She chuckled and said, "Maybe 3,000."

So they weren't all that ill except for some diseases that plagued them, such as malaria. Almost a third of the medical visits Cal saw involved malaria. It often debilitated the older folks for weeks so they couldn't work.

One thing he found medically interesting was that almost half the people Cal saw had toothaches, severely abscessed teeth that couldn't be saved; they needed to be pulled. This affected the children as well, notably because traders regularly brought sugar cane up the river and the children would suck on the sugar cane for hours on end. He felt relatively helpless encountering this on his first visit, because he could give them something for the pain, but little else. So, when he returned to Quito, Cal grabbed Ron Guderian, one of the medical missionaries whom he knew had taken special courses in emergency dental work, and asked him to teach Cal everything he knew. He taught Cal how to pull teeth with local anesthesia and allowed Cal to help with a few of the people he was treating.

Shortly after, Cal went to a local dental supply store in Quito and bought a whole set of dental extraction equipment. The next time he went up the river he was ready! He became famous in that part of the river. If someone had a toothache, Cal could give them an anesthetic and pull the tooth with hardly any pain. Since many, both adults and children, had suffered from rotten teeth and abscesses for months, they were most happy to have them out.

Thanks to Luis's helpful advice, the Onzole River opened for Cal the opportunity for the pioneer medical work and perhaps the spiritual work for which he had longed. Eventually Cal committed to visiting the river villages for a week of every month. Cal catalogued and kept records of the medical problems he encountered so he would know what medical resources to bring back up the river on the next trip.

CHAPTER 25

Mimi and the Handicapped

When Mimi arrived in Quito with Cal and the children and their 21 pieces of luggage she kept wondering what she was going to do in this place, since she did not speak much Spanish. She was going to have to think of something that was beyond the language. She wanted to make sure the children knew she was there for them, and that they could draw strength from her since Cal would be making regular trips into the jungle. She made life as fun as she could so they were not apprehensive. They did very well and began speaking Spanish far sooner than she did.

But Mimi was in an unusually free situation. The children were all in school and were doing well. They didn't need her to stay home and make sure they did their homework; they just did it. Her struggles with Spanish inhibited what would have typically been an active speaking ministry for her.

She basically stumbled into what became a very satisfying and meaningful involvement in the lives of others. It began with a blind boy in a piano shop. She learned about a boy around eight years old who had a gift for music. He was blind and so could not read music, but one of the premier piano teachers in Quito had seen his potential and taken him on as a student. The boy's family was poor and couldn't afford to buy a piano, so every day the mother would go from one piano store to another asking for the chance for her son to practice. One of the stores was located in the central mall of a modern shopping center in Quito. This little fellow made friends with the owner who gave him an open invitation to sit down and start playing right there in the mall. The owner considered it good marketing for his pianos. One of Mimi's friends witnessed this and told Mimi the story.

This so touched Mimi that she decided to hold a special concert just for the piano teacher and this boy. One of her Ecuadorian friends, Winnie Wright, arranged for an excellent concert venue. The boy would play first and then the maestro would play. And since Mimi would not consider putting the child on stage unless she could dress him as she would her own child, she hired a tailor to make him a little velvet suit, using a pattern similar to that worn by the Vienna Boys Choir. He tried it on and looked darling in it. She bought small glasses and glued pieces of x-ray film on the inside to simulate dark glasses. They charged a reasonable fee for the concert tickets, the venue was satisfyingly filled, and with the profit they were able to give the family enough to purchase a piano.

At the conclusion of the concert, Mimi held a reception at her home for the boy, his mother, and the piano teacher. However, Rosa was skeptical, as she was still getting to know Mimi and her motivations. In her experience being raised in poverty, most people only used the poor for their own benefit. Was this really going to benefit the boy? She asked the mother probing questions about Mimi's involvement in their family, which was interesting for Mimi to observe and realize there were many cultural issues and barriers yet to deal with. Years later, Mimi heard that the blind boy had received a scholarship for music training in Germany.

Mimi's dream was to help handicapped children like this boy come to the best of their abilities so people could see they were not incapacitated or disabled, but simply "differently-abled." She had never worked with the handicapped before, although her heart was always with them. With the help of Rosa and the women of influence whom she was meeting in Quito, Mimi became deeply involved with helping Ecuadorians develop their own ways of serving the handicapped.

It bothered Mimi tremendously that people with handicaps in Ecuador were described as *minusvalido*, which disturbingly sounds like "less worthy." She could see the potential of these people, and the idea that they would be called less worthy was more than she could bear.

She began to hear stories of families with a handicapped child, such as one with cerebral palsy. They were so ashamed of the child, believing he or she reflected poorly on the family, that they would keep the child confined, sometimes chained, to a bed in a back bedroom for basically their entire childhood. It didn't always happen that way, but it occurred often enough, especially in the poorer families who had few resources to even know where to look for help. Often the husband would not take any credit for the child's condition, blaming the wife for producing him a defective child. He would often leave the home, exacerbating the problem for the wife who now had to provide both resources and care for the entire family, including the handicapped child.

What could Mimi do? She wanted to present to the public the best that these handicapped people can do, so they would not be seen as a drain on the country. She began to imagine how she could invest in one child at a time, and bring out the best in this child. She had done it with the child prodigy pianist; that was a beginning.

One day the doorbell rang and Mimi answered it to find Rosa with two men, one of whom was carrying a tiny wisp of a person, a terribly misshaped girl with cerebral palsy. Rosa knew this little girl named Monica, who was around 12 years old and often seen at the village trash dump scrounging for food. Her mother had sold her into prostitution. She was filthy and horribly malnourished.

Rosa became aware that two men were in Monica's house that day, having their way with her. So Rosa quickly recruited two other men and went to the house, where they were told to "go away." The men with Rosa broke down the door, chased away the two abusers, picked up Monica, and brought her to Mimi's house. "Could you take care of her?" Rosa asked.

Mimi held the child in her arms as she listened to her story. She could feel the lice crawling over her from this child and could tell that the girl had not had proper care for many years.

What could Mimi do with her? The first thing she did was bathe her. She took all her towels and lined the bathtub with them. She filled the tub with warm water and gently lowered the little girl into the water. Mimi suspected this child had never had a warm bath, because she reacted as if the water was cold, but it was not.

At this moment Mimi found herself reliving a recurring memory from her childhood in Congo. She was considered an invalid as a child because she could not overcome the repeated cycles of malaria that kept her in bed for many weeks. One time she was so ill with a combination of strep throat and malaria that her mother decided to drive her to the doctor, a two-to-three-hour drive away. As they were getting ready to go, they received word that a missionary had been in a car accident and were asked to pick her up on the way and take her with them to the hospital. The woman lay delirious in the backseat of their car, conscious but very ill. At the doctor's home the doctor's wife was so gracious. She lined the bathtub with pillows, filled it with warm water, and settled the woman's sore body on the pillows. This image of the woman's kindness was one of the most impactful memories of Mimi's childhood.

"I want to have a big house, marry a doctor, and take care of sick people," Mimi told her mother during that visit. Her mother looked at her sickly daughter doubtfully. The next morning Mimi overheard her mother telling the guests at the breakfast table about Mimi's desire, and she could hear them all laughing in disbelief that this child would ever do anything like that. But here she was, married to a doctor, living in a big house, and caring for a sick child with the same level of tenderness that she had once witnessed. Only an eternal God could fulfill that childhood dream!

That evening Monica ate and ate. It devastated Mimi to think of this child being continually abused. As Mimi laid Monica on the bed, the girl suddenly became very frightened; Mimi put the mattress on the floor so she would not fear falling off.

Monica desperately needed a safe place to live, but there was no place for that level of care. This was the beginning of Mimi's understanding of the tremendous need for facilities and assistance for this type of child. She searched for some sort of permanent housing for Monica and other children who needed 24/7 care.

Through a generous friend in the US they were given $65,000 to establish such a place. Mimi found a woman named Elena Vasconez who played a significant role in a non-profit group called Camp Hope, that provided day care and rehabilitation services for disabled children. This group assisted in the renovation of a house that they called the *Casa* (house) *Hogar* (home), a Spanish play on words, and ended up incorporating the administration and care of the children at Casa Hogar into the services and work of Camp Hope.

After Rosa had settled Monica in bed, she began thinking about how she had been forced to break down the door to rescue her. Other people lived in this house. Rosa fixated on the fact that *Nobody should have a house that doesn't have a secure door and I've broken this door down.* So with her own money she hired men to fix the door.

Years later, at age 46, Monica was still living at Casa Hogar, able to dress and feed herself after occupational and physical therapy. Then, interestingly, Monica's mother came to Rosa, indicated that she was now following Jesus and was repentant of the grave harm she had brought to her daughter. She asked if Monica could come back to live with her. "I'm a different person than I was then," she told Rosa. As far as Mimi knows Monica is still living with her mother, who is now a changed woman.

Meanwhile, Mimi turned her focus to the large number of deaf children in Ecuador. Mimi's cousin-in-law Cindy Scott had worked with the deaf community in the US, and she told Mimi of a British woman, Dr. Morag Clark, who traveled the world demonstrating a method for teaching deaf children to speak. Dr. Clark was setting up national programs in various countries to continue this work. This resonated with what Mimi was trying to do, helping deaf children to be seen as contributing to society.

While serving as headmistress of a school for deaf children in England, Morag Clark had begun noticing that the few children who had been fitted with the best, most modern type of hearing aids often began to learn how to mimic some words. She found that if one took a child less than a year of age who was just in the stage where most children would be forming speech patterns and fitted those children with a hearing aid of sufficient power to overcome a good part of their deafness, those children would actually learn how to speak in a nearly normal voice.

She learned that the best way to teach a child to speak was simply to foster the manner in which parents normally taught their child how to speak. She began campaigning for a new system of dealing with deaf children, which included: 1) identify them early, 2) put hearing aids on them, make sure they're working, and keep them working; and 3) encourage the parents to continue the natural techniques they would normally use to teach their children how to speak—by prattling on to their children in the normal course of the day. More than anything she encouraged parents to simply spend time talking naturally with their child. With adequate hearing aids, these children would learn how to speak, and would integrate into their normal surroundings, the only difference from other children being that they had to wear hearing aids.

After 20 years as headmistress, Morag had been invited by the then-President of Turkey, who had a deaf child, to set up a program for deaf children in the capital city of Ankara. She worked there for seven years and was so successful she was invited to several other countries. Mimi invited her to come to Ecuador for the first of many visits with the Wilsons, funded by the British Council. Morag would come and consult, and then go back to wherever she was currently working in the world.

A new administration had just been elected in Ecuador, and one of the responsibilities of the president's wife was funding and administering the social action programs in the country. The incoming president and his wife were good friends with some of the influential people Cal and Mimi had come to know in their beginning days in Quito. The president's wife asked one of those friends, Winnie Wright, who had procured the blind boy's piano concert venue, to be her administrator. Within a few days of being named to that position, Winnie invited Mimi to meet with her at the presidential palace. Winnie looked at Mimi and said, "Can you imagine? Here I am in the position of managing the funds for social services all over this country! I have millions of dollars at my disposal, but I don't know where to start. Could you help me set some priorities?"

Mimi had just visited with Morag Clark and could see the potential for what could be done for deaf children in Ecuador. She suggested that Dr. Clark's program include as many of the deaf children in the country as possible and Mrs. Wright agreed. They set up a center for deaf children just outside of Quito, a large complex of buildings, and hired staff. They bought many hearing aids and started a national program to identify and treat deaf children throughout the country, especially the younger children.

Dr. Clark insisted they work with the parents to help them understand that their child may not be able to hear well, but they are not less valuable. With the use of hearing aid technology, most deaf children could be taught to listen and then speak, and could be integrated into normal schools and society, without the need for a sign language translator. The program became well integrated into Ecuadorian social services, and continues to this day.

There were other children in need as well. Mimi was contacted by the mission hospital at Shell, where a young Ecuadorian girl who lived on the edge of the jungle, had run out in front of a truck. The truck ran over her and crushed both of her legs. Both had been amputated, and the surgeon asked if Mimi could help her get artificial limbs. In Quito a couple of technicians knew how to fit and even construct artificial limbs. What they couldn't do was match the technology of a knee joint, which needed to be very finely machined. If Mimi could provide them a high-quality joint, they could make the rest of the prosthesis. So every time they visited the US, Mimi asked for donations of discarded prosthetic limbs. In returning through Ecuadorian customs, Mimi's duffel was full of artificial joints and limbs. She developed a little speech in case she was asked about it, "You just never know when you might need a limb!"

The little girl, about seven years old, came with a travel companion to stay at the Wilson's home while receiving her artificial legs in Quito. Using the prescribed exercises, Mimi worked with the child to show her how to transfer her weight to the two prostheses. Rosa watched Mimi's attempts and said, "This isn't working too well. Let me take her." Rosa took the child to her house and within one week Rosa returned with the little girl walking on her new legs. The doctor who fitted her was amazed at her quick progress, exclaiming, "I've never seen anything like it!" No one knows what Rosa put the girl through, but she learned how to walk that week.

Rosa was now an invaluable part of the family, and Cal and Mimi struggled with how to pay her what she was truly worth. They gave her a monthly stipend, which was on the upper edge of the accepted rate for a housekeeper among the expat population. But Rosa went so far above and beyond what was expected of a housekeeper. For example, when they'd go on a weeklong family trip, leaving the house empty, Rosa would move in to keep it safe and secure, bringing her own family over for the week. When her annual review was due, Cal realized that although she had done so much above and beyond what a housekeeper does, he could not raise her salary any higher. He was afraid he could be accused of distorting the traditional salary structure of the country. But there was another way to increase her pay, and that was to give Rosa a big promotion in job title.

In Spanish there's a special title, *mayordomo*, that goes back hundreds of years in Latin American and Spanish history. The *mayordomo* was the overseer of the entire ranch or farm, and was basically in charge of everything. He hired and he fired the other employees and was answerable only to the owner of the estate. "You've been working as a *mayordomo*, and because of that I'm going to pay you as a *mayordomo*," Cal said, and doubled her salary. Rosa wiggled in a very pleased sort of way but then looked around the house and said, "It's not much of a ranch!" Although Cal and Mimi wanted to recognize Rosa's value to them with the increased pay, they also knew that most of her money would continue to go where it had always gone—to meet the basic needs of the very poor in her barrio, all in the name and in the spirit of Jesus Christ.

CHAPTER 26

Pioneer on the Onzole River

*A*fter Cal's third journey up the Onzole River with medical and dental supplies, the traditional leaders of one of the larger villages, Santo Domingo del Onzole, called Cal to an evening meeting. They had built a big bonfire in the middle of the soccer field and the entire village gathered around, at least 200 people.

One of the spokesmen for the village elders gave a long speech on the health problems they were encountering, such as malaria and cholera, and insisted they needed medical care. "We are going to do what we can to make it possible," he said. "The first thing we're going to do is build a clinic and living quarters for the doctor and whomever he wants to bring up. It's going to take some money."

The spokesman ceremoniously pulled out his wallet and threw some bills down on the dirt at his feet. The night was pitch black except for the bonfire. "Now this is what I'm putting in. What about you?" He waited and slowly people got up, men and women, with money in their hands and ceremoniously threw it down on the pile. When the event ended, he proclaimed, "This is a good start." And it was. They began building that month.

In his visits to this series of villages, Cal had gained a good idea of what they needed. He accepted the offer of this village to set up a more permanent medical presence there. They were building a clinic, but it was going to take some real funding to make it functional, and with his commitments in Quito Cal wasn't going to be able to work full time in the jungle. One week out of the month was not enough to meet the medical needs of the population or get to know the people and be part of their village life. He would have to form a team of Ecuadorian health professionals who would be able to stay on the river long-term. The government was not interested in setting up a clinic in that part of the jungle, so he would need to provide support for the medical team.

During a six-week visit to the US that year, Cal had lunch with a successful businessman from their church. He asked Cal how he was doing, what was going on. Cal described how he had just started working in some jungle villages, that there were tremendous medical as well as spiritual needs, and that it was going to take a more permanent presence. The business-man, appreciating efficiency, focused on the fact that it took an average of two full days of travel each way to get in and out of that area: one day of travel by car, then at least another full day of travel by canoe. Cal was only able to be present in the village four to maybe five days per trip. The friend remarked, "Boy, that's a lot of time to travel!"

"Yes, that it is. But there's no other way. There are no roads, no nothing," said Cal. "You couldn't even cut an airstrip because it is hilly country."

"There isn't any other way you could get in?"

Cal said somewhat sardonically, "Well, the only other way I could get in would be by helicopter, but that's not feasible."

The friend became very quiet and finally said, "A helicopter, huh? I can get you a helicopter."

"Now wait a minute. A helicopter?" Cal did a quick mental calculation and said, "You know, it's going to probably cost close to a million dollars to buy and operate a helicopter in Ecuador! We'd have to hire a pilot to fly it. We'd have to have hangar space in Quito. There's going to be ongoing maintenance and so on. That's an incredible … no, that's not feasible."

The businessman said, definitively, "You need a helicopter. I'll get you a helicopter!"

Cal mentally visualized the impact a helicopter would have on the village people. He was trying to identify with them in their poverty and their need, but in this scenario he would descend from the clouds in this whirly-bird and be deposited on their soil to work his magic, only to be lifted up again a few days later. He thought *no, that's not the kind of image I want to leave with these poor village people.* So he said, "I really appreciate that. But look, for a quarter of what you're proposing to spend on a helicopter, I could do wonders in the villages there."

The friend said, "Okay, give me a proposal." So Cal did. He took the friend at his word for a quarter of a million dollars, outlining a five-year proposal that would shorten his travel time by using Mission Aviation Fellowship flights to the coast. From there he would meet the canoe. That would eliminate the drive, allowing him to get in and out in one day. In addition, the donation would allow for a sturdier canoe and the salaries and upkeep for the entire health team who would work there. The friend was true to his word and readily accepted the proposal. What was most wonderful to Cal was how they again saw the Lord supply what was needed in a clear and unmistakable way, just as the opportunity presented itself. It was yet another strong affirmation of God's direction and provision, even when a huge amount of funding was needed.

With this funding, Cal affiliated the project with a local Ecuadorian non-profit organization called CENAD that had similar goals and that had previously been involved in re-building activities following an earthquake on the coast, and included a spiritual focus in their development work. They were wrapping up those activities and were interested in getting involved in another area and could provide administrative help. They could hire the medical team so Cal didn't have to go through the legalities of being their employer. They insisted on a social worker as well, because they wanted to understand the whole culture. Under these auspices, Cal began the search for the medical team—a doctor, a dentist, and a nurse—in Quito. He looked for individuals who were more adventurous, who were willing to live for an extended period in primitive circumstances. Although it wasn't a requirement to be part of the health team, Cal looked for those he knew to be strong believers and capable teachers to include the spiritual development of interested villager when he wasn't there. He paid them a bit more than the government would pay them and was able to find some very dedicated people. A community-oriented nurse, Patty, quickly fell in love with the people and they with her. This caring was also evident with the doctor (Marcelo) and the dentist (Gabrielle) who were committed to community village work.

This new team's responsibility was to live in the village of Santo Domingo and provide ongoing medical care to the five primary villages of the upper river system. Cal told the village leaders that a full team of up to six people was coming, so they built a two-story clinic. The ground floor contained all the clinic facilities—medical room, storage, and dental suite, while the second story was living quarters for the team.

Cal discovered quickly in working with the medical team that they had all been brought up in the city with comforts and conveniences, and to live in such a rural, primitive area was as much of a culture shock for them as it was for any North American going to the mission field. It was a mission field for them as well. He had to help them understand the culture, and resolve that even though the people were different, the medical team could still relate to them. The team took this on well, but they also insisted they had to leave the village for at least a week every month to recharge with their families and feel some of the cool Quito air. That started a five-year preventive health development project in the northern jungles of Ecuador.

CHAPTER 27

Mimi on the River

In the beginning, Mimi didn't accompany Cal on his monthly trips up the Onzole River because she needed to stay with the children and had a full range of activity going on in Quito. She waited until radio contact had been established in the village so they could communicate with the children, and then she joined Cal on her first journey by canoe.

It was a huge canoe, four or five feet wide and 35 feet long, carved from one solid tree trunk, and outfitted with a small outboard motor. It held 20 passengers, and the custom on the river was that if a passing canoe was going your way and had space, they would give you a ride. There was a lot of sickness on the river, and Jorge, the boatman, would explain to the Wilsons why a given person wanted them to stop.

Mimi wore as much insect repellent and sunscreen as a body could take because her skin is so fair, and a big hat. Her bench seat was hard and uncomfortable, but she focused on the details of life on the river around her. One indigenous Chachi family came into view on the shore and Jorge knew them, because Jorge knew everyone on the river. The wife was four months pregnant and had symptoms of cholera. Could they take the family upriver and help her at the clinic? They took on the husband and wife as their children watched from the shore.

The mother was conscious but extremely dehydrated and barely able to walk. The primary symptom in cholera is extremely high-volume diarrhea, not just water but water and all the salts in one's body, which quickly produces severe dehydration and death. There was nothing in the canoe for her to drink, so Jorge pulled over to the side of the river and cut several coconuts, dumping them into the canoe. Another passenger pulled an envelope of rehydration salts from her purse, and Cal mixed it with the coconut milk. He explained to the husband how crucial it was that he keep pushing liquids. When he went back to check on the woman later, the husband hadn't given her any of the coconut to drink, so Cal stayed to get liquid into the woman's mouth. Suddenly Cal's jungle work came into sharp focus for Mimi, because this woman needed urgent help and Cal could give it.

When they reached the clinic, the villagers watching were visibly leery. They knew she had cholera, and that it was highly contagious. Cal started her on an IV, quickly pushing several liters of fluid, and was relieved they had gotten her to the clinic alive. She was now visibly more alert and improved.

Mimi was amazed at what Cal had done in the short time he had been making trips up the Onzole River. Here was a full-fledged clinic, and on the upper floor were the teams' beds. Having grown up in the Congo she knew what it took to get something like this going and she found it absolutely incredible. People came to the clinic and the team doctor patiently took them one by one, consulting with Cal as needed.

Cal went about his business and a half hour later Mimi went to check on the woman to find her kicking, restless and agitated. Cal came right away when Mimi called. He said, "She's dehydrated again and now in shock." Her blood pressure had risen with the IV but then plummeted to dangerous levels, which meant she had again lost a significant volume of her body fluids. Cal had left the husband with instructions to continue to give her sips of fluids–rehydration salts mixed with purified water– in addition to the IV every few minutes. Cal asked if he had given any fluids by mouth, and the husband responded, "No. She didn't want to take it." Cal knew that the Chachi people believed that if someone has diarrhea the best way to stop it was to stop taking fluids and food. This method may work well with simple gastroenteritis, but it is fatal with cholera.

Cal's response at that point was not delicate or empathetic. He hissed, "You may have just killed your wife by not insisting she take this fluid!" This shocked the husband, to see himself as personally responsible, and he again started pushing the fluids.

The woman stabilized, her pregnancy continued, and later when Cal and Mimi took their return canoe trip down the river the husband and wife were aboard. As they dropped off the couple at their village, Mimi saw a little boy on the cliff, his eyes pasted on the river. How many days and hours had he waited for his mother to return? It was a thrill to be able to return her to him, and to hear later that she had delivered a healthy baby.

Cal gave a large supply of tetracycline to the chief of the village where the woman with cholera lived, with instructions on its use, as well as advising boiling of the drinking water to decrease the risk of others contracting the cholera. In the past this group had been reluctant to accept medicine from the white doctor because they trusted more in their traditional beliefs. It took the close call of this young mother to convince them his ways might be acceptable.

Mimi's presence in Santo Domingo created quite a stir. Several of the villagers stopped Cal and expressed joy at being able to meet Mimi and finally see the doctor's wife. Then they'd ask how long they'd been married. "Twenty-five years? You can stay with the same woman for 25 years?!" It boggled their minds. A couple of young men asked Cal, "Well, you have other women on the side, don't you?"

"No, no, I'm very happy with her," Cal replied.

This was so shocking that it led to a group of men, especially those who were interested in spiritual development, to say, "You've got to talk to us about what the Bible says about marriage. We've never heard this before." Cal agreed to hold a meeting that evening.

In the culture of the blacks on the river they would typically start pairing off in their late teens. They'd stay together for two or three years, usually a child or two were born, and then one or the other would decide it was time to move on. More often than not it was the woman who basically said, "I'm tired of this guy" and she would kick him out, take her children, and go looking for another guy. The children always stayed with the wife, but the culture said the father of the children was responsible for paying for their care.

This started for women between 16 and 18 years old, and by the time they were 30, they had an average of eight to ten children and at least five to six fathers of these children. Every month the women would go around to the various fathers and collect what was due her for his children. As they became older, usually in their 40s, a man and a woman might choose to spend the rest of their lives together, with a lifespan that wasn't all that great. No marriage, no divorce, just this steady round-robin of partnering. The only major injuries seen in the clinic were those caused by a drunken brawl where two men who were fighting over the same girl would pull out their machetes and go at each other, then show up at the clinic to get patched up.

When Cal walked into the town hall for the meeting at 7:00, the hall was full: men and women, almost the entire village from the age of 10 and up. As he began talking there was dead silence. He read various Bible verses that talk about marriage and how God from the beginning had intended that the woman would stay with a man and the man would not leave the woman; they were truly one flesh that couldn't be pulled apart. He talked about the sanctity of the sexual act and how Jesus felt about changing partners. Then the questions started, all kinds of practical questions, like "What if she doesn't know how to cook? What do you do then?"

Cal said, "My wife didn't know how to cook when we were first married. And she learned. My mother taught her and she learned very well. She's an excellent cook now. In fact, she's published a cookbook." The meeting lasted for nearly three hours, leaving Cal exhausted.

The next morning Mimi asked Cal how the meeting had gone. She didn't attend, assuming it would be only men. "What was it you said?" she asked, because that morning the men in the village had been treating her like royalty. She couldn't walk down the stairs without one holding on to her. They thought Mimi must be very special to agree to stay with this man for this great length of time.

Cal hoped the meeting would create ripples of change, but it didn't. The culture was too strong for that. Only one couple appeared to stay together; the husband was the main shopkeeper who brought food and hardware supplies from downriver and sold them in the village. He had the only mobile phone that worked in the village and a propane refrigerator, which was uncommon. The woman was the teacher at the elementary school in the village and stuck with him for the sake of their three children. She had left the village early, obtained a good education, and returned to stick it out year after year. She became Mimi's best friend in the village.

Both the husband and wife were interested in following Jesus. Besides having regular Bible studies with them and trying to deepen their understanding of walking with the Lord, Cal talked to them about marriage and encouraged them to consider being the first ones in the village in generations to go through the marriage ceremony. They seriously considered it, but in the end, the woman said, "It's too great a risk; I'm not sure I want to stay with this guy my whole life."

Mimi was delighted to be able to sit around the table enjoying a meal with the medical team. It was apparent that Cal and Mimi lived in another world, but she thought of a way to try to bridge the gap. As she typically did with guests at home, Mimi suggested some table talk.

She proposed the question, "If you had been born the other gender, what do you wish you might have done?" Jorge, the huge boatman built like an ox, thought for a moment, and then snickered, "I would never think of that!" and that was the end of the discussion.

The villagers watched Mimi closely, and she knew she needed to provide a good example, including the use of the new latrine that Cal was trying to teach the people to use. He had had it constructed near the clinic a short distance up a hill so everybody could see it.

Mimi was watchful of and concerned about snakes. A six-foot anaconda had swum right alongside their canoe on the river, and she considered that far too close for comfort. As Mimi approached the latrine, she heard something swimming below. She wanted to go someplace else, but of course she couldn't put back the village's development with the rumor, "The doctor's wife didn't even use the outhouse!" So she waited, hoping the midday sun would cast rays such that she could see down to the bottom of the pit. She waited until the sun sent rays through a hole in the roof down to the bottom and she could see … frogs! Huge frogs. Well, she would not sit on an anaconda, but she didn't mind sitting on a frog, which was a great relief.

CHAPTER 28

Development of the Village Church

*C*al's goal as a believer was not just to provide medical care, but also to offer spiritual development to those who were interested. So while setting up the medical system for the upper river, Cal made it known to the village leaders that he was a Christian who loved God and was happy to teach those who were interested more about God and what the Bible taught about themselves and God's love for them.

When he offered a specific time and place for a Bible study, out of a village of 250 perhaps five or six showed up, most of them young men. Cal started the study in the Gospels and asked them to think about and comment on what they were reading, and how they might understand it more. When Cal wasn't there, Marcelo, the first team doctor, was happy to continue the discussions.

Three or four young men, all teenagers, showed authentic

interest in the Bible. One of them was Sixto, which means the sixth. His mother couldn't come up with a new name, so she just named him Sixto because he was the sixth child. He had never studied the Scripture for himself, but he was always interested in spiritual things. When Cal asked him how his spiritual interest began, he said, "As a child. I always wanted to know God. Even when the priest wasn't here, I'd go into the church to think and pray." There was a tiny Catholic church in the village that the priest would visit perhaps once a year. "I'd go into the church and just kneel down. I didn't know how to pray but I tried to pray and then I'd go about my day," adding, "I really want to know what the Bible says about God so I can follow Him better."

Lindon was another exceptional young man. Both Sixto and Lindon were among the stars of the village's soccer team. Lindon was the player that teammates and opponents alike referred to as *Abogado*, the Spanish word for advocate, or lawyer, because whenever there was a conflict on the soccer field, such as a disputed call, Lindon the advocate would step in, make peace, and encourage the game to go on. He was the peacemaker in the village.

At one of the town meetings, Cal proposed he train a few young people in the village to function as paramedics. When and if the medical team wasn't there, the paramedics could be the go-to people for immediate medical care. Eventually, when the team had to leave, the paramedics could take on the responsibility of public healthcare in the upper river area. Cal proposed a two-year training program for them and asked the village elders who they thought it should be. They considered this for two or three days and suggested Sixto and Lindon, saying that these two were by far the most responsible young people in the village, and they would like them to be their health workers.

So the two were trained in emergency medical care, preventive healthcare including how to give immunizations and how to talk parents into accepting immunizations, how to prevent diseases like cholera from taking hold in the village, how to sew up lacerations, how to treat infections especially in children, how to recognize problems that pregnant women might be having, and so on. Sixto and Lindon became the health workers of the village.

Cal had started the clinic by requesting five years of funding. His goal was to set up the infrastructure that would allow the village to continue on its own, maintaining the health not only of Santo Domingo, but the other four villages on the upper Onzole River. It was hoped that eventually the Ministry of Health would acknowledge the need for services in that remote area, even though up to that point they had failed to even visit this part of the river. Cal told the villagers at the very beginning that he was going to be visiting there for five years, and for five years only. At the end of five years he was going to be gone, leaving them with everything that he had brought in, especially the health training of the women and of Sixto and Lindon. After that period, they would have to manage on their own with the workers whom he had trained. The primary reason behind this emphasis was to avoid creation of a long-term dependence on outside funding and intervention, and to promote greater self-sufficiency of the village population.

Cal noticed that in the fourth year of the project the village elders were still suggesting new things that he could do or ways that he could continue the health work or expand it. He had to remind them, "You know, in one year I'm going to have to leave." They finally believed him, and that last year they accomplished far more than they had in the previous four, such as setting up a community trash dump and a network of latrines. Before that most everybody just dumped their trash out their window or used the river for their needs. The Ministry of Health was working on latrine development in the rural areas and provided concrete slabs to cover the hole of the latrine. Cal worked with the government to bring in many slabs for the village so individual houses could start building their own latrines.

Because of his contacts with the Ministry of Health in the province, Cal learned that the provincial Ministry of Health had agreed to accept the two men he had trained as health workers as official Ministry of Health employees. The Ministry of Health would supply them with the necessary medical supplies and medications, so Sixto and Lindon could continue applying their training. On that basis Cal felt comfortable leaving the jungle medical work to the villagers themselves.

Years later the government built a health clinic in that

village, with government-funded nurses and a doctor. On a return visit to Santo Domingo, Cal visited the new, nicely appointed, clean, and well-run government clinic. The nurses were solicitous and obviously capable and interested in working toward the health of the community. Cal asked them how Lindon was working out as the village health worker. They said, "Oh, Lindon, we could not exist here if it were not for him! He knows the people, he knows how to get things done, and he is extremely capable in terms of managing health problems. He is the axis around which this clinic revolves!"

Sixto had gone a different path. He worked as a health worker in that village for some time, but he wanted to continue his own spiritual development in full-time ministry. Cal had introduced him to his original mentor in Shell, Lloyd Rogers. Lloyd had the same passion as Cal did for equipping local people, so Lloyd had sent Sixto to a Bible school in Argentina for a four-year training program.

Upon his return to Ecuador, Sixto continued working with Lloyd, taking occasional ministry trips into the eastern jungle. But after the end of the Onzole villages project and his study in Bible school, Sixto spent most of his time in his home village of Santo Domingo. He continued teaching the Bible to anyone interested, and started a new church in the village that grew rapidly and became a major influence in the region.

CHAPTER 29

Growth of Family Practice Medicine in Quito

*D*uring the three weeks each month that Cal spent in Quito, he was intensely involved with setting up and strengthening a university-based postgraduate program in Family Medicine through the HCJB mission Hospital Vozandes. He worked to get all the stakeholders involved, collaborated with the university directors, and participated in curriculum development and active clinical teaching for the residents. He also coordinated with the directors of the Medical College of Ecuador to ensure they would accept the graduates in this new specialty.

Cal spent a lot of time talking to people, explaining what Family Medicine is and how it could improve primary health care across the country. For the most part, the medical and the university authorities accepted the new concept of Family Medicine. The postgraduate program began very small, with just two residents, Jose Eras and Susana Alvear. The following year it took on another three, and the next year another four.

The three-year program required extensive individual teaching and supervision on Cal's part. The residents trained in the HCJB Vozandes Hospital, although they attended other hospitals for specific training such as the National Pediatric Hospital for their pediatric rotation or the National Obstetric Hospital for their obstetric rotation. For rural and community medicine they went to the sister mission hospital in the village of Shell that worked with the jungle communities.

Cal particularly adapted the curriculum and focus of training to *not* look like a US residency program. He placed emphasis on a strong community focus and community development. He applied what he was learning on the Onzole River in many ways.

With the goal of training the new family physicians to work within the local community rather than in a hospital setting, Cal encouraged one of the two existing Ecuadorian family physicians (Dr Ritha Bedoya, recently trained in Mexico) to develop a private physician's office which could also serve as a training site. As the program progressed, the Vozandes Hospital realized it would serve their interests to have a series of local Family Medicine offices in Quito feeding patients to them. Consequently, the Hospital provided some of the funding to develop a new training clinic just a block from the Hospital.

Cal designed the clinic, which included one-way mirrors in two of the exam rooms that enabled a faculty member to sit behind the one-way mirror and observe the examinations and discuss the patient encounters with the resident later. Every patient was asked for permission to be observed through the dark glass mirror, and assured the curtain would be drawn if they were hesitant.

Jose and Susana, the first two Family Medicine residents graduated from the program in 1991 with a master's certificate from the Catholic University of Cuenca, to Cal's great delight. Shortly thereafter, the Medical College of Ecuador registered the first graduates as specialists in Family Medicine, which entitled them to practice; Susana working as an attending clinician and teacher in the Vozandes training clinic, and Jose beginning a private practice in Quito. As more family physicians graduated in the following years, the Vozandes Hospital continued to help establish additional Family Medicine clinics in other parts of Quito. The Hospital also paid a portion of the new graduates' initial salary until the patient population grew. Within a few years, each of the new Family Medicine centers was well established and self-sufficient, and the program grew to six to eight new residents per year.

The new family physicians gained quick recognition as outstanding clinicians within the medical profession and the general population. With a high level of quality, they could deal with a much larger scope of illnesses than many of the general doctors in practice at that time. Their initial patients brought their entire extended family for care, and word quickly spread about the "great doctors." Their affiliation with the respected Vozandes Hospital added to their reputation, along with their degree from the Catholic University of Cuenca. Another university, the Catholic University of Quito, was at the same time trying to re-orient their medical school curriculum more toward community-based medicine rather than hospital-based medicine. They hired Dr. Susana Alvear to serve on their faculty and later included several other newly graduated Family Physicians as well.

CHAPTER 30

Burnout

Life in Ecuador overflowed with activities, all of them fun and good and beneficial to others. As one of a limited faculty able to teach Family Medicine at the hospital in Quito, much of Cal's time went to teaching. Mimi was extremely busy running the house, hosting guests almost daily, and working with the handicapped, deaf and blind children. Cal and Mimi's weekly Bible study in their home expanded to three meetings per week to match the spiritual growth of some participants. In addition, they had to keep in touch with supporters and other contacts back in the US, including visiting teachers to teach elements of the Family Medicine curriculum, visitors interested in Mimi's work with handicapped children, and individuals interested in the work on the Onzole River. Including the monthly trips to the villages on the Onzole River … it was a lot.

Although neither Cal nor Mimi recognized it initially, they were both getting burned out. Part of the burnout showed itself in their marriage. They had a hard time feeling close to each other due to working in different spheres. Some interaction overlapped, particularly when they had visitors at the house, but they started to drift apart and to find fault with each other. Each of them was leaning on the other for support, and yet because they were both overwhelmed with tasks and responsibilities, neither of them could provide the kind of support the other needed. Cal began to think Mimi was not an appropriate match for what he was doing. At the same time, Mimi was beginning to think she had married the wrong person because Cal was totally into his work and new projects and had no time for her. Mimi described her life at that point as "like being caught in the wake of a speedboat!"

The situation finally came to a head while Mimi was in the States for several weeks helping Kyndra settle into college life. Cal had returned to Quito earlier because of the relentless demands of his multiple projects. Now, not only was the couple still overwhelmed, but they were physically separated for the first extended period in their marriage. Cal considered the thought that maybe this was for the better, that Mimi wasn't there to help him. *He had to handle everything on his own anyway, so why did he really need her?* Finally, Cal blurted out he wasn't sure she needed to come back to Ecuador, and at that moment, they both realized how dire the situation had escalated. Both were terrified at the potential consequences of such a discussion, and yet saw no immediate options.

This finally opened them up to their need for outside help. First, they talked to Glen and Shelly Volkhardt, their friends from the first day they had arrived. The Volkhardts exhibited a strong marriage in spite of similar pressures. Cal and Mimi haltingly told their story, Mimi speaking desperately and Cal secretly doubting whether this would really help. Shelly suggested that the best people she knew to help with this situation were her parents, Norm and Muriel Cook. These retired missionaries were respected for their experience and wisdom, and often counseled other missionaries who needed this kind of assistance and support.

Both Cal and Mimi had met the Cooks and agreed to see them for counseling. The Cooks were serving that summer as the official "grandparents" for a Christian camp in Northwest Oregon. Cal and Mimi flew to Oregon to spend a week with them at the camp, as part of a formal mentoring arrangement.

Life at the camp was very low-key. Nothing was expected of Cal and Mimi, and the Cooks specifically asked the camp staff to respect their privacy and not involve the couple in the program; to leave them alone. And gratefully, they did.

They sat down twice a day with Norm and Muriel and let their story unfold, along with their tension and pain. Cal and Mimi went on long walks, initially in silence, but then they began talking. It only took about two days of discussion for Cal to realize what a jerk he had been. He had so totally buried himself in the excitement of his work, the compliments of his trainees and those around him, and the satisfaction of watching the skills of others develop, that he had totally neglected Mimi and her unique skills and needs.

If they were to persevere with this kind of self-sacrificing work, Cal acknowledged he must draw limits around his involvement in new initiatives. He could not continue to accept responsibilities or new opportunities, even good ones, if his overinvolvement continued to pull the two of them apart. Currently, they did not have a good marriage; they were superficially getting by, mostly at the great cost of Mimi's long-suffering and patience. They realized the necessity of a different approach to their mission work. In other words, something needed to change.

Mimi and Cal took a walk after this rather sudden insight. It was the most glorious walk of their lives, in Mimi's opinion, because they were once again "one" as marriage should be. With barely a few hours of counsel they were acutely aware of what was needed in their lives.

So they spent five magnificent days making up and working through all the aspects involved in burnout: the depression, physical exhaustion, mental exhaustion, and the overwhelming expectations of others. Cal became deeply aware that their burnout was a consequence of his own ambition and drive, which could produce tremendous results, but at great cost not only to himself but to those closest to him. They got the rest they desperately needed and returned to the basics of their life and call together.

When they returned to Quito together, the first thing Cal did was take a solid look at all the projects in which he was involved and all the opportunities he had been considering—and drew a sharp line. In the jungle work on the Onzole River, for example, he transferred more of the responsibility for its administration to others. He asked the nonprofit organization (CENAD) to take a little greater role. He handed more responsibility to the team on the river which was appropriate since they had been there for some time and were stable enough to handle it.

More than anything, Cal began to explore his own drivenness, his secret need for the continual affirmation of his co-workers, associates, and friends, and his (up to now) insatiable desire to push himself to accomplish yet even more, all justified for the good and the spiritual development of others. He realized that he was involved in so many initiatives and was accomplishing so much primarily because he was unconsciously drawing on Mimi's strengths as well. This drain depleted her physical and emotional reserves and was not at all fair to her own needs and goals. All of this boiled down to one conclusion for Cal—he must return to the basics of a contented faith in God, who alone was the Originator of any positive results from his efforts. He needed to accept his own physical and emotional limitations, and the limitations of the spouse God had provided, content that his Father God would continue to bless their work even within those limitations. He accepted anew that the greatest impact they had as a couple was not so much dependent on their activities on behalf of others, but on their unity of mind and spirit sustained by their Father God Himself, and the love and peace that flowed from that relationship. Interestingly, following these insights, their activities continued much as before, but with a totally new attitude of dependence on their Father God for any results, and far less internalized pressure for visible evidence of success.

CHAPTER 31

Living on Missionary Support

Living on missionary support was a unique and stressful experience for Cal and Mimi, who were accustomed to paying their own way. Their mission sending agency, Christian Mission in Many Lands, officially supported them from the US by serving as a central point for funds donated to the Wilsons. Their local church, the Littleton Bible Chapel in Littleton, Colorado, contributed significantly to their support as well. No required threshold amount had to be raised. Consequently, before they left for Ecuador the only "support raising" they did was visit some of the churches around Colorado where they knew people, just to let their friends know they were on their way to Ecuador, their goals and proposed activities there, and asking for their prayers and advice. Cal deliberately avoided asking for money. On occasion, someone would approach him and say, "You're going to need some funds to do this with your family. Can we help with that?" and Cal would respond with gratitude, "Certainly!" and refer them to Christian Mission in Many Lands. He never wanted to give the impression that he was visiting simply to ask for money.

Cal believed with conviction that if God was directing them to go, He would supply what they needed. And that is exactly what they found. The one drawback was that they never knew each month how much they would receive. The amount always varied as it was dependent on strictly how much interested people could give.

They had never been in this position before. To Cal, it was a major psychological and cultural shift to accept funds from others who wanted to participate in what they were doing.

Both Cal and Mimi assumed incredible responsibility to be accountable to their donors. They felt the donors were essentially paying them to work, which resulted in an unconscious but very real internalized sense of obligation to produce results that added to Cal's drivenness. They could not allow themselves to rest and relax, but needed to be productive every minute of the day.

A good friend from their English-speaking church in Quito, a military liaison officer with the British Embassy in Ecuador, Tony Salter, asked Cal one day, "Why aren't you taking a day off? Why are you working seven days a week trying to get things going?"

Cal responded, "We have this tremendous responsibility to these people who are supporting us."

"Why don't you let the Lord take care of that? You need to learn how to relax," Tony replied. A short while later, he scheduled a weekend away for Cal, Mimi, and their family and he paid for it. That was their first relaxing weekend since they had arrived in Ecuador several months prior. Cal and Mimi realized Tony was right, so they adjusted their schedule to take a Sabbath as commanded in the Ten Commandments—one day each week of intentionally doing no work. It wasn't necessarily on Saturday; it was often another day of the week, but it was one day designed just to relax, rest, and reflect, all with God's delighted permission!

Over the years they came to rest totally in the confidence that the Lord was going to supply what they needed when they needed it. Every month the amount was different, and it often varied by several hundreds of dollars. In all the years they were in Ecuador, they never had a month where they lacked anything. The month they only received $200 was the month they had funds left over from the month before. Other months that ended up with lower funds, they had just gone to the market and stocked up on food so they had plenty for themselves and guests. When they had greater needs—such as when Cal's Chevy Blazer that he purchased for the trips to the Onzole River started falling apart, with metal fatigue setting in and various pieces failing—over two months they received multiple thousands of dollars without any mention of this particular need, some from people who had never donated before. They received enough to buy a new 4-wheel drive SUV with cash. This cycle of family need and God's generous response repeated itself time after time.

In addition, special funding, such as the huge grant Cal had received for the Onzole River work, formed a major element of the ability to serve as they did in Ecuador. In the early days following their arrival in Ecuador, their recruiter and mission mentor, Lloyd Rogers, had taught them one lesson that he had learned over the years: "If God is directing you into a particular area of work or service, He will pay the bills! And if the bills are not being paid, you must consider that God is moving you on!" Cal and Mimi took that to heart, and saw it come true on multiple occasions in their own life as well as in Lloyd's.

CHAPTER 32

The Children Go to College

*T*he three children were very much a part of Cal and Mimi's work and attention in Ecuador. They wanted to prepare the children for life in the US, or anywhere in the world, not just continued life in Ecuador. The Mission school they attended certainly helped with that, both in terms of companionship and the quality of the schooling. Plus, they were very grateful the school was within walking distance of their home, to Mimi's particular delight.

Kurt entered the 11th grade when they arrived in Ecuador, so he was only there for two years. Fortunately, he adapted well. While they were preparing to go to Ecuador, Kurt's high school year in Denver had been a shadow of what it might have been. He didn't get poor grades, but he didn't make many friends, didn't socialize much with classmates, and didn't get involved in any outside school activities. He simply went to school and came home, knowing he wasn't going to be part of the American high school scene since they would be moving out of the country soon. However, Cal and Mimi also observed that he was developing a quiet confidence, deep wisdom, and awareness of others that became stronger as he developed. When Kurt arrived in Ecuador, he threw himself into making friends, many of whom are close friends to this day and live all over the world. As he started looking at universities, Kurt's only criterion was that it had to be in Colorado; he loved the mountains and all they offered. He decided to apply to the same college Cal had graduated from, Colorado College in Colorado Springs, and was accepted.

The family traveled to the States for the summer after Kurt graduated in Ecuador, to help get him settled in Colorado College. He had the skills to make friends and had been well-prepared in Ecuador, so he didn't lack anything in terms of knowledge or social skills, and did very well academically and socially.

Kyndra entered the eighth grade in Quito, and her experience was quite distinct. She was three years behind Kurt so she spent five years in Ecuador, and quickly absorbed its culture and proficiency in Spanish. But in her junior year of high school, she rather suddenly announced she was not going to complete her senior year. She said, "It's not going to profit me anything and I just don't see a point in it."

Trying to understand her motivations, Cal asked, "What are you going to do then?"

She said, "I'm going to go to college."

Cal insisted, "Do you think any US college or university is going to accept you without a high school diploma? That just doesn't happen." (Of course, this was the father who had been accepted into medical school without completing his senior year of university or obtaining his bachelor's degree).

She said, "Well, I'm capable of doing it, and I'm going to do it."

So, Cal acquiesced, but he envisioned her applying to 14 colleges with application fees for each one. "All right, we'll do a test," he said. "You pick one college that you really want to attend. I will pay for the application fee for that one college, and we'll see what happens; any other applications will be your responsibility to pay," feeling confident that she was going to get rejected. Cal reasoned it was worth the money spent to convince her this was an overly ambitious idea.

Kyndra agreed, and because Kurt had had such a good experience at Colorado College, she chose the same college. She applied—and was quickly accepted, which blew Cal's reasoning to pieces.

Then the issue became how to pay for tuition, because Kurt was still attending and Colorado College was not cheap. However, Kyndra applied for and received a substantial scholarship, so she was off.

As soon as she arrived at Colorado College, Kyndra sat for a series of screening tests to test out of various courses. She tested out of Spanish and other courses as well, so that she started as a second semester freshman. She had wanted to move on, and that is exactly what she did.

In her first year, Kyndra had great fun, always loved a party, but managed to get good grades as well. But all were shocked to discover near the end of her first year that she had failed to apply for the following year of her scholarship. She had not submitted any of the necessary forms, and no one noticed until the deadline was well past, so she had no scholarship for the next year.

Cal and Mimi's income had been sufficient until now, with scholarship support of Kyndra's tuition and money they had saved, but only enough for one more semester of Colorado College at the full price. Doing a bit of research, Cal found that this same amount of money would cover in full the next three years at the University of Colorado in Colorado Springs. She would be able to graduate on the same amount of money as one semester at her current college. They presented that option to her, and she went back and forth until finally deciding she would switch to the University of Colorado.

However, after applying to the University of Colorado in Colorado Springs, she discovered she was not eligible for admission there because she did not have a high school diploma, in spite of her completion of a year at Colorado College. Again, in her mind, that was just a small hurdle. She researched what she needed to do to obtain a high school diploma, completed the necessary online GED courses in a couple of months, received her GED diploma, and was subsequently accepted at the University of Colorado.

A couple of weeks before she was to start she called Cal and Mimi saying, "I just can't do this! I want to take the next option, to go to Colorado College for the next semester with the funds that you have. I'll get a job while I'm there, drop out after that semester and continue working until I have enough money for another semester, and continue in that way until I finish. I am happy to pay my own way by working, as long as I can continue at Colorado College."

"Well, if that's your decision, that's fine," Cal said, actually feeling quite proud of his self-sufficient daughter. Kyndra had already started working at a pizza restaurant, and she really buckled down the next semester. She avoided the parties and divided her life between work and study, and did very well.

Interestingly enough, in the meantime, the Christian organization "Focus on the Family" had just purchased rights to publish a new edition of *Once-a-Month Cooking* and was distributing it. Mimi had just received her first royalty check, which more than covered a full semester at Colorado College.

Cal called Kyndra and asked innocently, "How are you doing?"

"I'm doing fine. I'm getting ready to drop out and start working."

"Well, we just got some funding that I think we can apply to one more semester," Cal announced, "but that's all."

Without hesitation, Kyndra replied, "All right, I'll take that." So, she continued with another semester. During each of the following four semesters, Cal and Mimi received enough in unexpected donations from friends in Colorado Springs and royalties on the cookbook that provided just enough to pay for the semester ahead. They went semester by semester with this same level of uncertainty and divine response. Kyndra graduated from Colorado College in three years because she studied hard and attended summer school sessions where the tuition was much less. With all of this, they were spared a fourth year's tuition; again, clear confirmation that the God they served was meeting their needs and those of their children at the time it was needed, generally not a moment earlier!

Kevin started in fourth grade in Ecuador and nine years later he graduated from the Alliance high school. By that point the entire family had made a lot of Ecuadorian friends, and many came to congratulate Kevin. To everyone's delight, ten awards were given, and Kevin received at least five of them. It was almost comical; he'd get an award, sit back down, then he'd get called up again. To cap the event, Cal had been asked to give the commencement address, and as the school principal introduced Cal, he jokingly insisted that the ceremony had not originally been designed to be a Wilson event!

Of course, having so many of their Ecuadorian friends present made the graduation very special. Kevin had also been accepted to Colorado College. The incredibly positive experiences of his two older siblings had convinced him Colorado College was by far the best option. Still, Cal and Mimi were concerned that after spending nine years in Ecuador, the transition to the US and American college life might be more stressful for him than it was for Kyndra or Kurt, who had spent less time in Ecuador. Kevin was such a steady, stable young man that it was sometimes hard for Cal and Mimi to know exactly how they might help him. He methodically completed almost anything he focused on, and he didn't ask for much help or advice or seem to need it. Cal and Mimi noticed Kevin's closest friends were often foreign-born. Given his extended time outside of the US, he naturally gravitated toward encouraging those who may have been feeling a bit isolated and alone.

This was one of the several reasons for leaving Ecuador and moving back to Denver at that time; to be more accessible to support Kevin's early years at college. Cal had been accepted on the faculty of the University of Colorado Medical School, so they bought a home near the medical school and set up a special bedroom for Kevin.

After they dropped him off at Colorado College, with great tears and heavy hearts, they were concerned when Kevin didn't initiate a call to them for the first six weeks. When they finally asked about this, he replied nonchalantly, "Oh, I'm doing fine. No problem." In his first year at Colorado College, Kevin came home to his special bedroom in Denver only two or three times. Their fears about his adaptation to US and college culture turned out to be totally ill-founded; Kevin adapted very well to US life and graduated from Colorado College with honors.

CHAPTER 33

Leaving and Legacy

*C*al and Mimi had decided very early that they would stay and work in Ecuador indefinitely. As long as they felt the Lord was using them and there were needs that they as outsiders could help with, they would stay. However, they had also determined that they would work toward enabling others to do what they were doing, and when that was evident, it was time for them to move on. Their primary goal was not to become indispensable or create dependencies, but to try to clone themselves so that capable Ecuadorians could carry on the work of developing and equipping others.

This principle guided them in every project they initiated. They designed each project to gain independence, to eventually operate without their involvement or continuous outside funding. For example, in the medical development work on the Onzole River, outside funding was initially required to begin the work, but much of the project activity included more than providing medical care. They trained local villagers in a new paradigm of preventive habits to improve their overall health, as well as educated health workers and midwives in how to provide basic primary care. Similarly, the deaf program was designed to be funded and administered by the social services of the Ecuadorian government rather than outside funds, and ultimately the Family Medicine postgraduate program was totally funded and administered by the Catholic University of Quito.

As they entered the eighth year of their work in Ecuador, Cal and Mimi could see that every single activity or project they were involved in now had someone very capable to take over that work. The Bible study that had begun with Nestor Romero had slowly grown over time to include a diverse group, all of whom wanted to know more of God and His nature. It was much more than a Bible study; it was now a friendship group that deeply supported each other.

Cal completed five years of work on the Onzole River and had formally left the area in the hands of the local leaders, the health workers the team had trained, and the Ministry of Health for support. The whole health situation had much improved in the village. Jungle residents were now following good public health practices, and the health indices were far better than they had been at the onset of the work. The incidence of malaria infection, for instance, had decreased by over 80% because of the control activities they had implemented.

Sixto and Lindon were trained to do the medical work in the village and the Ministry of Health had promised to support and provide supplies.

The work with the deaf was now funded by the government, run by government physicians, and was growing significantly. The home for severely handicapped people, Casa Hogar, was now managed by a group of Ecuadorians, with Rosa's continued active involvement.

The Family Medicine postgraduate program had just graduated twelve residents, who were now in the process of forming their own Ecuadorian Society of Family Medicine. Cal had moved the administration and primary funding of the residency program to the Catholic University of Quito, which was very interested in expanding the program, although they continued to use Hospital Vozandes and its clinics as their primary training site.

Most of the activities that Cal and Mimi had initiated were now able to be directed by capable, responsible Ecuadorians who had worked with Cal or Mimi for some time. Even more, it became apparent that if they did *not* step out of the picture, the further development of these leaders could be stunted; they would continue to look to Cal and Mimi for direction and help in difficult times. It was time to go.

But how could the family say goodbye to Rosa? It was so hard then, and Mimi says it's still hard now. She'll never forget watching Rosa walk down the street after they said goodbye to return to the US permanently. Rosa was so upset she could not speak; she did not think she would ever see Mimi again. Although Rosa would continue to work as a housekeeper for others, her primary passion was with the disabled, the very poor, the widows, and orphaned children, as well as the members of the small church she attended. Basically, Rosa helped anyone with a demonstrated need. The Wilsons made sure Rosa was protected financially for the rest of her life, to allow her to exercise this passion to her fullest capacity.

Denver, Colorado

1995-1999

CO-AUTHOR MARY BETH LAGERBORG AND MIMI, CIRCA 2000

KURT AND LORI, CIRCA 2000

KYNDRA AND TOM TRINIDAD, CIRCA 2000

SARAH AND KEVIN, CIRCA 2000

CAL WITH HIS SIBLINGS, 2002

CO-AUTHOR SHELLY VOLKHARDT AND MIMI, 2009

CHAPTER 34

Difficult Reentry

*A*s they repatriated to the US, Cal's interest continued to be in Family Medicine, especially after starting the Family Medicine postgraduate program in Ecuador. During that time, he observed how much he enjoyed training others in Family Medicine, and wanted to continue in that role as well as improve his skills. He had previously served as a volunteer teacher in the Department of Family Medicine at the University of Colorado while in private practice, so he contacted the department to see if he could be used as a full-time faculty member. The answer was a clear "Yes."

So, Cal returned to Denver to fill a faculty position at the university. His first meeting with the chairman of the department to define his role was a big surprise. Dr. Larry Green, the department chair, said, "You know, we've been trying to get a Family Medicine residency program started in the University

Hospital for ten years, but as a specialist hospital they had not been interested until just the past few months. You just started a new Family Medicine residency program from nothing in Ecuador; I believe you have the skills, so I would like you to start and develop this program."

The process of starting a new residency program was more structured in the US than in Ecuador, but the initial steps were basically the same—discuss the new program with various stakeholders and medical decision makers, calm the fears of certain specialists regarding potential competition, develop a consensus of support, and promote Family Medicine as a valued and important new specialty among the various clinical specialties of the hospital. With the help of the department chair, Larry Green, a development task force was formed, and Cal started hiring new faculty members and forming a team. Together they developed the new curriculum and training schedule, negotiated the development of a Family Medicine ward within the University Hospital as well as outpatient training space, and saw it approved by the American Board of Family Medicine. It required two years of work to reach the point of selecting the first residents for training.

Cal and Mimi's idea of a suitable home had been greatly influenced by their stay in the urban environment of Quito. Although they had previously lived in a suburban environment, they had come to value the convenience and neighborliness of an urban setting. In addition, their little nest was now empty. Kurt had recently married (Lori) and was working in Denver, and Kyndra had graduated from Colorado College three years before and was working in Colorado Springs. Kevin, the youngest, was just starting as a full-time college student at Colorado College. So, they took a leap of faith and decided to move to downtown Denver close to the university. Cal would be busy at the university and living close by would allow him to come home for lunch and be more present with Mimi.

After much searching, they found an incredible three-level condominium only a half-block from the university. It was totally new construction, and Mimi enjoyed selecting the appliances and colors and making it home. The condo had a small garden in the back and a two-car garage.

As always, they wanted their home to be a welcoming and restful sanctuary for friends and acquaintances such as interested medical students and residents, especially those who were spiritually minded. They had visions of starting a Bible study or a fellowship group among interested students and faculty. Hoping students would visit frequently, they had a room ready for them with coffee and drinks. However, in spite of multiple invitations and attempts, months went by and only one or two would stop in. Cal concluded that part of the problem was that these brilliant medical students, although they were sharp and had excelled academically, took little time for reflection or to simply enjoy life. If they did agree to stop by the condo, they would most commonly appear with a textbook under each arm. Mimi especially was most accustomed to dealing with very social people, and had a difficult time trying to relate to this level of focused intensity.

Mimi missed her friends in Ecuador very much. She was alone in this new place, including being without a car for the first few months. Not to be deterred, just as she had done after the earthquake in Quito, Mimi developed a plan to meet her neighbors and develop a community. She decided to host a Christmas luncheon for older women in honor of her mother, who had only recently passed away. She invited 12 women, encouraging each one to invite one other companion, so there would be 24 at the luncheon.

In her planning, she noted that the one-hour limit on street parking in front of her house would make it impossible for her guests to enjoy a leisurely afternoon. She waited until the assigned parking policeman began his rounds and ran out to meet him with a sheaf of hot pink pieces of paper in her hand with a proposal: the cars marked with a piece of the hot pink paper on the dash belonged to one of her guests, and would he please allow the guest to stay as long as the event lasted? Fortunately, he was in a merry Christmas mood and agreed.

The women arrived early, eager and with no other engagements on their calendars. As she was welcoming the guests, Mimi noted one woman on the sidewalk studying the arriving group. She was not dressed festively, and wore a simple tattered coat not designed for winter in Colorado. She stood watching all the women going into Mimi's house, and Mimi thought, *I have got to invite her*. So she ran after her down the street.

"You don't know who I am, but could you come to my

house for lunch?" Mimi asked her.

"No English," was the lady's short reply.

"Why don't you come eat with me?" Mimi said as she pantomimed her hand to her mouth.

That the woman understood, and she kissed Mimi on both cheeks.

Mimi brought her to the house and seated the woman next to her, so as not to embarrass guests who might not be up for a communication hurdle. The woman managed to convey to Mimi that she had four sons who lived in the area, and that she was visiting from Jordan. Mimi has forgotten how many times this little lady kissed her that day, but when Cal came home, she said, "I don't know anything about Jordan, but I sure love the people already!"

Not only were students reluctant to come to their urban home, but many of their former suburban friends also showed the same reluctance, and the wonderful time of reconnecting with old friends that they had anticipated was disappointing. The one-hour parking in front of their house was a barrier, and there appeared to be a subtle psychological barrier in visiting them in downtown Denver, a location many perceived as more remote and more complicated to negotiate. Although Mimi agreed that "Cal loves the high end of activity" and he was happily busy with the new residency, her concept of "home" was not going as anticipated.

Over the next three years, Mimi was able to host a few friends, and even host a Colombian medical student named

Pablo Moyano for several months. However, she was eager to have a home regularly filled with discussion, laughter, and the smell of good food. After much thought and anguish, she finally approached Cal with a big proposal. "I would like to look for another home, because very few are coming to visit, you are gone all day at the office or clinic, and I am very alone here. I know you are very busy and don't have any time to do this, but I will do all the legwork: find a suitable home, arrange for the move, and even look for a home that you won't have to spend time fixing up. I will do everything, so that one morning you will take your briefcase to work, and that evening you will come home to a new house!"

Cal clearly saw the anguish and passion behind Mimi's proposal, and easily said (quoting Capt. Jean Luc Piccard of the Starship Enterprise), "Make it so!"

As Mimi began house hunting, she rather quickly found a brand-new home in the western suburb of Lakewood that was everything she and Cal had wanted. Located 30 minutes from the Medical Center, it was still within reach. During the moving process, even before the move was completed, old friends started coming up the driveway to visit, and Mimi rejoiced. *"Yes! They're not afraid to come to Lakewood!"*

During these years in Denver and Lakewood, Mimi was occupied with writing and speaking. Both activities were nourished by a practice that had become firmly anchored in her heart over many years. She took time to come to know her Father God as He revealed Himself in the Bible.

She studied one character trait of God per year, such as His love, His mercy, His holiness, His justice, and His eternality (the conceptual implications of a God Who actively lives in eternity); and studied it deeply. Then she studied the significance of the different names for God in the Bible. She used several Bible commentaries, as well as the gracious help of a saintly old man at her church, who was Greek by birth, Mr. Tokatloglou, or "Tok" for short. He would read the passages she was studying in Greek, translate them for her, and add his thoughts as they came from the original Greek. She kept notes as she was learning, so that she could share with those around her what she had gleaned from this study.

Monday mornings were her time of prayer and meditation. When the children were younger at home, they knew Mom's Monday morning time was sacred. "We have to come in quietly because Mom's in prayer," they would say. She looked forward to offering the results of these studies to others, which became the core of the book *Holy Habits,* that she wrote with her friend Shelly Volkhardt, and was published in 1999.

Mimi was widely regarded as a Bible teacher and a speaker on *Holy Habits.* She also continued to teach the philosophy of *Once-a-Month Cooking,* which continued to find a wide audience in the US, and on *Table Talk,* that she wrote with her cookbook partner Mary Beth Lagerborg and was published in 1994. The latter book was an encouragement on the many ways people of all ages can be enriched and encouraged through guided conversations around a meal.

CHAPTER 35

Global Health

The development of the new Family Medicine residency program at the University of Colorado involved a number of major tasks beyond the development and official approval of the curriculum, such as the selection and remodeling of a new Family Medicine teaching clinic, the development of a Family Medicine hospital service within the University Hospital, the molding of new faculty members into a cohesive teaching team, and the selection of medical students who were comfortable with the challenge of participating in a brand-new residency program. However, this all fell into place, and the program opened with four capable residents in July 1997. As the program continued to mature with its capable teaching team, Cal considered ways to promote an increased interest in global health within the university. At that time only a few universities had developed a program to promote global health studies and activities, and yet Cal was encountering an increasing number of medical students interested in exploring medical service in the developing countries of the world. Students were coming to him asking where they could spend two or three months to explore and experience medicine in another country.

Cal brought up the idea with faculty members within the School of Medicine, and eventually talked to faculty in most of the other departments, like Physical Therapy, the Physician Assistant program, the School of Dentistry, and the School of Public Health. In each department he found at least one or two faculty members who had previous involvement in global work or interest in learning more.

Cal created an ad hoc group, calling it the International Health Consortium. They would meet to discuss what they might do as a group to encourage students to get more involved in global health work, how to facilitate that work, and who was attending upcoming meetings that were involved with global health. It was a simple beginning, but interest was growing.

Cal was named the first director of the Family Medicine residency and directed the residency for about three years. However, it became increasingly obvious, unfortunately to some of the faculty he was working with as well as himself, that he was not the best at administering an ongoing program. His real skills lay in starting a program, but when it came to meeting the consistent needs of an existing program, he found it more difficult to patiently deal with some of the necessary administrative details.

Larry Green, the chairman of the department, came to visit Cal one day. He pointed out a few of the comments or even complaints of some of the faculty members about Cal's manner of directing the program, and very kindly noted, "There are some people who are meant to be the pioneers and initiators and other people who are meant to be the ongoing stabilizers. Would you be interested in another type of work?"

Almost relieved, Cal said, "Yes, definitely. I would love to be able to do some international consulting and get back into global health work."

Larry gave him carte blanche to do that, so Cal embarked on a new search. One of the first prospects to appear was from a company called Abt Associates, who among other similar companies, had been issued an invitation by the US Agency for International Development (USAID) to develop a new program in the Middle East country of Jordan.

The scope of the project was huge. The five-year project was intended to improve the quality of primary health care and especially the accessibility to Jordan's reproductive healthcare services. One of the several required elements of the proposal was to provide intensive training to all the primary health care staff in the country, and Abt Associates invited Cal to propose a curriculum and training methodology. The Ministry of Health in Jordan employed some 650 doctors and 2,500 nurses and midwives scattered in clinics all over the country, and was concerned that most of them had a somewhat limited capacity in primary healthcare and needed to be trained to a higher level.

Cal agreed to write the proposal for the curriculum along with the training methodology element of the project, drawing from his experience in training family physicians, and submitted the completed proposal to Abt Associates. Although three or four other companies were also bidding for the USAID contract, Abt Associates ultimately won it. The understanding at the outset was that if they won the contract, Cal would move to Jordan and implement the training component of the project for the next five years; so Cal had tacitly already committed to this move, with Mimi's clear approval.

Since Cal was still an employee of the University of Colorado, he explained the situation to the Chair of the Department. The contract included a generous budget and salary for each of the key consultants such as Cal, so he was allowed to remain a full employee of the university while on loan to this project for the next five years. The budget allotted for Cal's services went straight to the university, which took a percentage for their administrative services, while the remaining funds covered Cal's salary, transportation, and living expenses in Jordan. This was actually a relatively common practice within the university, although most grants only covered a portion of the faculty member's salary.

Cal was pleased that this arrangement added to the university's claim they were involved internationally. And it was helpful for the USAID project to have a university professor providing training for the project. The opportunity also allowed Cal to remain fully employed by the university while working internationally, securing his benefits and promotion status.

Mimi was thrilled at the prospect of moving to Jordan. Would the people be like the dear Jordanian lady she had invited for lunch at Christmas? This was incredible. They had two months' notice to prepare to move to Jordan for five years, but they were ready for the task.

They gathered a smaller volume of belongings than they had prepared for Ecuador, in part because they had learned to pack better. Also, the three children were now on their own, starting careers, so it was just the two of them. Mimi packed her china dishes, silver, and glassware to ship to Jordan because she wanted to honor her guests at the table. They knew for certain they would be living in the capital city of Amman, which further refined their packing needs. Jordan was a middle-income country, so things like furniture would be easier to get once they arrived. They did take some major appliances specifically wired for 220 volts, such as a washer and dryer, because they had discovered that none of the available rental homes provided them. And yes, they took a freezer as well!

Once again Cal's mother joined them for the trip, together with Cal's father, Don. They wanted to visualize Cal and Mimi's living situation and help with the moving in.

They weren't quite sure what to do with their suburban house, until a dynamic woman, Marty Cooper, who had done periodic housecleaning for Mimi, asked if they knew of any housing possibilities because she had just been asked to leave the apartment that had been her home for several years. The timing couldn't be better. Cal and Mimi suggested that if she was willing to live in their furnished home and maintain it, they would accept a rental payment equivalent to what she had been paying recently. It was a win-win situation, and when they returned from Jordan after five years, the house was in better shape than when they left—spotlessly clean and totally functional.

They were now ready to go back overseas after a time at "home" that had confirmed for them that there were even greater needs and opportunities for relationship in other parts of the world. They were again returning to pioneer work and to hospitality in a new culture.

Amman, Jordan

1999 - 2004

MIMI IN AMMAN HOME, 2003

ANNIVERSAY DINNER EMBASSY, 2003

MIMI WITH
SANA DABABNEH

CAL, MIMI, AND VISITING PROFESSOR,
DR. LAURA BORGELT, IN PETRA

CAL AT THE
MONASTERY
IN PETRA

MIMI AND PEGGY GNEHM, WIFE OF
US AMBASSADOR, AT AMBASSADOR'S RESIDENCE

STUART BRISCOE AT AN INFORMAL
MEETING IN WILSON'S AMMAN HOME

CAL TEACHING DOCTORS IN BAGHDAD,
OCTOBER 2003

PHCI PROJECT COLLEAGUES

CHAPTER 36

Generous Hospitality

*D*uring a one month stay in a local Marriott hotel in Amman and with the help of local Jordanian staff with Abt Associates, Cal and Mimi found a very suitable home to rent for their five-year commitment in Jordan. As they had hoped, it was similar in style and taste to that of their Jordanian neighbors. The home consisted of the second and third floor of a duplex, with the owner living on the first floor of the building. It was lovely, with two separate seating areas in the living room for guests, one for the men and one for the women, as was the Arab custom. The living room was formal and ornate and meant to show to guests, and was furnished with massive, overstuffed furniture in silver and blue. The private living quarters, including bedrooms, a small office, and a guest room were up a flight of stairs. A narrow front porch and an outdoor yard were maintained by the owner, with a huge hedge of rosemary.

The house was nicely situated in a good, secure neighborhood. The policy of the Jordanian government was to have a mosque in every block of such neighborhoods, and the calls to prayer were synchronized across the entire city. From the first morning on, Cal and Mimi were awakened at 4:30 to an amplified prayer echoing off the stone walls of the neighborhood. Every structure in the city was by decree faced with white stone, providing a perfect reflecting surface for sound and an incredible echoing resonance to the prayer. Cal and Mimi rapidly grew accustomed to the frequent calls to prayer, and even came to enjoy it, as the calls regularly reminded them of their own personal need to pray more often.

The geography of Jordan is divided in three distinct regions, all running north to south. The Jordan Valley where the Jordan River flows along the west side of the country is extremely fertile and is where most of the vegetables and fruit are grown. The central region of the country consists of a series of hills that trap much of the rainfall and contain smaller gardens and pasture for sheep and goats. Millions of olive trees, one of their primary crops, thrive in this part of the country. The entire eastern part of the country is desert, totally arid. The city of Amman, and most of the population of Jordan, are in the central hills where water is more available, and it is cooler.

The dominant culture in Jordan is that of the ancient Bedouin. Until the early 1900s, Jordan consisted primarily of a collection of various Bedouin tribes with literally thousands of years of collective history. These Bedouin are much like

American cowboys. They live isolated from each other in nomadic family groups, and value hospitality and honor above all. For example, if a Bedouin found a member of an enemy tribe in trouble in the desert, who had run out of water and was dehydrated, he would take the suffering enemy into his tent and restore him with food and drink, treating him as a suffering individual and not an enemy. Their ancient code indicated that this period lasted for three days; however, following those three days of grace, the guest either had to leave or could be killed. These tribes collaborated some and fought much, but the Bedouin culture has many universal values that have been blended into Jordanian culture.

The Wilsons were overwhelmed with the hospitality of the Jordanians and quickly grew to love the people. Usually their conversations with neighbors and friends were in English, which is a common second language in Jordan. It is taught in the schools beginning in the elementary grades, so the younger people know it well. The older Jordanians, especially those who had migrated to the city from smaller villages in the countryside, spoke primarily Arabic.

Within the first few days of settling into their home, their neighbors across the street invited them to their home, eager to know what had brought them to Jordan. Mimi took over a plate of cookies as a gift to the hostess, only to learn it was considered unusual behavior to take food when invited to someone's home. Her hostess accepted it, however, understanding that the Wilsons were foreigners.

As Mimi visited with the women in the living room that evening, she was asked to share a bit about herself. She mentioned that she had written a book on how to cook one day for the month, and immediately there was stunned silence in both living rooms, because the men were listening in as well. One man said to the others, "I am so sorry. You know that I speak English, but I don't know what they're saying. She just said she cooks one day for the month!" Mimi tried to explain, but this was so out of their frame of reference that it became obvious they needed to move on to other topics of conversation.

This same evening Mimi came to believe what she had been taught prior to arriving in Jordan—that she should not compliment any individual on what they were wearing or their jewelry, because they would take it off and give it to her. One woman appeared in a dress decorated in solid cross-stitch. It was stunning. Mimi, who appreciated the Hmong embroidery, couldn't help enthusing on its beauty. At the end of the evening, she realized she had made a big mistake, as the woman reappeared with the dress in a large box and offered it to Mimi. Mimi was heartsick; she had not passed her first cultural test. She had assumed that surely her informant was mistaken; surely a person wouldn't really give their own clothes to her! Unfortunately, Mimi was not a quick learner in this area, and ultimately ended up with five additional gorgeous dresses in her closet!

The next morning a parade of women arrived from across the street bearing plates of food, including intricately made stuffed grape leaves about the size of one's little finger. As they handed the food to Mimi, the one who spoke the best English began an obviously well-rehearsed presentation: "Ma'am, we know that you may cook one day for the month, but we would like to show you how we cook a full month for one day." They all roared with laughter, thinking that this was the funniest thing they'd ever said. This became a significant bonding experience. A shared joke unites people like nothing else can.

This little episode pointed out one of the big differences in their cultures. When it came to food and eating, the Jordanians did not value efficiency as did the Americans. They honored their guests by putting their entire body and soul into the preparation of a meal, in many cases preparing for several weeks one special meal with guests or even with their own family.

These neighbors became friends. As Mimi would come and go, she would see the women sitting on their front porch, smoking their hubbly bubbly (the water pipe). They always invited Mimi to join them, and she always said the same thing, "I don't smoke, but if I ever did, it would be with you!" And again, they experienced the shared laughter. Whenever Cal and Mimi would be leaving on a more extended trip, Mimi would cross the street before they left to tell the old man sitting on the porch of their planned absence. He would respond by pulling down on his eye with one finger, indicating that he would keep a sharp eye on their property.

CHAPTER 37

A Most Pleasurable Work

*C*al enjoyed his work with Jordanian health professionals immensely; the pleasure of the interactions touched every bone in his body. It was new and innovative, and had not been done before to this extent. It involved getting to know an entirely new culture, new group of people, and it was well resourced. He started in, aware the work had to be done systematically and that the process must be appropriate for the people he would be training.

The Abt Associates project he worked with was known as the "Primary Health Care Initiative," and was massive in scope and funding. It was fully funded by USAID for five years, and its primary goal was a "sustainable improvement in the quality of reproductive and primary health care." The project consisted of six different components: development of a quality improvement process in each health center, training of all primary health care staff in reproductive and primary health care (which was led by Cal), improvement in health management information systems, research, improved techniques in health communication and marketing, and health center renovation and necessary medical equipment (involving 200 out of 360 health centers).

The rationale behind such an ambitious project was to provide all the necessary elements needed for a significant and sustainable improvement in primary health care and reproductive health, including medical records, health messaging, and renovation of older structures with necessary medical equipment.

The population Cal was asked to train totaled 650 primary care doctors and 2,500 nurses and midwives, who were specially included because reproductive health was to be a major element. He was also asked to develop some limited training for pharmacy technicians and laboratory technicians, although these were relatively short sessions. To understand the most critical elements of the training needs, Cal spent the first few months doing a needs analysis around the country. There were 360 community health centers in the country, and he visited representative health centers in small towns and larger cities. He observed their practice and what kind of patients they saw, reviewed their records and the central Ministry of Health records, and noted the most common conditions they treated. He then compiled a list of the 25 most common problems seen in the past year in each of these health centers, and the results were quite consistent across the country.

The most common problems treated were, interestingly, almost identical and in the same frequency as those seen in any family practice in the United States, such as headache, sore throat, abdominal pain, diarrhea, high blood pressure, diabetes, arthritic pains, and musculoskeletal injuries. There weren't as many sports injuries, because while competitive sports were certainly present in Jordanian culture, not many young people participated in them. Cal's assessment confirmed what he had assumed in the original plan he had previously submitted.

He also investigated the most effective manner of proceeding with the training. He was dealing with people who had been through reasonable training in a practical clinic setting. He knew that he would be expanding their knowledge, but in a few medical areas he would be contradicting their way of thinking about the management of some illnesses. New information and innovative treatment strategies had been published over the previous years. There was no way Cal could personally train 650 doctors and over 2,500 nursing staff by himself. The idea required scalability. He proposed identifying a group of capable, respected doctors and nurses who were interested in teaching and had shown some propensity for teaching in the past, which he termed master trainers. They would be chosen on a geographic basis, with master trainers from each of the 12 national governorates (the Jordanian term for a province). The plan was that at the completion of their training, the master trainers would set up a schedule of training for all of the doctors and nurses in their assigned governorate. Often several hundred medical staff needed training in each governorate, so this local training was not going to be a one-time event. Cal would spend most of his five years in Jordan with these master trainers.

Based on the conclusions reached in his needs analysis, he made some important initial decisions that he knew would be controversial. One major concept he proposed was to train the doctors, nurses and midwives at the same time with the same material. Because this was to be a rigorous training exercise, he would test the entire mixed training group on the same material with the same test. His primary reason for this was that in his visits to the various health centers during the initial needs analysis he observed very little professional interaction between the doctors and the nurses, as the nurses were primarily considered merely the handmaids of the doctors. They did only what the doctors told them to do, and were not considered capable of participating in medical decision-making or ongoing patient care. From his own experience, Cal knew that a collaborative, more equitable team approach to managing the patients resulted in much improved patient care and patient satisfaction, and he wanted to try to develop this attitude within the Jordanian health centers.

At the beginning of the training for the first group of master trainers, Cal proposed to the group that he wanted to show how a better sense of teamwork and efficiency within each health center could significantly improve the quality of their care, as well as the satisfaction of the patients. For this teamwork to develop, the nurses needed to know exactly what the doctors knew. This did not necessarily mean that the nurses would be doing the same things as the doctors, but that they could be more effective in helping the patient understand the disease process and the treatment the doctor was prescribing. In this way, the nurses would be more able to offer more effective counsel, guidance, and direction to the patient.

As expected, many of the doctors balked at this idea. Several of them, especially the older ones, felt demeaned and denigrated by the nurses participating in the same material as the doctors. They concluded that Cal should dumb down the material to the level of what they considered proper for the nurses. However, Cal persisted in this approach, trying to graciously honor the doctors without demeaning the nurses and midwives who were seated right beside them.

The training started at 8:00 a.m. and went until 4:00 p.m., five days a week. Since the trainees came from various governorates, they were allowed to go home on the weekends. After the first two weeks of training, they returned to work at their health centers for a week, with specific assignments and exercises that focused on practicing what they had learned the previous two weeks. This schedule continued for a total of five months.

By about the fifth week of training, Cal began to notice a genuine change in attitude among the participants. The doctors were much more engaged and involved, and their complaints of feeling demeaned disappeared, because it became obvious that Cal was legitimately teaching to the level of the physicians. The nurses and midwives absorbed the material like sponges, could be seen discussing various points during the breaks, and often asked very insightful questions regarding the physiology or management of a particular medical problem.

Cal was interested to see whether the nurses and midwives were able to fully process some of the complex material presented. He gave an exam at the end of each two-week period, just before they went home for a week. In the first few sets of exams he gave, to Cal's astonishment all did well and a few of the nurses consistently scored higher than any of the doctors. With some satisfaction Cal announced this to the whole group. This led to some grumbling among a few of the doctors, but it appeared that many of the doctors were secretly delighted as well.

Following the training, a formal graduation and commissioning ceremony, Cal started over with a new group of master trainers. He took no more than two people at a time out of each health center, and he relied on the district health directors to help him choose the most appropriate and capable professionals. During the off week when the doctors and nurses had returned to their health center with practice exercises, Cal caught up on paperwork and prepared for the next two-week training. When he had time, he would visit some of the health centers—just pop in. He'd ask the master trainers how they were doing and whether they felt the training was appropriate to what they saw in the clinic. He tried to gently find out if they had changed their patterns of approaching patients or how they were diagnosing or managing problems, all in a very collegial manner. Although change in the team's approach to the patients appeared to come slowly, it did appear that both the doctors and nurses were spending more time with the patients, especially in counseling and answering of questions, and that the doctors were more deliberate than before in their selection of medications and therapies.

CHAPTER 38

Driving and Taxis and Dinners into the Night

C al needed a vehicle since he would be driving to visit health centers all over the country. The project had hired a professional driver, a big, burly Palestinian named Hammad (one of the many shortened versions of Mohammed), who was built like a football player but had a very soft heart. He offered to take Cal to the economic free zone to buy a car because it was much cheaper out there, where he guided Cal on an appropriate model for the varied terrain of the country. Cal settled on a nice Mazda sedan.

It took Cal some time to learn to drive in Jordan, mainly because many of the men, and even some of the women, were very aggressive drivers. Very few had a sense of what it meant to stay in one's lane. Many of the streets in Jordan were well laid out with two to four lanes in each direction, but it was common practice to be cut off, especially at traffic lights. Cal spent the first six months of driving in Jordan in a perpetual state of road rage over the indignities he suffered. However, he began to notice that most of the Jordanian drivers were similarly ignored or cut off, and just seemed to shrug their shoulders and allow the other to proceed. This was something he could learn from them and he began to adjust his attitude.

When Cal started driving across the country, Hammad took him aside and advised, "When you go on long drives, there are two kinds of drivers you need to watch out for. If you see a woman driving the vehicle and her head is covered with her *hijab* (head covering for Muslim women in public), stay away from her. Because of their *hijab* they cannot see to their side, nor do they turn their heads to see to the side. They simply assume there's nothing there, so they are more likely to switch lanes in front of you as if you didn't exist. The other driver you need to watch out for is an old man in a *kaffiyeh* (Bedouin headdress) in an old pickup truck. Stay away from that driver as well—he just got off his camel two weeks ago!"

After thousands of miles across Jordan, Cal only had one accident—barely a tap. He never was in a serious accident or even had to have major car repairs, by the mercy of God.

Mimi, meanwhile, was having a delightful time getting wherever she wanted to go by local taxi. The taxi ride was often as fun for her as the destination engagement. Taxi drivers circled the area and often she would end up with ones she had ridden with before. The drivers always checked the center console to make sure Mimi was well stocked with cigarettes and water. They all had music tapes, and when they saw that Mimi was an American, they would put in American music. They rolled the windows down because it was beastly hot, and the music rocked through the neighborhoods. Many drivers tried to practice their English with her. One driver, as he stopped to let Mimi out, seemed to be wanting to say something, and finally came out with what he thought was an appropriate, but not flirtatious, comment, uttering, "Madam, twenty years ago your face was excellent!"

"Oh, thank you!" Mimi generously replied.

When Mimi got in the taxi with some drivers, she would be asked, "Shall we go to the same place as before?" Having gone to three places in a taxi that day, she would have to ask, "Where is that?" She kept finger puppets in her purse, so that at stop lights she could give puppet shows to the children in the cars pulled up on either side of her cab. When the light changed, often no one moved because they were watching the puppet show.

One time Mimi went by cab to a location where she was to meet Cal. They planned to drive the rest of the way home together. She got out of the taxi to wait. Cal was late and Mimi waited a half hour, with the taxi driver circling, obviously concerned. He finally had to leave, but before leaving he consoled her from the window, "Don't worry, Madam. You're safe in the Middle East!" Indeed, Amman was safer than many American cities, and Mimi never felt afraid in Jordan, including on her many taxi rides.

The Wilsons met a wide variety of people in Jordan. Cal's work on the USAID project included at least five other American expatriates. The company hired a large staff of Jordanians as well, all of whom spoke good English. Cal and Mimi spent most of their time over the five years in Jordan with locals. With the training sessions five days a week, seven to eight hours a day, they got to know each other quite well, and in many cases were introduced to their families.

Many of the master trainers, both doctors and nurses, started inviting Cal and Mimi to their homes, sometimes in the city or a few hours' drive to their farm or their ancestral home. The trainers came from all over Jordan, so this involved quite a lot of travel, but Cal and Mimi loved it. The Jordanians invariably wanted the Wilsons to come to their house because they wanted to introduce them to their whole extended family. When the Wilsons invited people to their home, often the guests would refuse until the Wilsons had first been to their place. These people considered it a joy, an honor, and a privilege to have guests for a meal.

Cal and Mimi learned many of the Jordanian customs. They learned it was unthinkable to cook enough food for just one meal. Jordanian thinking was that there should be enough food on the table not just for the family and invited guests to eat their fill, but for them to do it all over again. A guest would express appreciation for the food by eating lots of it.

Cal and Mimi noticed that often a family member would be stationed next to each of them with the primary responsibility to be sure they never saw the bottom of their plate. As soon as they had cleared off a little bit of their plates, there would be another spoonful or two added on. Having grown up being taught to clean his plate, Cal kept trying to, but it never happened. Within their first year he gained 35 pounds! The invitation to a meal usually started at seven in the evening and went late into the night: they rarely got home before 11:00 p.m., or even 1:00 a.m.

The women, especially the younger ones, made an effort to watch their weight. But in Jordanian culture a big man, especially with a big face, is considered a powerful man, so the men don't mind being overweight. However, this has tragic consequences, as many die early. As a physician, Cal observed that the incidence of atherosclerotic heart disease in Jordan was astounding. Very often, males between 40 and 50 years of age would fall over with a sudden death heart attack.

Cal and Mimi eventually discovered polite ways to decline food, but it had to be declined at least three times. Finally, the host would admit, "Okay, well, I guess you may be serious about this," and then move along to three different kinds of desserts.

CHAPTER 39

In Jordan on 9/11

September 11, 2001, began as a normal day for Cal and Mimi, until a friend and neighbor called in the early afternoon with the astonishing news of the coordinated attack, inviting them to come to their house to watch the scenes unfold in their Jordanian family home.

Among the images splashed all over the world was one of a group of young Arabs dancing and singing in the streets, rejoicing that America had finally been humbled. However, this video was not taken in Jordan, but in the Palestinian territory in Israel. There was nothing but grief and sadness among the Jordanians in Amman. Every flag flew at half-mast.

Almost immediately, a growing line of people formed outside the American Embassy in Amman to personally pay their respects. A Jordanian custom when someone dies is for the family of the deceased to set up a tent in a large area with many seats. Friends and members of the community come from all over and just sit; not to talk, but just to sit and wait in silence as a way of showing their support and grief for the deceased. The American Embassy in Amman set up an official register for visitors to sign and huge tents on the embassy compound to accommodate all the people who came.

The Sheikhs who represented each of the many Bedouin tribes came. Government officials came. The king himself came. But the largest group to show their grief were the average Jordanian businessmen and businesswomen and workers. This went on for several days, and at times the line to sign the register stretched for two or three blocks outside the embassy with both dignitaries and working Jordanians waiting to sign the official register and sit with the others.

Cal and Mimi knew that millions were grieving in the US, but it was incredibly comforting for them to share their grief with the very people group who were supposedly the aggressors. Even the grocery store remained solemn and quiet when Mimi entered. No one would speak loudly because they didn't want to disturb her grief.

CHAPTER 40

Petra and Friends

*C*al and Mimi's favorite site in Jordan—without question—was the ancient city of Petra, which they visited many times. Whenever they had visitors from the US, they were sure to take them to Petra. They would walk the initial two kilometers through the natural slot canyon (called the Sik) and be amazed as they faced the entryway to an elaborate, giant tomb carved in the side of the sandstone cliff, the Treasury building made famous by Indiana Jones. Civilization in the Petra area dates back to around 7000 BC. At one time, the historic city served as a bustling trading center. The scale of the entire area is massive, filled with several valleys lined with unique tomb structures carved out of the natural sandstone of the massive cliffs of the valley. As in all ancient sites, archeologists have identified several layers of civilizations are present simultaneously, from the magnificent Nabatean carved tombs to an ancient Roman amphitheater and city structure to one of the first Christian churches of the Christian era with intricate mosaic floors. This UNESCO site is unique in that many Bedouins once lived in the sprawling city of ruins, before being relocated to a newly constructed village overlooking the site. The Wilsons often encountered boys herding goats or men loping through the valley on their camels.

On one of their initial visits, Mimi struck up a conversation with a young Bedouin man named Issam Majali, who ran a small refreshment area selling soft drinks right in the heart of Petra. They chatted easily about everything, and every time Cal and Mimi visited, they would stop by his kiosk and buy a Coke. One day he promised, "Someday when we close up, I'm going to come and take you to see the area around here."

Mimi felt badly because they had only purchased Cokes, and his gesture felt extravagant. Finally, after several visits in which they kindly declined his offer, Issam insisted, "Tonight's the night! I'm going to take you out tonight to see some parts of Jordan few have ever seen. I have a friend who has a Jeep, and we're going to take you out into the desert." Cal and Mimi had run out of excuses, and so agreed to go.

Just as the sun was setting, he took them to the edge of the mountain range from where they could see the entire Jordan Valley south of the Dead Sea, an extremely dry, desert area known as the Arabah. They could look across the valley to the Judean desert of Israel, a magnificent view in the gathering dusk. On their return they stopped at a sandstone rock face where Issam had placed several *lumiéres*, a candle in a bag with a bit of sand, all over the rock face. The effect was magical, mysterious, and relaxing. Here the two Bedouin men barbecued several kinds of meat over a small charcoal grill, and they all ate their fill and drank Cokes. When the meal was over and they were lounging in the sand on blankets, Issam announced that now was the time for the evening's entertainment.

Petra draws tourists from all over the world and working in Petra these men dealt with people from many cultures. Even the young children in Petra learn four or five languages quickly. They could speak a bit of German, Japanese, Korean, Spanish, and English, matching their discussion to whatever nationality they thought you might be. The entertainment the men offered was mimicking their impressions of tourists from various nationalities, all of it highly stereotypical, but absolutely hilarious.

"Now this one is Chinese, oh, he has a big camera, he wants to go crick, crick, crick," they mimicked, complete with formal bowing. They cycled through the Germans, the French, and the Egyptians. However, they saved the best for last, presenting with great bombast, "Now, here's an American Marine from the embassy in Amman!" With that, Issam and his friend launched into a continuous barrage of swearing, cussing, and some outright profanity, all shouted with a deep southern accent. Cal and Mimi were so weak with laughter they couldn't stand, and a little embarrassed as well that this was the enduring impression of our nationality.

As Thanksgiving plans began to unfold, the Wilsons contacted Issam and invited him and his friend to share this traditional meal with them, just the four of them, in order to honor them. Mimi tried to make her invitation as gracious as their prior invitation, explaining, "One thing that is important to us is that we share this meal with family and close friends, and we would like to share it with you." The two men made the four-hour drive from Petra to Amman, delighted to find the feast ready. Apparently, some previous expatriates had invited them to Amman, but had never followed through. Issam said to Cal and Mimi, "Isn't it interesting that our cultures are so different, but our hearts are the same? Next time you come I want you to stay at my hotel." Until then, they had no idea he also owned a hotel near Petra.

Even if they didn't have guests to bring, Cal and Mimi would sometimes drive down to Petra so Cal could get out from behind a desk and get some exercise. At an absolute minimum they would walk five miles in Petra. They explored every corner of it, and by the time they left they counted that they had visited it 35 times. Each time, they made a special point of finding Issam and getting caught up on his life.

Although there were a modest number of Arabic Christian churches in Amman, there were very few Christian churches that held an English-speaking service. However, the non-denominational Amman International Church held all of its services in English, was pastored by an American couple, and welcomed believers of all nationalities and Christian denominations. Cal and Mimi attended regularly and became part of a real community involving many of the other members, including the US Ambassador, Skip Gnehm, and his wife Peggy. They became very good friends with the Gnehms, and frequently visited Petra with them. The ambassador was quite knowledgeable about the history and archeology of the area and would invite a knowledgeable person to be their guide on their walks through Petra. There were active archaeologic excavations in Petra at the time, and the project director would take them around and explain what was being found. Skip and Peggy would invite the Wilsons to visit various other tourist sites in Jordan, many of which were ancient biblical sites. Because this was often a semi-official visit, various dignitaries would accompany the group, such as the head of the directorate and other local officials. This was great for all, as the information shared by these local leaders was often more extensive than that known by an average guide. The Wilsons have continued as close friends with the Gnehms long after both couples left Jordan.

Some of the expatriate American consultants attending the Amman International Church formed a midweek Bible study group that met in the home of a USAID couple named Charlie and Nancy Crane, which Cal and Mimi were invited to join. This also developed into several lasting friendships, not only with the Cranes and some of their children, but also several other long-term expat workers. Even after leaving Jordan, Cal and Mimi visited the Cranes in several of their subsequent assignments, such as the Dominican Republic and Tanzania. Their daughter Pam completed a doctorate in water management and joined the Wilsons several years later in Rwanda as part of a multi-country program to develop potable water sources for isolated villages.

CHAPTER 41

Bringing People to the Next Level

C al's work left Mimi with the time and opportunity to invest in the people around her. One new involvement for her that she thoroughly enjoyed was to help house workers advance to the next level of their specialty. These house workers were almost always long-term expatriates from countries such as Sri Lanka, the Philippines, or Thailand. Soon after they were settled in Amman, Mimi invited over ten house workers who were employed by people she knew and taught them the next level of service: a butler, for example, or a maid. She identified these candidates by asking when she had lunch with a friend, "Is your maid at the end of her capability, or is there more that she could learn?" Mimi would go downtown and purchase the required uniform for these individuals, so they didn't have to pay for it themselves, and would hold training sessions. At the conclusion of the training, she held a formal graduation ceremony, complete with a certificate with their name on it. They were overjoyed with the training and a formal certificate, as these humble workers had never experienced anything like this. Mimi was thrilled each time she heard of the positions they were offered and how far they progressed with the training they had received.

Mimi found a soulmate in a new friend, Sana Dababneh, who was equally devoted to working with the poor and disadvantaged. Sana was the sort of person who would line the inside pocket of her car door with cracker packets so that when she stopped at a stop light and children gathered around the car, she could give them crackers. Sana was a Jordanian nuclear pharmacist trained in the US, married to a big bear of a man with a gentle heart named Amjad, and had two children. Her extended family was well-known in Jordan as part of the Christian community, which has persisted since the apostolic times, even though they are now a small minority of the predominantly Muslim country. Mimi and Sana met in a women's Bible study, organized by the Amman International Church. The Bible study was open to anyone, so the great majority of the attendees were English-speaking Jordanians. Mimi had been asked to speak, and she presented her thoughts on *Holy Habits*, the book she had published with her co-author, Shelly Volkhardt.

Sana sat right in the front of the group so as not to miss anything. As a devout believer as well as highly intellectual, she asked the most incredible questions. Mimi and Sana became close friends and Mimi decided to look for something they could do together to show the love of Christ.

Every Tuesday the two went to an orphanage in Amman and simply loved on the children. The nuns of the orphanage would spread a clean blanket in the center of the floor and place the babies and children on it and wait for them to arrive, just to love on them. Both women loved to tenderly hold these small children.

One visit that Mimi will never forget was when one of the young children was extremely ill. Mimi held her and had the sensation that she needed to love that child. But it was like the Lord was saying to her, "No, I'm loving *you* through this child." She held her in her arms and realized that the Lord had blessed this child with his love, and that she, holding the child, could get the same blessing. Although the child died the following week. Mimi learned how through blessing the children, she received blessing herself.

Cal and Mimi had become acquainted with an American special forces soldier who had the unenviable job of clearing out land mines that Saddam Hussein's forces had placed along the border with Jordan to prevent the people from leaving the country. Although he was a rough individual, Mimi tried to figure out how to capture his heart, and persuaded him to come to the orphanage with Sana and her. He said of Mimi, "She has a way of being very persuasive, especially after she's fed me a couple of times!" Mimi coached him, indicating, "I want you to take that baby and that child and that one." He threw them over his shoulders like they were sacks of potatoes, but it won his heart. He hadn't been touched in months and here the children were touching him and climbing on him. It softened him, and he came back several times. She realized that the nuns created these "blanket times" so that other people could be blessed. They soon discovered that several of the children were both deaf and blind, and the caregivers didn't know what to do with them. Soon after that eye-opening conversation, a special house was built for these children with specially trained caretakers, so Mimi knew that Sana had both the resources and contacts to make things happen for the benefit of others.

Mimi heard many stories that confirmed that Sana's mother was of the same spirit as her daughter. One story with long-term results involved one of the itinerant sellers of flowers commonly found at major intersections in the city. Sana's mother regularly stopped at a corner where she noticed the same man had been present for several weeks selling flowers. She began to talk with him and found that his name was Mohammed. On subsequent stops she inquired about his family, and of course bought some flowers during the long red lights. After several such visits, Sana's mother asked Mohammed if he had any ambitions for doing more than selling flowers. "Oh, absolutely," he said. "I'd love to have my own shop. I'd sell vegetables."

With little fanfare, Sana's mother set him up with a small vegetable stand. Years later, when the Wilsons arrived in

Amman, he was doing very well with a vegetable market in a major shopping center of the city. Although the shop was small and absolutely packed floor to ceiling with various fruits and vegetables, they were fresh and the smell was delightful. This became the place where Mimi purchased her weekly vegetables, and she also developed a close relationship with Mohammed, not knowing until he told her that his success was in large part due to the kindness and generosity of Sana's mother. When Mimi came to shop, Mohammed would set her up on a stool and offer her some tea, while she would indicate from this perch how many of which vegetables she would like to buy that day. When she returned to America, one of her most significant episodes of reverse culture shock was walking into Safeway and finding no stool or tea ready for her.

When Cal and Mimi visited Jordan again after being away for several years, Mimi went to the vegetable market to greet her friend. Mohammed looked up at her when she entered and exclaimed with delight, "Has the light come back into my shop again?"

Mohammed now lives in the US. He is retired and several of his children have attended American universities. Even before moving to the US, he faithfully called or texted Mimi on most major holidays, especially Easter and Christmas, because he knew those are Christian holidays, and also on Mother's Day, just to wish her a happy holiday and find out how she was doing.

CHAPTER 42

Clinical Training and Transformation

*C*al was very clear about his goal with the USAID project in Jordan: to provide a broad-based scope of knowledge to the primary health care staff, with which they could treat almost anything that came into the clinic in a very capable and evidence-based fashion. Unfortunately, this goal conflicted somewhat with a subgroup of USAID managers and workers who were part of what was described as the population control group. Their goal was for the training to focus on reproductive health, which in their minds primarily meant the improved use of birth control methods.

Jordan's birth rate was an average of well over six children per marital unit when the project started. The population control group wanted to see the average drop below three children per family. Everyone knew the challenge they were dealing with, and USAID knew it as well. They were dealing more with Jordanian cultural concepts regarding the family structure than a lack of clinical knowledge of birth control.

Cal dealt with this controversy by not targeting the ancient cultural concepts, but by taking a scientific point of view, trying to point out to medical providers the medical, social, and psychological advantages of having fewer children. Around that time some credible studies were available showing that if a woman could space her pregnancies apart by about three years, her overall health, even in the poorest countries in the world, was far superior than if she had a baby every year until she was exhausted.

With the blessing of USAID, Cal tried not to attack the cultural problem of having large families, but to encourage the women and their husbands to space out the pregnancies for the sake of the mother's health. The average childbearing span of a woman is about 20 years, basically between ages 18 and 38, with some flexibility, and the size of a family will vary significantly if a child is born every year compared to every three years over these reproductive years. Cal focused on the positive issues of a smaller family size, such as their ability to devote more attention to each child, and the lower economic burden of university tuition for fewer children. This latter argument was especially important, as modern Jordanian families will sacrifice anything to allow their children to attend a good university.

As it worked out, the population control group within US-AID was so strong that they were the ones who often controlled much of the USAID funding, so Cal needed to meet at least some of their expectations. He had no objection to teaching birth control principles that included a good knowledge of the various options, proper judgment in their application to the various conditions and desires of each woman, in addition to knowing how to appropriately counsel a woman. This teaching was especially important in the training of the nurses and the midwives. Abortion was absolutely prohibited at that time in all Arab countries, including Jordan, so that was not part of the curriculum.

The primary difference between the USAID population control group and Cal was one of focus; the USAID office wanted 50 percent of the training to be on reproductive health, but Cal felt that although it should be a significant part of the training, it should probably be no more than 15 percent of the actual content. Cal went back and forth with the USAID director stationed in Jordan, a Jordanian woman who had worked with the USAID for many years. She knew the political issues inside and out, but also knew the country and its cultural values, and Cal felt she was probably more in favor of his approach than she could publicly say.

Most of the time, Cal had no problem. One or two times a director from the population health office in Washington came to Jordan, examined the training, and complained about the insufficient emphasis on reproductive health. This was based primarily on the amount of time spent on the subject, not the quality or comprehensiveness of the training. The Jordanian USAID office usually managed to placate the population control group with measures such as the appointment of a gynecologist (also an Arab) to work on the training team.

Some of the master trainers were outstanding individuals—among the nurses and midwives as well as the doctors. This was evident from their concern about their patients, the depth of their questions, and their desire to positively impact the lives of the families in a holistic manner. Cal spent a bit more time with these individuals than with some of the others.

Cal had identified in his needs analysis that most of the general practitioners working in the community health centers had not been trained in Jordan, which had a fairly high level of medical practice overall. Instead, most had received their medical training 10 to 20 years before in one of the Soviet republics such as Belarus or Romania. The extent and style of medicine that they learned was modeled on the Soviet training that focused only on the clinical situation and not the whole-person-centered care that every patient longs for. Most of these general practitioners had little understanding of the current evidence on best practices for medical care, for instance, in the control of high blood pressure or diabetes.

Five years before Cal and Mimi arrived in Jordan, the director of Family Medicine from Brown University, Dr. Vincent Hunt, had come to Jordan at the invitation of one of its primary universities to start a program in Family Medicine. At that time, the medical training in Jordan was relatively small and rudimentary, and King Hussein determined he needed many more health professionals, especially doctors, to work in the communities. Dr. Hunt had been instrumental in starting two separate Family Medicine training programs. By the time Cal arrived, there were approximately 60 practicing family physicians in the country.

The major difference between the general practitioners in the community health centers and the family physicians was the scope of their medical training. A general practitioner had basic rudimentary medical training (as noted before, often in a former Soviet republic), trained primarily in hospitals, and started practicing straight out of medical school. This often led to difficulty in effective functioning in a community setting, which requires a long-term perspective of patient care, a broader knowledge base, and a different set of tools in dealing with patients. The family physicians, on the other hand, received three years of training after medical school, similar to other specialties trained in Jordan.

The actual training process of the master trainers occupied only half of the training component of the project. Cal spent about two years training three different groups of master trainers, with each group spread out over a five-month period. The unique third group of master trainers consisted of only 20 selected, residency-trained Jordanian family physicians. To promote longer-term sustainability of this type of primary care training, the country needed a stable group of qualified trainers, not only clinically competent and up to date, but experienced in effective teaching techniques. Cal devoted significant training time to pedagogical instruction (the use of various teaching methodologies), in the curriculum of all three groups of master trainers, but focused especially on this in the last group of Family Physician master trainers.

After completing the training of all three groups of master trainers, these trainers were divided into geographic teaching teams, consisting of a doctor, nurse, and midwife on each team. Their new job description within the Ministry of Health was now to teach this same material to select groups of doctors, nurses, and midwives in their assigned governorate. The master trainers taught the same material that Cal had taught, but in a more condensed time frame (six to eight weeks instead of five months), which meant that some subjects were not quite as in-depth. In addition, because the curriculum had been taught in English (in which all of the master trainers were fluent), the material had to be translated into Arabic for presentation to their colleagues in the governorate. This was done entirely by the master trainers, with the various sections of the curriculum reviewed by capable translators (provided by the project) for accuracy before compilation into an official Arabic curriculum handbook.

Working together as a training team fostered more teamwork. Participants had to learn how to divide up the topics and support each other in the training. Cal made it quite clear that the doctor would not be doing all the teaching; the nurse and/or the midwife would also take part in that role. Because the groups for training had to be carefully chosen to avoid extracting too many health workers from each clinic at a time, the groups were small (often 12-18), and each governorate required up to 8 different groups to cover all of the health center workers in that area.

Cal visited each of the 12 training teams several times a year. On these all-day trips, he would drive to the governorate and locate the site of the training, then simply walk in, sit down, and observe. Jordan is a small country with Amman in the center. Cal could drive to Aqaba in the far south, arrive by 10:00 or 11:00 in the morning, sit through several hours of training, and still get back home that evening. Although he did not speak much Arabic, he could follow the discussion by the trainer's use of key English medical words (because there was no commonly known equivalent in Arabic), and especially by noting the non-verbal communication demonstrated by both the trainer and the participants.

Not surprisingly, the same battle noted earlier, with the doctors taking offense at being taught together with the nurses and midwives, surfaced repeatedly with each group of community health professionals in the governorates. Cal instructed the trainers on how to deal with this issue. Primarily, he advised them to reflect on their own attitudes and feelings when they started the master training, and to simply share with their colleagues their own changes in attitude. Some of the complaints went all the way to the Minister of Health, who was willing to go against the objections of many of the doctors. He was adamant that, if this method was going to improve health center teamwork, he wanted it to continue. So, Cal's training was reinforced at the highest level.

After each small group session in each governorate, Cal asked the participants in the community-level trainings to give an evaluation of the course. Almost universally, the comments were very positive. Cal also reviewed the evaluations that the master trainers completed near the end of the project. Now at least two years removed from their own training, experienced in the training of others, and again working in their individual clinics, their responses validated Cal's process. In response to questions such as *What have you learned from this? How do you feel this can move forward?* the most frequent comment stated, "I have come to greatly value the contribution of the nurse and the midwives, and we are working together as a team!"

It thrilled Cal that the participants recognized an improved attitude in the health centers, and especially improved teamwork between the male doctors and the female nurses. Although the training may not have turned mindsets 180 degrees, it did steer them toward more evidence-based medicine with a greater level of empathy and perceived care for individual patients.

Formal graduations were held at the end of each training period in each governorate, usually held in a local hotel. With great ceremony, each participant received a gold-rimmed certificate printed with their name. The event almost always included the traditional feast meal, a Jordanian dish called *mensaf,* (a huge plate of rice with saffron, roast lamb, or sometimes goat, with the whole plate doused in a slightly bitter liquid yogurt).

The traditional way of eating *mensaf* is for the men to gather in a circle around a huge tray of *mensaf*, with washed hands. Each man mentally designates a sliver of the rice and meat in front of him as his, and with his right hand, he scoops some rice with a piece of lamb and compresses it into a sticky ball the size of a large marble. He then sets the ball on top of his thumb as if he were about to shoot a marble and shoots it into his mouth; the key point of etiquette being that none of his fingers could touch his mouth, which is considered very unhygienic. The women eat *mensaf* in a more conventional manner, with spoons and a plate.

Cal became expert at eating *mensaf* this way and grew to love the traditional dish. He *had* to love it, because sometimes he attended a graduation ceremony every day for 10 days in a row.

CHAPTER 43

Into Iraq and a Difficult Farewell

*D*uring the Wilsons' last two years in Jordan, following 9/11, the US administration suspected Iraq to be one of the great destabilizing forces in the world due to Saddam Hussein's unpredictability, his buildup of weapons, the threat of development of weapons of mass destruction, and his invasion of Kuwait. These fears led to what is now called the Second Gulf War, where the US launched its attack on Iraq from various points—including Jordan. That fact was hidden even at the highest levels of the Jordanian government; only the king and a few of his confidants knew the US was staging a base of operations to attack Iraq from deep within the eastern Jordanian desert.

During the build-up to the Second Gulf War, the US Embassy became very concerned about possible repercussions and terrorist activity in Jordan, because of its close ties to the US and immediate proximity to Iraq. Because of these tensions, all non-essential US citizens were advised to evacuate from Jordan, and since USAID was an official government agency, all of its employees were ordered to evacuate. So, with about a week's notice, Cal and Mimi found themselves back in Denver for an undetermined period of time; still part of the project, but instructed to continue their work virtually.

Since their Denver home was rented to Marty Cooper and her family, they could not just move back home. Fortunately, USAID had anticipated that and provided the funding for Cal and Mimi to rent and furnish a small condominium near their home on a short-term basis. Because the expectation was that the basic work of the project would continue in Jordan under the Jordanian staff, Cal developed a virtual work schedule to connect via the internet (prior to the days of Zoom) with his co-workers. Given the time-zone difference of nine hours, he began the connection at 4:00 a.m. and continued working through to about 11:00 a.m., with most of the conversations occurring between 4:00 a.m. and 8:00 a.m. Denver time. This turned out to be a very relaxing, even reflective time for Cal and Mimi, in that the work pressures were much less, and since no one in Denver had anticipated their return, their social schedule was quite light. With the exception of waking up at 4:00 a.m., they felt almost as if they were on a paid vacation.

The evacuation order was lifted shortly after the Second Gulf war ended, about two months after arriving in Denver, and Cal and Mimi returned to Jordan. As it turned out, Jordan was spared retaliation for their role in the war, and their security forces were able to control most of the anticipated terrorist activity. So, Cal and Mimi again stepped into the work, the visits, and the enjoyment of Jordanian hospitality with the evacuation months only a pleasant memory.

With the Second Gulf War, Saddam Hussein was kicked out of Iraq and forced into hiding. The country was declared to be "liberated," at least by the US. Almost ten years of sanctions against Iraq had already crippled its economy and created the inability to access outside information and equipment. With this "liberation," Iraqi life turned much more chaotic. Iraq was in dire straits.

The Iraqi Ministry of Health expressed a desperate need for more primary care physicians to deal with the large numbers of people who had not been able to get proper medical care during the war, or were already in poor health because of the shortages imposed by US sanctions prior to the war. The Iraqi Ministry of Health concluded that the only way to develop effective primary health care workers as quickly as possible was to follow what had been done in some former Soviet countries: to retrain existing specialists as generalists. They selected a group of existing specialists, such as internists, pediatricians, and obstetricians, and offered them additional training in primary health care. Basically, they said to the pediatrician, "You may know how to deal with children, but now you are going to learn how to deal with common problems in adults" or to the obstetrician, "Learn how to deal with men's health issues in addition to women's."

Cal was still working with USAID in Jordan when health officials in Iraq approached USAID for help with the initial retraining of Iraq's primary healthcare workers. Since Cal was doing this very thing, USAID requested he participate in the Iraqi training as well. He agreed, and adapted a shortened version of his Jordanian primary care curriculum for use in Iraq. Cal traveled to Iraq three times in the immediate post-war period, for a week to 10 days each time, and each time was a real adventure.

His first visit to Iraq was six weeks after the end of the Second Gulf War. Cal saw first-hand the jubilation and euphoria of the country because the war and the strict sanctions were over. Saddam Hussein was gone, in hiding at the time, and most Iraqis were looking forward to a whole new future. Cal felt privileged to be part of that positive vision. However, significant risks still existed, with long-standing tensions between the Sunni and Shia branches of Islam, ongoing terrorist activities and multiple bombings.

The Baghdad training team consisted primarily of former professors in Iraqi medical schools who were no longer able to work because of the chaos. Because of the ties to US assistance, the training team had to maintain a low profile in a small non-descript office, and conduct training in a small, non-pretentious hotel tucked on a side street. The group of specialists to be re-trained had been selected by the project director and numbered about 20. Because of the strict pre-war sanctions and the war itself, most of them had not participated in any continuing education for many years other than what they could find on their own. These specialists were as eager to hear about some of the newer ways of dealing with common problems as the general practitioners were.

One morning as Cal was teaching, a loud *Boom!* rattled the windows, the impact so massive that they all felt a shockwave hitting their bodies. Everybody fell silent—a bomb had gone off relatively close. Two or three of the Iraqis muttered under their breath, *"Masha'allah,"* the Arabic term for "God bless them," because they knew that people had died.

After the moment passed, Cal looked around the room. No one had moved. Everyone wanted to keep going, so he continued teaching. A few minutes later, a cellphone rang, and Cal watched one of the doctors answer the phone, say a few words, and quietly get up and leave. A few hours later he was back sitting with them to finish the day's training. The Red Cross building, which was not far away, had been bombed that morning, and this doctor's home was directly across the street from it. The bomb had blown out every window and many of the doors in his house. Fortunately, only one or two family members were present in the home, and none had been hurt. So, the doctor surveyed the damage, noted that no one had been harmed, and came back to the training.

Because Cal's visits in Iraq were limited and his movements strictly controlled, he did not have the opportunity to follow this early group of specialists-turned-generalists as they began training the young physicians assigned to various community health centers, many of whom were recent graduates from Iraqi medical schools. However, he heard they were teaching effectively as well as providing updated knowledge to those they trained. He felt privileged to be able to participate in a slight way in the rebuilding of a torn nation, even though it would be torn even more by violent terrorists over the following years. He was left with an indelible impression of the generally optimistic spirit and resilience of the Iraqi people. In addition, he became close friends with at least two of the Iraqi medical school professors in Baghdad, and communicated with them for many years after. Cal would go on to make several more visits in later years to continue to try to help re-develop their broken health system.

As mentioned earlier, the goal of the training program in Jordan was to form master trainers in reproductive and primary health care. After the project ended, the Ministry of Health recognized members of this group of master trainers as experts in primary healthcare training. Cal also hoped and anticipated that some of them would become leaders in the Family Medicine movement in Jordan, and he wanted to see that thrive as well. On subsequent return visits to Jordan, even years after the project termination, Cal was overjoyed to find that most of the trainers he had mentored were still active in teaching and providing a good example of high-quality primary health care, and some of the Family Medicine trainers were active in existing Family Medicine postgraduate programs.

Cal and Mimi would pack and return to Jordan tomorrow if they could. They loved the place and the project, and it was very hard to leave. There were many factors that sealed Jordan in their hearts, such as the depth of relationships with many Jordanians, the sense of acceptance that they both felt, and the opportunity to positively influence the health development of an entire country. There was a deep sense of history permeating the entire land, which included not only Petra but many Roman ruins, sites important to the ancient Israelites on their way to their Promised Land, such as Heshbon and Mount Nebo, and later Crusader castles built by European knights. They have tried to return to visit almost every year; it's their favorite place to relax and meditate.

Lakewood, Colorado

2004-2010

TOM, KYNDRA, JORDAN, AND HUTSON, 2009

PIERCE AND MIRIAM ON HADRIANS WALL,
ENGLAND, 2005

KEVIN AND
SARAH IN LIMA,
PERU,
DECEMBER 2004

KURT, LORI, MIRIAM AND PIERCE, 2009

JORDAN
TRINIDAD, 2007

KEVIN AND SARAH AND MIRACLE BABY, KYLE, 2006

MIMI SPEAKING AT A CHURCH
CONFERENCE IN LIMA, PERU, 2004

COMMUNITY CONSULTATION IN GHANA, 2008

CHAPTER 44

Catching Up with the Children

*C*al and Mimi always considered their roots to be in the Denver area. Beginning with their work in Ecuador and continuing through the work in Jordan, they returned home for a visit every year for at least a month or two. While it wasn't the same as living full-time in Denver, it allowed them to maintain at least some of their close relationships and renew contacts.

When they returned to Jordan after these visits, they always felt there was so much more they could have done at home if they had stayed a bit longer. But on the other hand, the time spent was sufficient to permit a sense of some continuity with friends and family. In addition, international calling was becoming more efficient and cheaper, especially using the internet, which they greatly used in Jordan to keep in touch with family and friends in the US and in Ecuador.

Since Cal's brother and sister-in-law, Kirk and Dawn, now owned their former home on the family farm, they were welcomed right in with them, in their old house, whenever they came home to visit (leaving the house sitter in place in their current house.) This made it feel like they were indeed coming home.

Prior to returning from their five years in Jordan, they gave six months' notice to Marty Cooper, who had been living in and caring for their home. They were able to move back in, with all their own furniture, dishes, and belongings already in place. They found the sparkling clean house looking better than when they had bought it brand-new five years before. Even the little things that sometimes malfunctioned had been well maintained, for which they were incredibly grateful.

Their first priority upon returning home was to reconnect with their adult children and grandchildren. Over the past five years of absence much had happened. During a downturn in the economy, Kurt, their oldest, had lost his job managing the philanthropic portfolio of the family friend who had originally funded the work on the Onzole River in Ecuador. He worked as a roofer while he searched for another job, and after waiting 14 months, was offered the directorship of a media production organization called Compass Arts in Grand Rapids, Michigan, that produced high-quality videos and books for the Christian community. Kurt had earlier been involved in the initial development of this organization while managing the philanthropic portfolio. Kurt and his wife Lori and their two children, Pierce and Miriam, relocated to Grand Rapids, where they stayed for almost 15 years. Lori assisted Kurt in the business from the home, as she felt that her children were her primary responsibility. The media production company thrived under Kurt's leadership, adding a training institute for young media students such as those studying at Calvin College. When Kurt left the company 15 years later, the company was split into three separate companies to help the new management cope with the diverse structure that it had become.

Their daughter, Kyndra, had married a fellow Colorado College student and friend of Kurt's shortly after graduation. Her husband, Tom Trinidad, became a minister with the Presbyterian Church of America, and continued with his doctoral degree in ministry at Notre Dame in South Bend, Indiana, where Cal and Mimi visited them upon their return to the US. Kyndra obtained a job in a bank while Tom was at Notre Dame. With her trademark self-confidence, she had responded to a help-wanted notice, and easily convinced them she was the best person for the job. As she started the job, she asked for a policies and procedures manual, but the bank director responded, "Well, we don't have one here, but I can tell you about it," leaving Kyndra to learn how to do her job by asking lots of questions and making some initial mistakes. In an attempt to help her co-workers and those who would come after her, she wrote a full policy and procedures manual in her spare time, and presented it to her supervisor when she resigned two years later. They were very sorry to see her leave.

Kevin had graduated from Colorado College about the same time Cal and Mimi left for Jordan. Before he graduated, he was recruited by Anderson Consulting, Inc., specifically for their "Change Management" program, designed to help companies through various transitions. Shortly after, Kevin married Sarah, a schoolteacher he had met at church, and they stayed in Colorado Springs. After a year of working with Anderson Consulting, Kevin noted the lifestyle of most of the partners required an average of 14 hours/day of work, and total dedication to the company. Kevin held different priorities than this type of lifestyle, so despite an outstanding evaluation at the end of his first year, the generous salary, and corporate benefits, he gave his notice to quit that very day.

Kevin and Sarah had been considering mission work for some time. Now that Kevin was unemployed, they decided to enter into missions in a full-time capacity with the Youth for Christ organization. They were recruited to start a computer laboratory and learning center in Lima, Peru, for street children in the most poverty-stricken area of north Lima. Unfortunately, because of significant misunderstandings with the director of the Lima Youth for Christ, Kevin and Sarah began to explore other opportunities. After a difficult two months they joined an association of Christian Missionary Alliance churches in the north of Lima. The young couple fit the association's vision to set up a computer learning center for the poor young people of that area, to provide them with more marketable skills for the Peruvian job market, as well as encourage participation in their church activities. After setting up the computer center and training not only young people but also many of the pastors of the church association, Kevin and Sarah were integrated into the pastoral staff of the Alliance Church.

One of Kevin's great advantages was that he had grown up speaking Spanish in Ecuador for over nine years, so his Spanish was flawless, and Sarah spoke very good Spanish as well. Kevin was often asked to translate for visiting English-speaking pastors. On one occasion, the visiting pastor began illustrating a sermon point with a story that was very culturally American, and not easily understood by the majority of the relatively poor church members. Kevin quickly noted the problem and developed his own illustration that was more appropriate to the audience, pausing to let the pastor continue in English, but delivering his own story in fluent Spanish. A few bilingual members of the congregation began chuckling, but Kevin didn't think the visiting pastor was aware of the switch. Kevin also did some of the preaching among the five churches of this Association.

CHAPTER 45

Mimi's Writing and Speaking Activities

Returning from overseas and re-establishing their roots proved difficult for the Wilsons, in part because they had so loved living and working in Jordan. Mimi had pictured lots of time with old friends, only to concede that many old friends were in a different stage of life. It was very difficult to re-invigorate some relationships, in part because she assumed the relationship would be similar to what she had left, but it was not. She had to make a new life, and she did.

Mimi had started writing a new book, *Trusting in the Goodness of God*, with her friend from Quito and former co-author, Shelly Volkhardt, who was still in Ecuador and later moved to Miami. They had frequent phone conversations at 6:00 a.m. to review the material each had written, and to decide how to integrate it into the book. They had been prayer partners for 30 years, and each knew the other well enough to decide instinctively whether they should use Shelly's illustration or Mimi's.

Her book, *Holy Habits,* was selling well and had been translated into several languages, and *Once-a-Month Cooking* was also selling well. Her book success led to speaking engagements for Mimi at many women's conferences. Typically, Mimi was able to choose her topic and she would preferentially speak on the nature and character of God, using material from her current year's personal study which provided a constant joy to her. In addition to several speaking engagements in Colorado, many conferences were in different states, requiring quite a bit of travel.

Mimi loved speaking to women's groups, especially when she could stand close enough to see the participants' faces and receive feedback from them. By the end of a conference where she may have spoken four times, she had developed relationships with many of the ladies, greatly nourishing her spirit and creativity. As the frequency of speaking invitations increased, the need for her to prioritize her time also increased. She decided to prioritize weekend conferences or women's retreats where she could speak several times, develop a theme, and get to know the women along the way, rather than accepting single, one-time events.

Her pattern in organizing a weekend speaking event became relatively standard. Beginning on a Friday evening, she allowed time for the women to simply relax. They usually traveled from a distance and were road weary, so she didn't introduce any new material that first evening, but focused on entertaining and impactful stories. By Saturday morning the women were ready to listen. She would begin by providing examples of how she began studying the goodness of God and His eternality, and then expand on other aspects of God and how they impact our lives. There would typically be two more Saturday sessions, and on Sunday they would commonly end with a communion service.

Women signed up on a schedule to spend individual time with her, so Mimi made sure she wasn't tired when she arrived at the event. It was time-consuming, but thrilling to see where individual women were in their spiritual journey. They would come to Mimi's room and chat, often about the topic just discussed or about something in their life that they regretted. They would say things like, "I was part of a Bible study once, but I gave it up years ago. How do I begin again?" and Mimi would offer some counseling. It could be draining at times, but she usually found it invigorating.

Mimi's study of the character of God spanned many years. It provided the foundation for her books, *Holy Habits* and *Trusting in the Goodness of God,* and much of her speaking ministry. She constantly grappled with how to take these concepts and make them applicable to the current culture.

One of the illustrations that she took around the world when she spoke was that of tiny boxes of thankfulness, to illustrate the idea that God is eternally good, even if we do not always see it. She would teach that in our humanness, our tendency is to drag God down into our world, a time-bound and performance-driven world. When Mimi would ask a woman "How was your day?" she would often reply, "Exhausting!" But days are not exhausting to an eternal, loving God! Every day is His gift. To highlight this concept, she encouraged women to take a small square paper box (which Mimi gave to each one) and put it by their bed, representing a single day, open and ready to receive God's goodness. However, each woman needed to identify something to put into the box. For example, she might awaken and simply thank God for a comfortable bed, symbolically putting this gratitude into the box. Or, "Thank you, God, for shoes." "Thank you for ice cream." "Thank you for my children." She could continually be putting into her box the multiple good things God had provided for her. At the end of the day her she could close her symbolically full box and give it back in thankfulness to her loving Father, a day full of His goodness. The next morning, she would open her box again and start filling it. Mimi's primary point of teaching was to arrive at a place where we consistently notice God's goodness and respond to it in thankfulness and worship.

Cal had grown up in a church in Littleton, Colorado, the Littleton Bible Chapel, that generously supported them during their nine years in Ecuador. While in Jordan, he received his faculty salary from the University of Colorado and USAID agreement, and needed no outside support. However, the church continued to support them emotionally and with prayer. Upon their return they resumed attending the Littleton Bible Chapel, although they quickly realized that they were again in a different culture. Cal described the first few weeks as, "We felt somewhat like Rip Van Winkle awakening after years of sleep, to find that we did not know almost 50% of the people in our church, that we startled our guests by moving to kiss them as we did the Arabs, and that an evening with friends often required two weeks advance notice instead of a casual "How about coming over tonight?" In spite of these adjustments, they quickly resumed feeling right at home, appreciating the value of many relationships that went back 20 or 30 years. Many couples had children approximately the same age as theirs, friends they had known years before and with whom they had shared the joys and trials of childrearing. These friendships were among the most stabilizing influences in their lives. Several of those couples had come to visit them on the mission field, and having shared international experiences greatly solidified those relationships.

Of course, Cal and Mimi had guests in their home regularly, which for the Wilsons meant much more frequently than for most families. One signature dish that Mimi loved to prepare, and that she could provide very quickly, was a head of fresh cauliflower, surrounded by cooked peas, baby shrimp, and hard-boiled egg in a cream sauce. This was presented on a large platter with the cauliflower in the middle, and the shrimp in cream sauce all the way around it. Mimi found it to be an easy, one-dish meal. Homemade bread was always ready in the freezer, as was dessert—always chocolate, dark chocolate.

One new discovery was that she now had to learn to accommodate diet preferences, food intolerances, and allergies. Suddenly, many people could now only eat certain things, which after years in poor, underdeveloped countries, was something she had not dealt with before. But Mimi took on dealing with dietary restrictions with her typical determination, not wanting anyone, old friends or new, to miss out on a shared meal at the Wilson table.

CHAPTER 46

Change in the Focus of Family Medicine

A short time after moving back to the US, Cal reported for work at the university. He had been part of the University of Colorado Department of Family Medicine throughout their time in Jordan, receiving his normal salary with USAID funds routed through the university. He basically stepped back into the Family Medicine teaching program that he had started before they left for Jordan, this time as an associate professor. The residency program was moving forward nicely, and those who had taken over the program were leading it well. The residents were happy with the program, and they now had a custom-built new clinic in the Stapleton area of Denver. Cal settled back into teaching in the residency and seeing some patients.

Stepping back into a practice after five years of absence, he saw mostly new patients. But some whom he had cared for in private practice fifteen-plus years before heard he was back and slowly drifted back under his care. He enjoyed reconnecting with them.

Still, Cal experienced significant culture shock. He had become accustomed to the Jordanian Muslim's extremely conservative way of thinking. Their thought process was much more intuitive than Americans', forcing him to make some adjustments in his discussions with the Family Medicine residents and other faculty.

He also noticed that his perspective was now much broader, having spent significant time both in Ecuador and the Middle East. He had a hard time identifying with some of the local issues that seemed to consume many people. He identified more with global issues around the world, that in most cases were far more severe and far more problematic than many of issues that consumed those in the US.

An example is the HIV epidemic that had begun in the late 1990s and exploded in the early 2000s. He had not seen this as much in the Middle East. Their conservatism, especially in extra-marital relationships, was in a sense protective. This was not because Jordanians didn't fool around sexually, but they didn't do so to the same extent as in Western countries. As Cal returned, the HIV epidemic was in full swing in this country and consuming an exorbitant amount of medical attention, and rightfully so. Yet, Cal compared the medical situation in the US with that of most of Africa, where there was very little treatment, or in Asia where the treatment was inaccessible even if it was available. He was committed to try to do what he could to help improve the health situation in his own country. At the same time, his heart went out to many other countries where poverty trapped people who had little recourse to anything that might prolong their useful life when faced with problems like AIDS or chronic diseases.

One local situation did strike Cal deeply. When he left the University of Colorado Hospital to go to Jordan, the entire Department of Family Medicine was oriented toward care of the underserved in Colorado. It was their goal and their mantra to prepare doctors to care for patients in areas with limited medical service, for example, in rural areas and the poor within cities. Over the years the department, long before Cal joined them in 1995, had been committed to trying to reach the poor around them and provide them with appropriate medical care.

When Cal began the residency program, although it was affiliated with the University of Colorado, the teaching clinic of the residency, A.F. Williams Family Medicine Center, operated primarily through significant grants from a private foundation and the income that it generated. While Cal was in Jordan, the University Hospital began expanding its footprint, and evolved into University Health, a full healthcare organization that is now widespread throughout Colorado. It started purchasing private practices, which was common in those days, and one of the practices they acquired was the A.F. Williams Family Medicine teaching clinic of the Department of Family Medicine.

So, Cal came back to new owners and managers of the Family Medicine clinic. The University Hospital now provided the clinic management staff, so the Department of Family Medicine was no longer involved in the selection process. The new owners provided many helpful services such as billing and bookkeeping. However, as Cal sat in one of the faculty meetings listening to the new clinic manager from University Hospital describe upcoming changes in scheduling and seeing patients, it became immediately clear to Cal that the clinic would no longer treat any patients who had difficulty paying.

In the past the Family Medicine clinic had a fund it could draw on if patients were unable to pay their full fee. The clinic also tried to keep their fees at a reasonable level as much as possible. But all of that went away. Basically, the new management did not allow the clinic to take on patients without adequate insurance, meaning many of the impoverished patients they had been caring for over the years could no longer be seen at the clinic.

Cal raised his hand and asked the new clinic director, "Well, if this is the case, and we're not going to be seeing uninsured patients, what about all of the uninsured patients we've been taking care of up until now? Or what about the needs of the poorer communities here in Denver or around the state? Our clinic has been viewed in the past as part of a social safety net for people who needed medical care but couldn't afford insurance or big bills."

The new clinic manager curtly replied, "Dr. Wilson, don't try to impose your values on us!" His remark implied a veiled reference to the known fact of Cal's work as a missionary physician and implied that his Christian values were interfering with business and outside the current thinking of University Health. Cal's heart sank. One of the primary foundations on which the clinic had been built, to reach the poorer people who had difficulty finding appropriate medical care, was now gone. The new management appeared to be entirely centered around making a profit and working only with patients who could afford good insurance.

Cal tried to understand the new reality, as it didn't look like there was much he could do about it anyway, other than look for ways to provide some supplemental help from other sources. He turned his focus to training the residents and providing them with a more global perspective, including caring for those who needed help but had limited financial means. He believed that if those in training could begin to consider the social and economic aspects of medical need, they would also be sensitive to primary healthcare needs on a global basis, and work creatively toward helping to meet those needs.

CHAPTER 47

Coats for Afghanistan

*C*al and Mimi hosted a variety of guests in Jordan, including an internationally recognized pastoral couple who had a fun sense of humor and loved to sit around the table telling stories of their adventures from many parts of the world. In these conversations, the wife shared something she had recently experienced in refugee camps in Afghanistan.

In the refugee camps of those displaced by war with the Taliban and various insurgencies in the mountains of Afghanistan, the conditions were so dire it was common for babies under two years old to freeze to death at night. Mimi didn't know when anything had hit her with greater sadness: to wake up and find your baby frozen because the huddled family was not able to generate enough warmth —it was incomprehensible. The wife indicated that she had heard that there was not a single baby under two alive in several of the refugee camps during the winter.

Mimi thought, *Well, I can't bring those babies back, but I can help make sure it does not happen to more babies.* How could she get them something warm? While in Jordan, Mimi began collecting coats for children, a project she intensified when she returned to the US. She asked friends for used children's coats and scoured thrift stores for them, looking for coats in very good condition with lots of insulation. As she washed and prepared the garments, Mimi inserted a small heart-shaped piece of felt into a pocket with a safety pin, trusting the recipient would understand that the warm coat came with love. Whenever she heard of someone going to Afghanistan for contract or military work or mission work, she talked them into taking a bag of coats to pass along to one of the agencies serving displaced refugees.

As Mimi continued with this mission, it became apparent they would soon be moving to Rwanda, where she would be unlikely to find warm coats, and even if she found any, it would be impossible to effectively ship them to Afghanistan. She prayed and watched as her Father God began to open doors for this small ministry to continue. She had at that point accumulated and prepared more than 100 coats, with no visible way of getting them to the most needy. After a visit to their children in Grand Rapids, Michigan, they were sitting in the waiting room of the airport when Mimi overheard a man near her talking about going to Afghanistan. She immediately wondered *Will this be the one?* With some trepidation she approached the man and shared her story. With a smile, he said, "Yes, I will distribute them for you," and gave her an address to which the coats could be sent. The man was a colonel who was helping to plan the American response to the refugee crisis in Afghanistan and was specifically involved in the distribution of supplies such as clothing through military channels.

What a joyful wonder! At a family meal, shortly before leaving for Rwanda, Mimi shared her Afghan coat story, including her heartbreak at having to potentially abandon helping out these refugee children. After the meal, a distant, yet close in heart relative, Debbie Perry-Smith, offered to see how she could carry on with the vision. Through her various relationships, Debbie was able to connect with several other non-profits that would sustain Mimi's dream for eight years. Good friends and partners of the non-profit organization H.E.L.P. International from Loveland, Colorado, were receiving "retired" United States ski resort uniforms that had to be repurposed out of the country, and they were at a loss as to how and where they could distribute such warm bounty to reach the most needy. These were high-end winter clothes and coats manufactured by the best names in winter wear, which were now at their disposal to literally save lives among the families and children of Afghanistan. Although the biggest need was for children's warm coats, Mimi reasoned that since these parkas were very well insulated coats, they could also be used as a large sleeping bag for small children by zipping them into it.

During this process, Debbie was introduced to a retired US

Air Force General and his wife, founders of the Lamia-Afghan Foundation, who were already doing humanitarian relief work with Afghan refugees. This general had served during the height of the Afghan war, and had developed a heart for the people, especially the children. Since their foundation had an existing relationship with the US Air Force and the USAID Denton Program, Debbie and the H.E.L.P. team dovetailed into the process of this relief work and started preparing the first load in the winter of 2010.

Preparing the donated winter gear for shipment was no small task with existing military shipping protocols. Preparation of each shipment required sorting out garments too worn out to send, preparation of a detailed inventory, taping, labeling and weighing of the boxes, and then stacking them on pallets within a specified height range. After inspection, the pallets were shrink-wrapped for trucking (via donated services of a large trucking company) from the H.E.L.P. warehouse to one of the two Air Force bases in Colorado. One of the loads of 27 pallets was delivered in the middle of a heavy snowstorm with the assistance of a nearby construction company who offered special equipment to load the truck in spite of the snow.

Between 2010 and 2018, seven loads of winter clothing for all ages, comprising well over 7500 boxes with over 150,000 pieces of winter clothing, were sent to the mountain refugee camps of Afghanistan. As an example of the scope of each shipment, in early 2018 over 650 families together with 300 students received winter coats in three different provinces, all due to the shared dedication and collaboration of multiple small non-profit groups such as the Lamia-Afghan Foundation and H.E.L.P. International, together with the US Air Force.

As circumstances in the country changed, decisions were made to scale back the delivery of aid. However, just before one of the final loads was to be flown to Afghanistan, Mimi (who by then had returned from Rwanda), Debbie and the H.E.L.P. International team were invited to Peterson Air Force Base in Colorado Springs to watch the cargo plane be loaded, to board and tour the aircraft and then witness the take off. Mimi's heart was bursting with gratitude and thanksgiving as she praised God for making all of this possible over eight years, involving a significant number of key individuals, all for the sake of providing a warm coat to thousands of those who were freezing in the cold of a war-torn nation!

CHAPTER 48

Center for Global Health Goes Live

*C*al continued with his dream of setting up a system within the University of Colorado structure to promote involvement in global health activities. Before he left for Jordan, he had begun to coordinate what he called an International Health Committee, consisting of interested faculty members from various medical departments and even various schools, such as dentistry and physical therapy, to talk about what they could do to provide more of a global perspective on healthcare to their students. However, when Cal left, that committee faded away.

Upon returning from Jordan, Cal reconnected with some of those interested faculty members and learned that many were still interested. They discussed setting up a formal, ongoing Center for Global Health within the university structure. As Cal pursued this endeavor, he discovered that less than a year before, a business professor, Dr. Blair Gifford, had set up a Center for Global Health within the School of Business at the downtown University of Colorado campus. Dr. Gifford had noted that several of his students were interested in healthcare administration, so he set up the Center to provide some global context to their training, since health is universally one of the greater needs around the world.

Cal met and began collaborating with Dr. Gifford. This innovative business professor was interested in a much broader scope of business concepts and ethics than many in his field. It became obvious to both Cal and Dr. Gifford that a functioning Center for Global Health within the School of Business limited the involvement of many interested healthcare professionals. When Cal suggested moving the Center to the Health Sciences Center, Dr. Gifford totally agreed. He understood that he could continue to use the Center for business students, as Cal's vision was to make it as broad based as possible for those interested in global health.

With the Center for Global Health at its new location at the Health Sciences Center, Dr. Gifford suggested that Cal assume the direction of the Center. Cal began having serious discussions with the various stakeholders involved, all the way from the upper administration level to the staff who were actually going to do the work. He talked with the chair of his Family Medicine department and with the Dean of the Medical School, who had worked with Cal when he was an intern, and both were very much in favor of it. Cal went all the way to the Chancellor of the University to talk about it, and again found a receptive ear.

He formed a Board of Directors of interested stakeholders and faculty members, and in 2005 formally organized the Center for Global Health within the Health Sciences Center. It was strong in concept and scope, but unfortunately weak in a consistent source of funding, but benefited greatly from the interest and contacts of the Dean of the Medical School.

At a reception for businessmen, the Dean of the Medical School met the CEO of the Newmont Mining Company that was headquartered in Denver. The CEO mentioned to the Dean that in the company's large-scale mining operations in various parts of the world he was concerned about the well-being and health of the communities who lived around the gold mines, usually in isolated areas in poorer countries. He wanted to see if there were particular issues with their health that could be attributed to the nearby mines, and if so, what might be done to help them.

At the conclusion of several subsequent meetings, the CEO signed a memorandum of agreement to do a needs analysis in every one of their larger mines, which at that time involved three different countries: Peru, Indonesia, and Ghana. Newmont was willing to pay for a multi-disciplinary health team to perform a thorough health needs evaluation and propose appropriate recommendations. The funding for that contract was routed through the university and became the first major funding available to start the Center.

Cal put together a needs analysis protocol based on his past experiences in poor, isolated communities, and organized teams of four to five interested faculty members from various medical disciplines. Over a period of about two years they visited each of these mining sites, spending time in the communities surrounding the mining area to better understand the health issues present and their possible relationships to the mining industry.

A team would spend 10 to 14 days at one site, the maximum time that could be spared away from their jobs at the university. They had the opportunity to not only identify the most significant health needs, especially those needs that were exacerbated or created by the presence of the mine, but also to provide recommendations as to what might be done to address them. These teams were not only observant, but innovative. For instance, in the highlands of Peru around Cajamarca, the mine was situated near 11,000 feet elevation. There were only a few roads in the area, so many villages and households were semi-isolated. The people complained that because of the geography they had always had difficulty getting their farm products such as sheep or chickens to market. One of the ideas that emerged from the team's brainstorming was a recommendation to place a cell phone tower in a strategic location to cover many of those households that were otherwise totally isolated, following the principle that improved and consistent communication among themselves and the outside world could promote improved access to more distant markets.

When the team traveled to West Africa, a place Cal had never been to before, he was amazed that Ghana was such an overtly Christian country. The churches are extremely vibrant and most of the government officials are very active in their local churches. In one meeting between the Provincial Director of Health and all of the tribal chiefs in that area to discuss their health issues and needs, the Director stood up at the beginning of the meeting and said, "As is our custom we would like to open with a word of prayer," and then called on one of the local leaders to offer the prayer. After a productive and very respectful meeting, they then closed with prayer.

Often when Cal and his teammates approached a village in Ghana, he noted a small handwritten sign on the side of the road that read something like "Ebenezer Prayer Center This Way – All Welcome," pointing to a faint path leading off into the bush. On the other side of the village, he often spotted another sign pointing to the "Praise God Prayer Center –Off This Way."

As the team surveyed these villages to get a sense of the kinds of health problems they were suffering, Cal consistently noticed that none of them talked about mental health issues, whereas mental health issues are usually in the top ten of issues that most healthcare providers see in primary healthcare around the world. He regularly asked local healthcare providers, "What about people who are depressed? Or people who come in with anxiety or panic attacks? Do you see anybody like that?" The nurse or health officer would scratch their head and say, "No, we don't have anybody like that here." Cal knew statistically their answer was probably not correct. Finally, Cal met an elderly and experienced health officer who had been working in the village for many years, and asked him the same question.

The old man responded, "Yeah. We have some people who are depressed or ridden with anxiety. But that's not a medical problem, they do not want to talk to me about it; that is a spiritual problem. This is the role of the prayer centers. When they are suffering these kinds of emotional struggles, their family will take them to the prayer center."

The prayer centers turned out to be little retreat centers, usually just one or two houses, where people from the nearby village could come and rest, meditate, pray, and receive spiritual counseling. People would stay at the prayer center for as long as it took until they could be reintegrated into the village again. It struck Cal that in a country where there is much less division between the secular and the sacred, some of the deeper problems that people suffer, like depression or anxiety, can be dealt with very effectively with local counseling and spiritual guidance.

Sadly, just as the teams were finishing their reports, the price of gold dropped drastically and Newmont Mining faced substantial cutbacks. Economic realities prevailed, and the local mine managers were reluctant to implement the health team's recommendations. To make matters worse, the CEO who had been so supportive was fired. The new CEO was more attuned to the economic health of the company, and much less to helping the poor people around the mines.

Although health assessments halted, at the same time this endeavor by a concerned businessman provided the initial financing that allowed the Center for Global Health to get off the ground. Over the next few years, the Center for Global Health continued to be financed in large part by consulting contracts for similar kinds of situations, by groups who wanted some sort of evaluation of a particular country or a specific intervention in a country.

For example, the American Academy of Family Physicians was formally approached by some senior health officials in Albania to provide guidance and training on how to improve the quality of the primary health system in Albania. This small country had been the only truly communist country in Europe for many years, influenced initially by Russian Communists and then by the Chinese, and had been totally closed to any outside interaction for several decades. The dictator of Albania had for over 30 years prohibited any outside contact with the Western world, permitting only contact with Russia and later China. Albanian doctors were prohibited from reading Western journals or from listening to or attending medical conferences. This lack of continuing education led to a critical withering of the professional aspect of medicine over time. If doctors needed training they were sent to Russia, and the Soviet health system was very fragmented.

When this dictator died, the floodgates opened, and suddenly Western information and news from the rest of world came flooding into the country. The health system leadership of Albania suddenly became aware of the many inadequacies of their healthcare knowledge and system, and were struggling to raise the level of healthcare. They wanted to start with a good primary healthcare system, so they asked the American Academy of Family Physicians to send a consulting team to work with them to help do that. One of Cal's colleagues from Shiprock Hospital days, Dr. Daniel Ostergaard, had been working with the Academy of Family Physicians ever since he left Shiprock, and had been put in charge of international relationships within the academy. He called Cal and said, "We've got to put together a team to respond to this."

That began a series of six consultative trips to Albania to identify the issues; complete a basic analysis of their needs within the health system, especially primary care; and propose appropriate training processes. Over the next two years several teams, which included Cal and others from various universities, visited Albania periodically to help formulate specific policies. These included required continuing medical education for the existing physicians, and training key primary healthcare doctors in various parts of the country in skills and medical concepts that had not been part of their training over the previous 20 to 30 years. The Albanians' desire to learn was incredible and rewarding. This contract allowed the Center for Global Health to continue to be involved in global work and provided ongoing funding for its staff and programs with students and residents.

CHAPTER 49

A Premature Birth in Lima

*W*hen Cal was working with the Newmont Mining Company, although the mine was in the Peruvian highlands above Cajamarca, the portal of entry for Peru was Lima, the capital of Peru where Kevin and Sarah were working with a group of Christian and Missionary Alliance churches. They had been there about four years, and Sarah was pregnant in her sixth month when Cal came to visit them in conjunction with a trip to the Newmont mine.

Kevin and Sarah had decided that because the work and pregnancy were going so well, she could continue with the pregnancy and delivery there in Lima. So, Cal scheduled an additional few days in Lima on their way home.

Cal's team was comprised of three other faculty members from the University Hospital, one notably a pediatrician who was the director of the neonatal unit at Children's Hospital.

Years before, one of her residents had been a Peruvian pediatrician who had come to learn neonatal intensive care at Denver Children's Hospital. He was now working in Peru and she wanted to see him as well as meet Kevin and Sarah.

Cal scheduled a meal in a nice restaurant for the whole team from Colorado, plus several medical guests, including the local neonatologist. At the end of the meal as they were saying goodbye, the Peruvian neonatologist happened to look down at Sarah's very pregnant belly. He handed her his card and said, "I hope you don't feel that I'm being forward in this, but if for some reason you feel like you need help with the baby after the delivery, please give me a call."

Sarah ended up going into labor and delivering almost two-and-a-half months prematurely in Lima. The baby, named Kyle, weighed no more than three-and-a-half pounds, presenting many potential risks. Sarah pulled out the neonatologist's card, called him, and he transferred the baby to the hospital where he was working. Knowing that for many women the care that was available for a baby that tiny was somewhat minimal in Peru, Kevin and Sarah now had the assurance the baby was going to be attended by a doctor who had been trained in the best of Denver Children's Hospital. They all saw this as God's hand and thanked God for it.

The capable care Kyle received was not the only blessing, however. He did beautifully, started eating right away, never became seriously jaundiced, and never came down with any type of infection. He just ate and grew. He stayed in the hospital for about a month until he reached at least four pounds, the weight at which he could be discharged, and came home to a very grateful family!

CHAPTER 50

Mimi's Diagnosis of Parkinson's Disease

After returning from Jordan, an occasional friend would comment that Mimi's handwriting was getting smaller. She was still active, and she had the same amount of energy and creativity as always. She was feeling well and doing well, so she dismissed the issue as unimportant. But about five years after returning to the US, it became apparent that she was beginning to move more slowly on occasion, often when tired or fatigued, which usually resolved within a few days. In addition, she began noting other symptoms, like losing her sense of smell, which for someone who likes to cook is a disturbing development. The changes were not abrupt, but were a gradual progression of certain symptoms.

Mainly because of the slowness of movements and a few

other changes that Cal had noticed, they decided to have her evaluated. The evaluation confirmed she had Parkinson's disease, although very mild at that point. She was a bit slower, but it didn't affect much of anything, including her creativity and general energy. They were making plans to move to Rwanda full-time, and Mimi felt that she was totally up to the challenge.

About two years later, however, in Rwanda the frequency of the episodes of slowness was increasing, and they began to explore possible treatment options. On her birthday, Mimi said to the Lord, "Could you help me find a doctor who is interested in my full capacity—not just the old woman in Room Seven?"

Shortly after this prayer, she and Cal went out to get donuts, and a man they had recently come to know came up to Mimi and said, "I hope I am not overstepping my bounds, but one of my best friends is a researcher in Parkinson's disease, and I wrote to him this morning to see if he would take you as a patient." Cal and Mimi contacted the recommended doctor in Cleveland. He was a neurologist involved in researching new therapies for the disease, and he was very happy to consult with Mimi long distance. Mimi marveled that she had just prayed for the Lord to provide someone who was interested in maintaining her high level of function, and here he was!

Much later, while they were visiting Kurt and his family in Michigan, they were able to meet the doctor in person. He was indeed a kind and sympathetic individual, especially interested in finding appropriate medications that would maintain a high level of function with minimal side effects. He recommended a new treatment, a medicine available in a skin patch. Mimi began the patch treatment, and it effectively controlled many of the symptoms, so she continued with the patch for several years. At one point, the patch was not available in the States, and could only be purchased through Canada, but they were still able to acquire it. Eventually, however, the patch began to lose its effectiveness, and she had to move to another form of treatment.

One of the most difficult aspects of a progressive disease such as Parkinson's is the conscious acceptance of the slow but steady deterioration of physical functioning. Cal identified two things that he thinks genuinely helped Mimi deal with this disease. One was the medication that kept many of the symptoms under relatively good control. It was easy to adopt an attitude of, *Well, I've got this problem, but it's not too bad.* The second positive factor, Cal felt, was Mimi's attitude. She refused to allow the disease to make her feel depressed or useless, or to define her. She maintained a positive attitude about it; in fact, she would joke about it. And she would continue to push herself, like refusing the wheelchair when they were in an airport, because it honestly was more helpful for her to walk.

"I think the only times I can feel overwhelmed is when I realize that everything I do takes longer to complete, such as when I make bread," said Mimi. "I will think, well, that shouldn't take four hours. Mentally I still see bread making as something that goes fast, but in reality, I'm slower and less efficient. That's the difficult aspect that is hard to get used to."

Kigali, Rwanda

2010-13

MIMI AND JOLLI, ONE OF 25 TOP ACHIEVING
WOMEN IN AFRICA

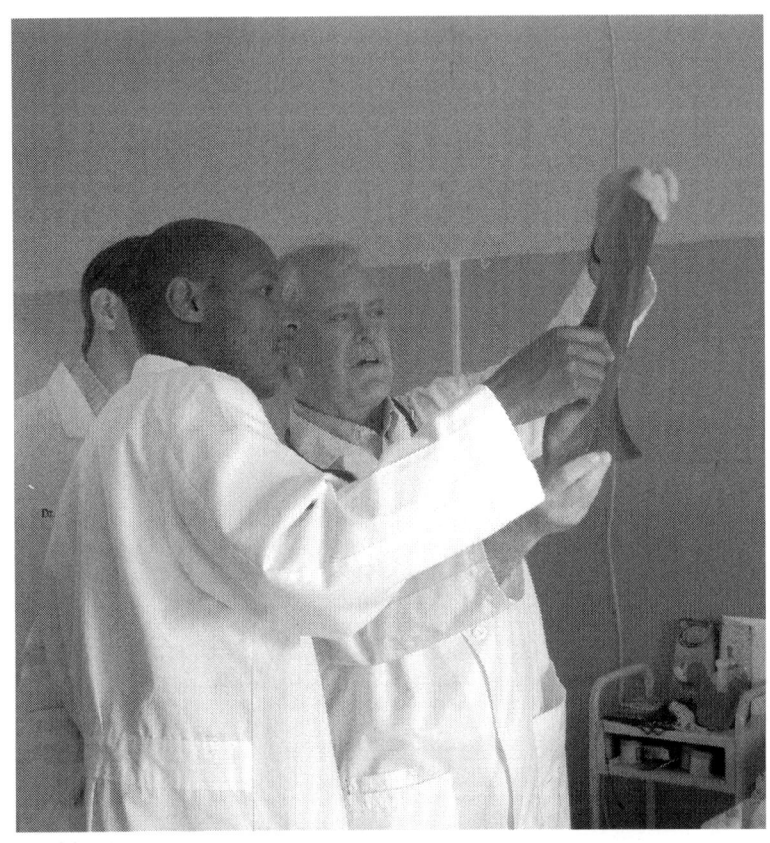

CAL AND MICHAEL MILLER REVIEWING PATIENT
WITH FAMILY MEDICINE RESIDENT

DISCUSSION WITH FAMILY MEDICINE RESIDENTS
AND DR. MICHAEL MILLER

FIRST SPECIALISTS TO GRADUATE IN FAMILY AND
COMMUNITY MEDICINE, 2012

HOUSE IN RWANDA, 2010-2013

John   John   Theo   John Paul Solange
Whatever you do, work at it with all your heart.. Col.3:23

HOUSEHOLD STAFF

MIMI AND JOLLI, ONE OF 25
TOP ACHIEVING WOMEN IN AFRICA

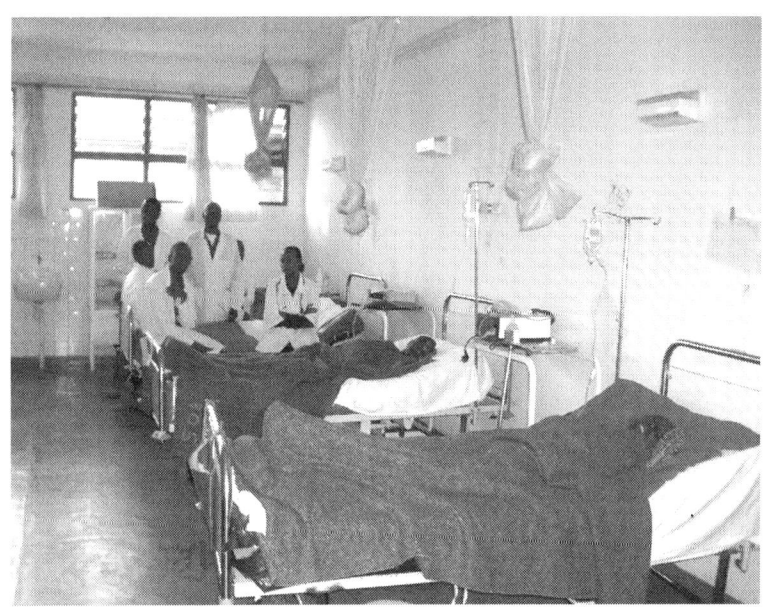

HOSPITAL WARD AT DISTRICT HOSPITAL

UNIVERSITY OF RWANDA SCHOOL OF MEDICINE, 2010

SPARROWS

MIMI IS READY FOR THANKSGIVING
GUESTS, NOVEMBER 2012

CHAPTER 51

Help for Rwandan Doctors

*A*s director of the Center for Global Health, Cal received all the communications from the university related to global health activities. One day in 2005 he received a call from a man who introduced himself as Greg Hodgson, Director of Global Health Initiatives for Centura Health, one of the hospital health systems in Colorado with a network of multiple faith-based hospitals, most of them Catholic or Adventist. Centura Health had developed a program to encourage its employees to be involved in global health outreach activities with the support of Centura Health. Three to four times a year Greg led a team of health workers to provide ancillary services and short-term training at one of their sister Adventist hospitals in another part of the world.

On a previous visit to an Adventist hospital in Rwanda, Greg had a revealing conversation with the Deputy Director of

Health for Rwanda, indicating that Rwanda was in the process of restructuring its medical school and restarting the process of postgraduate training (known as specialty residencies in the US) in several of the major specialties, all having been dormant following the genocide of 1994. The Deputy Director of Health revealed that at that time there were only six qualified surgeons in the entire country, eight internal medicine specialists, and the same number of pediatricians. Most of the specialists in the country had either been killed during the genocide or had fled to other countries and become employed there. The remaining specialists were expected to provide consultancy services for complicated cases in a population of over 10.5 million, and they were not physically capable of taking on the additional task of training new specialists. The need for medical training was urgent, both at the medical school and the postgraduate level, and the Deputy Director specifically asked for visiting specialists from the US to come and help in this new training process.

Greg called Cal at the Center for Global Health and asked if there might be some resources within the university to help restart the residency specialty training programs in Rwanda. He offered to fund Cal's expenses to accompany the team to Rwanda and explore the situation firsthand. This was an offer Cal could not refuse. And, of course, Mimi, as always, was on board.

Upon arriving in Kigali, Rwanda, they visited Mugonero Hospital, a Seventh Day Adventist district level hospital on the shores of Lake Kivu in the north of the country. For Cal this was a good introduction to the current realities of Rwandan hospital care; it was very basic, with one US trained missionary physician and a few Rwandan physicians, nurses and other health workers.

Cal met with the Deputy Director of Health in Kigali who had made the initial contact with Centura Health. At the time there was approximately one Rwandan physician for every 30,000 Rwandans, compared to about one physician for every 100 people in the US. The medical school was currently functional and graduating around 70 students per year in the traditional Francophone methodology. At the conclusion of this exploratory visit, Cal confirmed that the pressing need was for visiting specialists to help train their specialty students, primarily to help fill the gaps in the curriculum that Rwandans were not able to meet with their own resources, essentially for the surgeons, internists, pediatricians and obstetricians in training.

Back in Denver, Cal investigated and located within these specific specialties a number of doctors, both within the university and in private practice, who were interested in approximately two weeks of collaborative training in Rwanda, as long as their costs were covered. Several months after the initial trip, Cal again traveled to Rwanda to set up this process, stopping first at the US Agency for International Development (USAID) office which was part of the US embassy in Rwanda. He knew USAID had a special fund that was used for internal projects, and Cal suspected funds might be available for this ancillary training. He presented the current situation and need with a short proposal, focusing on the fact that this had originated at the request of the Rwandan Deputy Director of Health. Cal happily received word that his proposal was accepted and funded. USAID agreed to provide funding for a total of 25 US specialty physicians to Rwanda each year for three years, with the objective of supplementing the training that new specialty residents were already receiving, as well as to provide new information and therapeutic techniques currently in use.

From 2006 to 2010 Cal supervised this project from Colorado, but also visited Rwanda two to three times each year, usually accompanying some of the doctors and monitoring the effectiveness of the collaboration with the National University of Rwanda School of Medicine. Initially he went with every group of doctors who volunteered, but over time he was able to develop support within the National University of Rwanda to receive these volunteers and work with them. One of his initial contacts in Rwanda became the newly installed Dean of the Medical School of the University, Professor Herbert Nsanze. The President of Rwanda personally brought Professor Nsanze from Uganda to begin the conversion of the entire teaching curriculum and methodology from the traditional Francophone standard to an international English standard for medical training. Cal and Dean Nsanze became good friends, together with his very capable assistant, Jovin Akana Bakunzi, who had originally trained to be a priest, but had such tremendous administrative and people skills that Dean Nsanze persuaded him to be part of the medical school reform process.

As the program progressed, Cal came to know the various specialists in the two major teaching hospitals in Rwanda, as well as the medical culture of care. There were a lot of logistics with each visit, such as where the visiting doctors were going to stay and eat, and how to keep them healthy, but in general there were very few problems.

During his repeated visits, Cal began to comprehend the health system and the situation more clearly in Rwanda. Clearly primary care physicians needed improved training as well. With the scarcity of referral specialists and the geographic difficulties of transport, primary care physicians were often required to deal with many complicated cases. At that time, the primary healthcare in the country was severely limited, and was provided mainly through a system of community health centers that fed into local district and provincial hospitals. A cadre of nurses (with little physician support) provided a rudimentary level of primary healthcare in the community health centers, but in many cases, up to 70% of patients were referred to a district hospital primarily because the nursing staff were not trained or equipped to deal with many common problems. Even at the district hospital, the doctors had not been well-trained in providing good ambulatory healthcare but focused primarily on the hospitalized patients.

Cal began to discuss with Dean Nsanze and other faculty doctors the possibility of training a new type of primary healthcare worker for Rwanda, a family physician trained in a broad scope of primary ambulatory, community-based care in a formal postgraduate residency training program, very similar to the new programs for the other specialists, who could effectively supervise the nurses at the community centers and manage the more complex cases in the district hospitals. He also discussed this idea among the various stakeholders within Rwanda, from the Rwandan Medical Society to the Ministry of Health to the various directors of the teaching hospitals. As he laid out the concept, there appeared to be much enthusiasm for it.

So, Cal moved ahead and started developing a Family Medicine training program, which became known in Rwanda as Family and Community Medicine (FAMCO). It took about a year to develop a curriculum and a program in collaboration with the Rwandan medical and educational authorities, which included the approval not only of the National University of Rwanda, but also the Rwandan Parliament. As Cal continued visiting Rwanda to not only help with training the specialists but also to begin working on this FAMCO program, he determined there was much to be done that required a more consistent physical presence. Fortunately, he was able to find a Family Medicine faculty member from the University of Colorado, Dr. Inis Bardella, who was willing to move to Rwanda for a year to help get the program started. She did a tremendous amount of work in selecting the first of a capable group of physicians for the training, and overseeing the first year of training. In addition, she developed some new initiatives for the residents, such as a personal data device (a "Palm Pilot" at the time) with ancillary medical data and formulas to help with medical decision making. Although Inis had to leave after that year, another colleague from Colorado, Michael Miller, an extremely capable family physician and the son of one of Cal's former partners in private practice, volunteered to fill the gap. Michael moved to Rwanda with his wife and three boys and remained there for four years overseeing the FAMCO program.

As an example of the residents chosen to be pioneers in this new program, Theoneste Rubansabigwa was among one of the first group of residents selected for training as a family physician. He was a follower of Jesus, had been working with two missionary physicians in a secluded district hospital for several years, and was especially interested in working with the more disadvantaged Rwandans. He was bright and possessed such leadership skills that he could have gone anywhere, but he chose to stay in the area where he had grown up, just to be able to provide quality medical care.

Even though Michael Miller was capably leading the FAMCO program and interfacing with key authorities on a regular basis, he sensed there was even more that could be accomplished if Cal and Mimi were to join him. So, Cal began the process of finding a new director for the Center for Global Health, and again approached the Chair of the Department of Family Medicine, now Dr. Frank DeGruy who had succeeded Dr. Larry Green, about spending some years in work in Rwanda rather than in the Department.

Cal and Mimi's goals were similar to those when they had moved to other countries - they wanted to be active in developing the medical capabilities of the country, especially in primary healthcare. But at the same time, they wanted to get involved with the people, helping with spiritual development and meeting other needs. Dr. DeGruy agreed wholeheartedly with the concept as long as Cal could find the funding to support his university salary.

At that time, Cal and Mimi transitioned from USAID funding, which was limited to three years, to a partnership with a group working in Rwanda out of the Department of Public Health of Tulane University, directed by Dr. Laura Haas. The Tulane group was looking to develop closer ties with the National University of Rwanda Medical School and saw it to their advantage to partner with the University of Colorado Center for Global Health since the Center had already developed the close relationship with the University they were looking for. Through a three-way contract (Tulane University, University of Colorado, and the National University of Rwanda) they were able to arrange sufficient ongoing funding for both Cal and Michael to stay in the country, as well as to fund the FAMCO training program.

As new specialists graduated from the residency training programs, they immediately started training the younger residents. Cal and Michael began to transition out of helping to develop the other specialty programs and focused on the FAMCO program.

CHAPTER 52

A Country Healing

*T*he genocide in Rwanda took place in 1994 and Cal started working there in 2005, so 11 years later the wounds were healing but still fresh. The genocide was not carried out from the outside. Almost every village in Rwanda had integrated the Hutu and the Tutsi groups. The two were not separate tribes as is commonly thought, rather only slightly different ethnic groups who had been totally integrated together for generations. The Rwandans note that prior to colonization by the Belgians, then the Germans, and then the French, the very names "Tutsi" and "Hutu" did not exist. The colonists invented the names to help them distinguish between the tall, thin Tutsi with a finer bone structure that resembled Europeans and the stockier Hutu, who the colonists imagined were more stereotypically African.

Initially, the colonists continued the existing social and governance structure of the reigning Tutsi monarchy with the Hutu performing most of the agricultural work. However, with the transfer of colonization power from the Germans to the French following World War II, the more egalitarian French assisted in the dissolution of the monarchy and insisted that the majority population of the Hutu (close to 70% of the population) should lead the new democratic government. This decision led to nearly 30 years of conflict and growing hatred between the two groups, culminating in the assassination of the Hutu Rwandan president, together with the president of neighboring Burundi, by still unconfirmed perpetrators in 1994, which triggered the onset of the genocide within days. For 90 days, the Hutu basically surrounded the Tutsi families and systematically killed well over 900,000 of them, neighbor killing neighbor.

The genocide ended abruptly following the assumption of power by the previously exiled Tutsi general Paul Kagame, who immediately launched a democratic government with himself as elected President. In an effort to provide justice for the destroyed population, a two-tier system of prosecution and justice was set up. Since so many thousands of Hutu had participated in the killing, it was virtually impossible to officially prosecute every suspect through the existing legal system. As an alternative, the newly-formed government started collecting evidence to find the most egregious offenders. Basically, if a suspect had killed fewer than 12 people, he or she was deemed a minor offender. Those who had been involved in the murder of more than 12 individuals were prosecuted through the official legal system.

The minor offenders appeared before a local village tribunal that consisted of elders from each individual village, together with one or two local individuals who had been given a brief course in basic legal principles. Each individual village identified those who had participated in at least some of the killing. The smaller villages joined together, mostly on Wednesdays, to judge those who had killed their people. The primary goal was for the victims' remaining family members to tell their stories and to provide an opportunity for the perpetrator to repent and ask for forgiveness.

The tribunals were closed to outsiders, as this was considered a private, shameful event that was not to be publicized. They functioned in a traditional Rwandan manner, all conducted in the local language, Kinya-Rwandan.

Most of the perpetrators confessed they had been wrong in participating in the killing. Many of them felt pressured to do so by their surrounding neighbors, by the newsfeeds that were coming over the radio, and by the general atmosphere of hate and mistrust that had been generated in the country. Frequently, offenders said, "I really didn't want to, but I felt compelled to do so" or "I got caught up with it." If killers appeared to show any sincere repentance and were willing to apologize and exhibit evidence of grief, they were given lesser sentences and ultimately accepted back into the community.

Some incredible stories emerged from this post-genocide time of mourning, reconciliation, and reconstruction, such as the wedding of one of the killers to the ex-wife of one of the men he killed. The level of forgiveness offered was often amazing. The church in Rwanda—involving many denominations—actively helped promote this cycle of repentance, forgiveness, reconciliation, and acceptance, insisting this was the very pattern shown by Jesus Christ.

For the most part, Cal and Mimi observed extraordinary healing on the individual Rwandan level during their time there. Certainly, great healing occurred on the national level. President Kagame and the Parliament passed a law making it illegal to even refer to the terms "Hutu" or "Tutsi," insisting "We are all Rwandans."

The reconciliation councils continued until 2011, the second year Cal and Mimi were there full-time. Having served their purpose, these tribunal councils were disbanded. In reality, some undercurrent of resentment still existed, especially on the part of the former Hutu, but the resentment was now more based on socio-economic factors.

During the leadup to the genocide and certainly during the genocide, huge numbers of "Tutsi", especially the more educated with some economic means, left the country and disbursed as refugees all over the world. Regardless of whether they settled in a nearby African country like Uganda or Tanzania or made it to Europe or the US, many enrolled in a university and obtained a degree.

When President Paul Kagame invited this Rwandan diaspora to return to the new Rwanda, they came home by the hundreds of thousands. It is estimated that well over a million of the former Rwandan "Tutsis" have returned, most of them now well-educated, and with a global awareness of the rest of the world. The members of this reunited diaspora fit nicely into a key element of the new government—no more nepotism, no more favoritism in government positions, with favored positions assigned to the most trained, experienced, and capable individual—a government of meritocracy. These mostly young, ambitious individuals became the new leaders of Rwanda.

The former "Hutu," who never left the country and had been educated under the Francophone system of education were being left behind, generating some of the resentment noted in Rwanda today.

CHAPTER 53

A Big House and Filling It

God provided a special house for the Wilsons' three years in Kigali, the capital city and center of everything in Rwanda. Since they loved hospitality, Mimi expressed her desire to the realtor as they began the search. "I want the biggest house you've got for rent." He took Mimi to a huge old house that had just become available. The current renter, a distinguished Rwandan, had just been named by President Kagame as ambassador to South Africa, and was wanting to sub-lease the house while he was gone.

As they walked through the extensive house, Mimi asked the realtor what a particular room was for. "It's for your ironing, ma'am." Mimi had never had a separate room for her ironing and hadn't seemed to need one. The house had so many bedrooms there was one wing the current renter never used, and the giant back porch was large enough to serve 100 people.

It all seemed grand to Mimi. The new ambassador intended to leave within a few days and he was leaving behind the magnificent wood furniture and furnishings acquired from all over the world.

For three grand months they lived in this enormous place, long enough to realize the profound amount of work required to keep it up. The back garden was nicely planted with all kinds of trees and flowers, but it hadn't been attended to for months and was severely overgrown. In a corner of the garden lay a huge pile of trash. When Mimi asked the gardener, who came with the house, to clean it up, he said, "No, I can't do that."

"Why? Do you need some help?" Mimi asked.

"No," he said, and told this story. The house sat immediately below a bluff where the Parliament building was located. During the end of the genocide and factional fighting with armed groups in Kigali, the rebel group turned this house into their headquarters. They shot at the Parliament building on the bluff above them, and Kagame's forces returned fire—directly at Mimi's grand house. The gardener was concerned that unexploded artillery shells might still be in the backyard, and some might be underneath the pile of trash.

Eventually the area was cleaned out (except for some of the lingering trash pile) and became a gorgeous backyard. Looking at the house from certain angles revealed multiple pock marks of bullet holes. Thereafter, when children played in the backyard Mimi would pray, *Oh Lord, keep them from being blown up*!

However, three months after moving in the Wilsons were abruptly evicted. Unbeknownst to them two brothers had inherited the house and had been fighting in court for several years over who would own it. One managed the house and had leased it to the Ambassador, and then approved a sublease to the Wilsons. The second brother finally managed to legally gain full control of the house and immediately informed the Wilsons they had to move out.

Fortunately, in the interim their realtor had located another house, somewhat smaller but brand new, on the outskirts of Kigali. Mimi could actually count the bedrooms in this house; there were six and another two rooms that could be used as bedrooms, with five bathrooms. It had a huge, gated yard and garden around it and some back buildings. The new house was ideal for hosting groups and for entertaining.

As they were preparing to move to the new house, they heard from the Rwandan ambassador to South Africa who had previously rented the grand house. He said, "The new owner has evicted me as well, and I don't have any place to store all this furniture. Would you mind taking it with you to your new house?" The new house was totally unfurnished; in fact, the kitchen and some of the cabinetry was not yet finished. So, with great exuberance they packed up as much of the fine furniture as they estimated they had room for and it fit beautifully. The dining room even had enough space for the massive dining table. Made of solid wood, the tabletop displayed intricate carvings over the entire surface. A thick sheet of glass lay over the top to reveal and protect the carving. The dining room chairs were similarly carved and richly upholstered.

When the Wilsons moved into their new home, the kitchen was an empty space. The owner, who claimed the house was ready for occupancy, explained he wanted the kitchen to be built "to American standards," because he wanted the house to be comfortable for foreigners. He took Cal and Mimi to the kitchen supply store and asked them to choose whatever Mimi wanted. So, they had the privilege of designing the kitchen, including cabinets and appliances, to American standards, and within ten days it was operational.

Of course, Mimi fed the 12 workmen who came each day to work on the kitchen. At first she served them with her silver-plated flatware, until she discovered that 12 pieces were missing after they slipped them in their pockets. She had wanted them to feel special, and she guessed they did, but it was plasticware from then on.

To make the house feel like home, Mimi had brought with them to Rwanda an "instant bedroom"—a quilt, pillows, lamp, everything needed for the master bedroom, plus mosquito netting around the entire bed. She slowly added to her supply another five bedrooms' worth of coordinated quilts and bedding.

As with their previous extended international stays, the Wilsons opened their home to almost anyone the Lord brought their way who needed a meal, or a bed for a few nights, or even for a more extended stay. Some friends came and went intermittently the whole three years they were in Rwanda. One single Rwandan woman, Jolli Dusabe, was the project director for the Ministry of Agriculture. She would call Mimi and simply say, "I'm dead tired," which was Mimi's cue to prepare a tray from the leftover food they'd just had for lunch, make a bed for her on the sofa, and cover her with a blanket. She would eat, sleep soundly for an hour, then jump up and go back to her work.

Jolli was from a large Rwanda family who had migrated to Uganda prior to the genocide and she had completed a university education. At that time, foreign donors favored Rwanda, affording the Ministry of Agriculture millions of dollars to apply towards improving the local agricultural yields. Jolli loved the Lord and focused on the needs of the farmers themselves. She took very seriously the tremendous responsibility of managing millions of dollars each year.

Once, when she called to ask if she could possibly take a nap, Mimi inquired, "What is going on in the office?"

"I just put all my directors into a big circle and gave them three questions to work on over the next hour," she said. "And when I finish my nap, I'll see how they did."

When Jolli was named one of the ten most influential women in Africa by the *Manchester Guardian* newspaper of the UK, Cal and Mimi held a celebration to honor her. They invited everyone who might appreciate the incredible work this young woman was doing, including many expatriates who were also working to support Rwanda, as well as the American Ambassador to Rwanda and his wife.

In the early days of frequent visits to Rwanda, Cal visited a dynamic Anglican church with an English-speaking service, well attended by many English-speaking Rwandans as well as expatriates. When they settled in Kigali, Cal and Mimi attended regularly and came to know many in the congregation. They joined a midweek Bible Study group from the Anglican church, held in the home of one of the ministers, Adriaan VerWijs, and his wife Lizette, missionaries from the Netherlands. The group included some of the expatriate businessmen in the church as well as key Rwandan young people, such as Nicholas Muneeza, one of the exceptional young men of their church. Nicholas also started a Bible study group of young men in the church and eventually was asked to study for the pastorate. This wonderful connection with some outstanding individuals became their second family in Rwanda, and correspondence with many of them continues to this day.

A dynamic young woman, Sheila Mutesi, led the choir at the church. She had a wonderful voice and a special talent for leading the choir and the congregation in honest worship. After a few months at the church and after chatting with choir members, especially Sheila, Mimi got the idea that the choir needed a night out just to be able to have fun in a safe environment, so she invited them over for an evening of dinner and fun. Perhaps 15 came, including some hangers-on, all young women. The first thing they did when they came in the front door was kick off their shoes, leaving a mountain of shoes by the front door. They made themselves at home, some helping in the kitchen with the cooking, and others with setting the table. Everyone, wherever they went throughout the house, was either dancing or singing or both; they just couldn't hold still. The entire evening was so much fun. A few stayed overnight, they so enjoyed being together and being able to let off steam in a safe environment. They just curled up on one of the rugs or three or four on the sofa, not minding being cuddled up to each other. They just wanted to be together. Years later, Sheila met an African-American young man working with USAID in Nigeria, and they were married in his home town in Alabama. Cal and Mimi were able to attend the wedding, and share Sheila's joy.

Another frequent guest was a young graduate engineer, Jesse Thornburg, from Asheville, North Carolina. Jesse volunteered with a small organization in northeastern Congo to rehabilitate an old hydroelectric power plant that had stopped working. The plant had been donated to the Congo in the 1930s when some hydroelectric dams and plants were decommissioned in the Pacific Northwest of the US. Since the equipment was so old Jesse found it nearly impossible to get necessary parts, so he had to improvise many parts from local African supplies, such as using a local jungle hardwood to replace the bearings for the turbine (they actually worked!). The plant was located in an area of the Congo just across the border from Rwanda near the town of Goma, in a region that was surrounded by several local militias who were fighting for control of the area. Jesse was frequently stopped by one group or another, and several times his life was truly in danger. He stored his belongings at the Wilsons' in Kigali and would visit periodically to get some rest or to wait out current hostilities between two or more of the local militias and the Congolese army. Jesse was one of their most regular visitors, and was always welcome.

At Thanksgiving, the Wilsons' house always overflowed with eager guests, which usually consisted of Rwandan friends and expatriate workers from various countries, such as Rohith Peiris from Sri Lanka, the manager of a large tea factory, Dr. Phil Cotton from Scotland, who ultimately became the Vice-Chancellor of the redesigned University of Rwanda, and various American consultants such as the two young agricultural consultants, Ben and Eli, who supplied the turkey one year. Ben and Eli were originally from the midwestern US, but were working with farmers in eastern Rwanda to improve their yields of corn. A week before Thanksgiving, they sent a video of the turkey to be served at their holiday meal—demonstrating how the bird had learned to play soccer. The turkey stood in the farmyard carefully watching the movements of a soccer ball. Whenever it was kicked, the turkey went running toward the moving soccer ball, and with one of its claws gave it a big kick and sent it flying in another direction. Then he chased after it, and gave it another kick, gobbling loudly all the way.

"Do you really want to eat this bird?" Ben rhetorically asked.

When Mimi asked him the same question, he answered,

"Well, it's not going to be easy this time, but yeah, this is the best turkey for the meal."

For fun, Mimi devised a raffle for guests to guess the final pre-oven weight of the turkey. A chocolate bar went to the guest with the closest estimation. Although each guest invariably had meaningful stories to tell and was often making appreciable contributions to the development of the country, they also craved a traditional holiday celebration with a bit of silliness, which Mimi was happy to provide!

Fortunately, because the cost of employment was so low in Rwanda, Cal and Mimi were able to employ a solid staff of helpers. Mimi hired a young woman, Solange, to cook and clean the house. An unspoken but culturally strong requirement was that every house with a gated enclosure should have a doorkeeper/guard who spent the night and watched the place, so Cal hired two guards, Jean Paul and John (known for convenience as "Little John" because Jean Paul was so much taller) who alternated shifts. They also hired a highly capable gardener, Theo, who turned out to be a wonderful and ambitious young man.

Early in their stay in Rwanda, while still in the first grand house, a young man in his late teens showed up at their gate. He shared his story of his parents being killed during the genocide, making him a genocide orphan. His name was John, and he was trying to find a job. Mimi wasn't sure what to do with him at first, so she brought him into the house and gave him something to eat. As they were walking out, John noticed that Mimi had set up an ironing board and had been ironing. He enthusiastically chirped, "I know how to iron!"

"You're hired," Mimi said, "on Thursdays." So, he became their do-it-all fellow, and followed them to the second house.

Cal and Mimi encouraged most of their staff to advance to a higher level. Since most of them had graduated from high school, Cal and Mimi paid for their ongoing education, either night school in a specific trade or even university if they were willing to put in the effort. It gratified the Wilsons to see how often these young people would step up to a much more sustainable life situation.

Their efforts weren't without disappointments, of course. John, the young man who began with the ironing, did not complete the university studies they had paid for and suddenly disappeared. He later appeared on Facebook asking them for large amounts of money, raising a strong suspicion that he had become involved in an organized gang.

One of their later house staff, Grace, was the 18-year-old sister of Jean Paul, one of their night watchmen, and had been abused at her last place of employment. She was a beautiful, sweet girl, who loved the Lord with her heart and soul, and Mimi loved her dearly. When they walked down the street, Grace would put her arm around Mimi, which may not have been totally culturally appropriate for Rwanda, but it was an expression of their love for each other. The thought of her having been abused was more than Mimi could stand. Grace did the cleaning and some cooking, and did it well, so Mimi also taught her recipes and sent her to English classes so she could eventually be on her own. Mimi believed she could prepare Grace for a much better position than she had previously known, potentially as a cook for a reputable expatriate family. Also, since Grace also loved children, Mimi suggested she might be able to find a longer-term position as a nanny, an idea that excited Grace.

Like John, one housekeeper, Solange Nyuraramera, followed Cal and Mimi from the first big house. The manager of the house had sent over a small team of people to clean the first house after they moved out, and Mimi noticed that one young woman, Solange, really put her heart and soul into the work, staying several hours longer than her colleagues and being very thorough in her cleaning. Mimi talked to the manager and asked if they could continue to hire Solange, and he was agreeable to that.

Solange quickly demonstrated that she was not only a good housekeeper, but also a good cook. After working for them for about two years, and learning many new recipes, Mimi noticed the young woman becoming withdrawn and almost depressed. She asked her if there was anything wrong, and Solange initially said no. But a day or two later, without saying a word, she handed Mimi a slip of paper, revealing the positive results of an HIV test. She said, "I didn't want to tell you this because I know that you'll fire me, but you have to know the truth."

Mimi looked at her and said, "That doesn't mean we have to fire you. Are you under treatment?"

She said, "Oh, absolutely. As soon as I got this test result, I immediately began the Rwandan HIV treatment program. I'm taking my medicines every day now and feeling well."

"Great, that's all we need to know," Mimi assured the worried girl. "No, we will not fire you! We'd love to have you continue to work with us." With this, Solange's depression cleared and she continued working for the Wilsons until they left Rwanda.

Mimi has enjoyed markets wherever they lived. She regularly took Solange and Grace to the local market to show them what she liked to buy and the vendors Mimi bought from. She also introduced the women to the young boys and girls who watched the parking area and came running whenever they recognized a regular customer like Mimi, who paid them with treats in exchange for carrying her shopping basket.

Mimi got their groceries from a couple of small grocery markets within a short distance from their house. There was also a larger market close by for when she needed other things such as fabric or sewing supplies. She went and also took guests there often enough that she became well-recognized. She loved to take guests to the market because this was one of the best ways to get a feel for a country.

Through Cal's relationship with the University of Colorado Center for Global Health and his frequent speaking at national global health conferences, he received inquiries from young physicians around the country who were interested in becoming more familiar with the intricacies of global health.

These interested students and doctors became an almost steady stream of young professionals, married or single, who wanted to see what medical care in Rwanda was like and how they might fit into it. Because of Cal's work with the National University of Rwanda, its training programs and several of the teaching hospitals, he was usually able to place them in a spot where they could work with FAMCO residents or other Rwandan physicians to better understand the medical system and medical culture there, as well as many common tropical diseases and their management.

As a result, the Wilsons had the privilege of meeting some incredible physicians. One couple from Leeds, England, Peter and Katie Cartledge, who were both doctors, lived with them for six months and became very close friends. They later returned to Rwanda with their children to work another five years participating in the medical training. Another couple from Denver, Caleb and Ellie Van Essen, had just gotten married and Caleb was about to start medical school. They came to visit because Caleb wanted to prepare himself for practicing in an underserved and global environment. Interestingly, he had grown up only a few blocks away from the Wilsons' church, the Littleton Bible Chapel. The newlyweds stayed with them for two months and are still close friends, as Cal and Mimi have prayed for them through medical school, surgical training, the arrival of three active children, and Caleb's installation in a surgical practice in Grand Junction, Colorado.

For missionaries who lived in other towns of Rwanda but

came to Kigali periodically, Cal and Mimi opened their home for an overnight stay or as a place to collect their things. So, a steady stream of missionaries enjoyed the Wilsons' hospitality, such as Drs. Caleb and Louise King, who worked for many years in a relatively isolated district hospital affiliated with the Anglican Church. Both were brilliant individuals, have both graduated from Harvard Medical School, and Caleb continuing with a doctorate in engineering from "across the street" at the Massachusetts Institute of Technology (MIT). In spite of their academic achievements, they both devoted themselves to the care of poor rural Rwandans for over 10 years, sending their equally brilliant children to Kenya for middle and high school. Louise also volunteered as one of the FAMCO instructors when they moved to a more accessible district hospital in a nearby province.

It got to be so busy that Mimi started getting calls from people she didn't even know, saying, "We heard you're running a boardinghouse. I'd like to reserve a room for about three weeks." They were a bit chagrined to hear this, because they had always treated their home as a gift from God to be offered to those in need, not a commercial enterprise.

CHAPTER 54

The Sparrows and a Roadblock

A mong the guests that found their way to Mimi's table were three older Rwandan women who had previously attended a spiritual conference given by Mimi and had some questions for her. In the course of the meal, they related a story of their recent activities that had a profound impact on Mimi. Sometime earlier, leaving the soccer stadium after a game, they noted an entire line of women just outside the stadium, obviously selling themselves.

They were so distressed by this that they began considering how they might best help these women find employment that did not involve selling their bodies. They developed an interesting strategy. One of them had connections with the Rwandan Police and asked them to round up as many of these women as they could on a particular day. The police obliged by rounding up at least 60 women, who assumed that they were being arrested, but in reality the three older women simply wanted to interview them to find those who genuinely wanted to change their lifestyle if the opportunity were provided.

They identified about 20 women who desperately wanted out of this lifestyle but could see no other alternative. Many were not literate and had their own children whom they needed to feed. These three older women offered to teach them skills that could bring in some funds, in exchange for a commitment to not prostitute themselves. They rented a home in a quiet neighborhood that served as a gathering place, classroom, and workshop, and began teaching them how to make paper beads and simple sewing using spare scraps of fabric collected from the dirt of the market floor. Mimi began visiting this group, initially offering just love and tenderness. But she also began searching for outside markets for the handwork that the women were producing, as well as for ideas for new and attractive items to make. Her guiding motto in this was "Women heal better when they can create beauty." Just as Mimi began to work regularly with these women, the three older women who had started the effort found that each had to move to another country. Another Rwandan woman, Jane Usanase, was found to help coordinate this work and provide a liaison with the group.

One early question that arose among the gathered women was what to call themselves. They had formed a legal cooperative but could not settle on an appropriate name. In an effort to teach them their intrinsic value before God, even if they were not appreciated by men, Mimi showed them Jesus' teaching "Are not two sparrows sold for a penny? Yet not one of them will fall to the ground apart from the will of your Father. So don't be afraid; you are worth more than many sparrows." These poor women took this to heart, and began calling themselves the Sparrows Cooperative, because they could rest in the fact that they were indeed valued by God.

Mimi began talking about this with her network in the US, and a variety of women from the Littleton Bible Chapel offered to help as well. One couple, John and Kathi Pitzer, visited the Wilsons and Kathi spent time with the Sparrows, producing patterns for new items to sew and making quick repairs on items that had not been completely finished. She helped them with new patterns such as a cloth bird stuffed with cotton and hung with a string that could be used as a Christmas tree ornament. Mimi noted that some of the early birds produced looked more like dolphins, but interestingly, they sold anyway, and improved with time. Another woman from the Littleton Chapel, Annie Phillips, offered to help sell the items produced by the Sparrows via an internet website, which became quite effective. Other women took up a collection to purchase sewing machines for the Sparrows, which greatly increased their output.

One beautiful result of the Sparrows Cooperative was the development of a real mutual interdependence for basic needs. For example, many of the Sparrows had AIDS and were under regular treatment in the government HIV program. However, the drugs used often caused significant nausea if taken on an empty stomach. The Sparrows periodically pooled a bit of their spare change to buy a small stock of food which was available to any woman who needed to get something into her stomach before leaving to take her medication.

As their economic situation improved, the Sparrows became visibly more active and cheerful, their children began to thrive, and they even began purchasing clothing that made them feel beautiful. They would often break into exuberant song, and dance around the small workshop with little provocation. Over time, Annie Phillips, working through the capable manager and translator, Jane Usanase, and Laura Sager, a long-term expat resident, helped them develop a varied line of handmade products that sold well through the website. She continued this work long after Mimi had left Rwanda, developing a sustainable and effective market for their creations, until eventually the Sparrows Cooperative developed their own outlets, such as Kuasa Collective in Kigali, Godwin in Tanzania, and even Manos Emprendedoras in Denver.

As Cal and Michael Miller were in the process of choosing a third class of residents to begin training in Family and Community Medicine in Rwanda, the ground shifted. A new Minister of Health was appointed, a very capable woman who had big ideas as to how she was going to renovate the Rwandan health system. Her philosophy encompassed the idea that what the country needed was more specialists. She began negotiating with the US Department of State for a sizable grant that would provide for visiting specialists from the States to train a whole new cadre of Rwandan doctors in the four basic specialties along with emergency medicine; ear, nose, and throat; orthopedic surgery; and neurosurgery. They were all needed without question, but she did not feel that primary health care needed any further support, or trained FAMCO generalists.

Cal ran into a major roadblock as he talked with her. He pointed out that the University of Rwanda and the Rwandan Parliament had already approved and was moving forward with the FAMCO program and that this was another group of specialists who could really help to transform the primary healthcare sector of Rwanda. However, she did not understand the concept of Family Medicine or primary healthcare. She viewed primary healthcare as merely the pass-through to get to the specialist. However, the US Department of State team insisted that Family and Community Medicine be included in the list of residencies to be developed and supported through the funding, which resulted in its inclusion in the $50 million aid package that was approved by the US Department of State for the Rwandan Ministry of Health.

At the same time, for the one of first times in its history, the US Department of State agreed to transfer this money directly to the country of Rwanda, in large part because Rwanda had such a clean reputation for transparency and lack of corruption. However, shortly after the money was transferred to Rwanda, the Minister of Health cancelled the FAMCO program and applied that portion of the budget to the training of other specialists, in spite of the attempts by several physicians whom she respected to convince her otherwise. Cal was forced to cancel the third group of FAMCO residents who had already been selected. The Minister allowed training to continue for the two cadres who had already started, but when they graduated, all with good marks and full honors with the National University of Rwanda, there would be no further funding for Family and Community Medicine forthcoming.

In Cal's opinion, any new funding would need to come from within the country, motivated by a desire to help improve the quality and scope of primary healthcare. Interestingly, the University of Rwanda medical school (now with the name newly changed to reflect the ongoing reform process) continued the curriculum of basic Family Medicine for medical students within the School of Medicine, as the current Dean (Dr. Patrick Kyamanwya, a young surgeon) and the new Vice Chancellor (Dr. Phil Cotton, a general practitioner from Glasgow, Scotland) both deemed the Family Medicine concepts of comprehensive patient care and community-based medicine critical to the formation of high-quality physicians. In addition, the School of Medicine added subjects such as patient communication and biomedical ethics to the curriculum. Some of the newly graduated FACMO physicians as well as two volunteer trainers from the Netherlands stayed on with the University of Rwanda and continued much of the Family Medicine conceptual training in the medical school, which continues even now.

CHAPTER 55

The Two Month Farewell

Cal and Mimi foresaw the end of their time in Rwanda as Cal's work was being closed down. Drawing on their experience in Jordan, they decided to spend the last two months saying goodbye to their many friends and colleagues. They had been a big part of the lives of many diverse individuals, and these friends had been a large part of theirs over many years. They wanted it to end properly. They scheduled a full two months for having people to the house for a meal to review their time together, say goodbye, and plan for the future. They all could mourn together the reality that they were not going to see each other as frequently.

Mimi loved the rhythm of planning party after party. Cal and Mimi distributed many of their own family pictures, because Rwandans especially appreciated pictures that included the Wilson children, as the family structure is so important to them. In one house where they had left their family picture, they noticed it hanging on the wall—just the picture by itself—with the purchased frame containing the stock photo hanging right next to the picture. Cal and Mimi suspected their friends wondered why on earth they had given them this picture of a dog, but years later they saw it was still there, the stock picture of a dog and their family photo hanging right next to it.

Saying goodbye at their church was very moving. Some of their friends had come to recognize how much Cal and Mimi loved one song that was particularly meaningful to them: "I Then Shall Live" by Bill and Gloria Gaither. As a surprise on their last Sunday at church, Nicholas and another friend from the choir stood apart and sang that hymn for them, an extremely meaningful experience!

A big part of preparing to leave a country involves not just emptying the house, but deciding what will be taken back and what will be left. Cal and Mimi had brought a containerful of appliances, supplies, and furniture to Rwanda, and they didn't want to take any of it back. So, with the help of some of their many friends, they held an old-fashioned yard sale, selling the appliances and other unneeded items. There was no problem finding interested people because almost all of it had come from the US. Cal and Mimi made sure everything sold at a price appropriate to the Rwandan economy.

Mimi also continued a tradition that she had begun in Ecuador years before, which was to carry with her a set of fine china for special events and meals, simply because she has always loved to set a beautiful table. As in the previous countries where she lived, from the moment she entered the country she had begun looking for an appropriate person with whom to leave her china. She watched for someone who loved hospitality and whom they had hosted for dinner various times throughout their stay, so the dishes would provide sweet memories.

Mimi had chosen that person almost a year before leaving Rwanda but kept her plans a secret. The woman Mimi selected, Bernadette Kabango, came by the house to see what they were selling as they were packing to leave. Mimi prepared a special luncheon for the two of them, and as they ate, Mimi informed her that the dishes on which they were eating were now hers, together with the glassware and silver. It took a moment for Bernadette to grasp what Mimi was saying, but she was almost overwhelmed with pleasure at the thought of inheriting Mimi's treasured set.

Bernadette was a native-born Rwandan whose family had fled Rwanda some years before the genocide when there was already active persecution against the Tutsi. She was just a little girl at the time, but she remembers a mob coming for her family and the hurried trek in the middle of the night to enter neighboring Uganda. They escaped on a harrowing nighttime walk over a key border bridge guarded by Rwandans eager to intercept them. In God's mercy, they crossed at a time when every one of the guards was asleep, and not a single one awoke as over 50 parents and children quietly crossed the bridge. Eventually, the family immigrated to Canada, together with many other

Rwandan expatriates. Bernadette met and married her husband and lived in Canada for 25 years, raising their family there.

After her husband, Francis, also a native Rwandan, retired from his work in Canada, they decided to return to the new Rwanda to retire. They were both very dear believers, and Francis had gone through some theological training, as he had always wanted to minister in Rwanda. He was ordained as a minister in the Anglican church upon his return, and was assigned a new Anglican church in Kigali.

Cal and Mimi very quickly felt a special bond with Francis and Bernadette, not only because of their common interest in the spiritual development of themselves and others, but also because the couple were also quick to offer their home to others in hospitality. Mimi also wondered what to do with a collection of antique tablecloths she had been given a few years before, all spectacularly embroidered and collected from a variety of countries. Knowing that Francis often ministered in smaller village churches as well as in Kigali, Mimi reasoned that each of these white tablecloths could be used to cover the local communion tables for their services. So now 15 gorgeous, hand-embroidered, antique tablecloths are sprinkled among the various small villages where Francis ministers.

Finally, the day came for them to go. It was difficult to say goodbye … and say goodbye … and say goodbye as various groups came and went. Mimi knew there would be people at the airport to say goodbye, so she brought a box of chocolates to pass out, which converted the experience into a picnic.

Mimi's Parkinson's didn't seem to affect their life in Rwanda much at all, especially with the treatment she had started; the disease was simply something to put up with. It was marvelous how the Lord allowed her to have the strength and agility to do all that she did.

Cal could see evidence of her Parkinson's from time to time, but it was very mild and almost intermittent to where it really did not affect her energy level or daily functioning. She did have to take medication, but they were blessed that she went through almost four years of active Parkinson's with some medication, but at such a controllable, mild level that most people did not know there was anything wrong.

Interestingly, the Rwandans were very attuned to episodes where she could use a bit of help. If one saw her having some difficulty walking on the street or carrying something, they would run over, grab her arm, and walk together to her destination. This occurred as often with total strangers as with close friends.

A few years after leaving Rwanda, Mimi again saw Rosa in Ecuador and told her she had Parkinson's disease. Rosa looked closely at her, recalling all the time they had spent together in Ecuador prior to her Parkinson's, and said, "There's nothing wrong with you, you're just slow!" describing the very essence of the disease. It was only the goodness of her God to give such a long-standing period of mild and controllable symptoms.

When Cal and Mimi left Rwanda, they knew that they just had to continue to return, and God permitted them to return regularly, every year or so for many years.

Lakewood, Colorado

2013 – PRESENT

CAL AND MIMI AT ECHO LAKE, COLORADO, 2021

VINCENT CUBAKA, RWANDA, 2018

VISITING NESTOR AND SUSANA IN QUITO

NESTOR ROMERO AND FAMILY VISITING
CAL AND MIMI IN LAKEWOOD

WILSON FAMILY IN CANCUN, 2018

CHAPTER 56

Awards and Redirection

The Wilsons returned from Rwanda as Cal turned 65 years old. He didn't want to officially retire, especially if that implied a rocking chair, because his perspective on life had broadened tremendously. He wanted to continue in global health work and to remain affiliated with the Department of Family Medicine at the University. But at this stage of life, he also felt that he needed to focus on the nurturing of relationships already begun. For both Cal and Mimi this meant not looking to innovate new projects, but to work with and behind others as they developed. Their intentional role in retirement was to continue working in relationships to help bring people to their best.

Cal reviewed this idea with Dr. Frank DeGruy, the chairman of the Department of Family Medicine, who agreed with his plan. He said, "We'd love to have you continue to be an adjunct member here," which meant as a volunteer clinical professor. "We're sorry to see you go, but we understand."

The Department of Family Medicine held a big farewell party for Cal with the whole medical and ancillary staff. Some of Cal's closest colleagues in the department were doctors whom he had hired to be part of the new Family Medicine residency at the University Hospital back in 1995. Most of them had continued in the Department and had matured, and it was most rewarding to see them still involved and active in new teaching initiatives. For example, Cal had hired Dr. Mark Deutchman from a busy rural Family Practice in Idaho, and had watched him greatly enhance the training of the new Colorado program, especially in areas like general obstetrics and office procedures. However, Mark began noting the great dearth of qualified family physicians in the rural areas of Colorado, and so devoted himself to not only actively recruiting physicians from those areas, but also establishing a career pipeline in which capable high school students were given the opportunity to work with some of the existing rural physicians, in the hope of encouraging them to follow this path.

Over his career of many years, Cal had received many awards and globes (in honor of his global health work), but he was perhaps most honored, and also most conflicted, over receiving the 2005 Humanitarian Award of the American Academy of Family Practitioners (AAFP). The AAFP is the second largest medical professional organization in the country with tens of thousands of members, second only in size to the Academy of

Internal Medicine Physicians. The Humanitarian Award is a national-level award that is presented at the annual conference every year, and Dr. Frank DeGruy had nominated Cal in 2005.

While in Rwanda, Cal had had several productive conversations with the American Ambassador to Rwanda. The Ambassador regularly referred to the nonprofit groups operating in a country like Rwanda as "do-gooders." He did not necessarily use this term in a pejorative manner, but simply acknowledged the purpose for which the nonprofit organizations were there—to do good. Cal and Mimi knew their presence and work in a country was about far more than just doing good. Their goal was to identify areas in which the people themselves wanted to change and improve, to help them achieve their own goals, and to do so in a sustainable manner that would continue long after Cal and Mimi were gone. They wanted to be agents for desired change, not only in the medical field, but also in the social and spiritual realms as well. Although this could certainly be considered humanitarian work, there are many lesser activities that fall under that umbrella as well.

While Cal could not fault the AAFP for choosing the term "humanitarian," he tried to address the issue in his acceptance speech, not negatively but positively. Cal and Mimi walked down the aisle, Cal was presented with the award with the usual kudos, and he opened his acceptance speech with a story about a young boy who asked his father, "Dad, I can understand that vegetarians eat only vegetables and pescatarians eat only fish, but what do humanitarians eat?" They loved that, and it cleared the atmosphere. He first introduced Mimi as the instigator of many of the projects they had completed, and then went on to explain that the award was a bit of a surprise, because "Our practice has been to simply draw a circle around ourselves wherever we are and offer ourselves to those individuals who happened to be in the circle at that time. We are especially drawn to those with physical, emotional, or spiritual needs that are not being met by other resources. That is why we have spent so much time in the resource-poor areas of the developing world." Cal's "humanitarian" work, as well as Mimi's had been much more than just going into a country and handing out things, but they had both invested in people and worked to achieve lasting change.

CHAPTER 57

Syncing with the Children's Lives

By now the three Wilson children had married and had children of their own. When Cal and Mimi returned from Rwanda to Lakewood in 2013, both of their sons, Kurt and Kevin, were living in Grand Rapids, Michigan, where they had found a much better job market than in Colorado. Kurt had accepted an invitation to lead a new nonprofit startup that he had originally promoted, called Compass Arts, which developed and distributed books and video productions primarily for Christian nonprofit organizations. Kevin had taken additional training while in Peru in computer program coding and development, and after unsuccessfully looking for a position in the Denver area, found a great position in a small commercially-oriented company in Grand Rapids, the city where Sarah grew up.

Both of their son's families had evolved their own lives

in Michigan and had developed a whole set of friends and church affiliations. The long distance between Denver and Grand Rapids necessitated strong intentions to spend time together, which they tried to do several times a year in addition to phone calls.

Kyndra and her husband, Tom Trinidad, stayed in Colorado Springs. Tom had completed his doctorate in theology and was now the senior pastor at the Faith Presbyterian Church in Colorado Springs. Kyndra was in the process of building a business as an independent consultant in marketing and branding of organizations, with the focus especially on colleges and universities. Cal and Mimi loved having them so close. They could pop down to Colorado Springs periodically and take them out to dinner or Kyndra and Tom could drive up to Lakewood and they could do things together in Denver. The geographic closeness gave Cal and Mimi a good level of contact with their two grandchildren, Jordan and Hutson.

When granddaughter Jordan said goodbye to Mimi for one of their return visits to Rwanda, she was heartbroken because she and Mimi had had so much fun together, so she gave her a parting gift: a boxed set of tiny, little bones. Mimi looked at them and wondered how to say thank you for a little set of bones. She was thinking, *Please give me a little tip…..!* Jordan quickly explained that the bones were the contents of the stomach of an owl that she had dissected some time before and was one of her treasures. Now this *was* a unique gift, and became one of Mimi's treasures as well. She kept it with her jewelry so she could be sure to show it to Jordan when she returned from Rwanda. She still keeps it with her prized jewelry.

To celebrate Cal and Mimi's 50th wedding anniversary in 2018, all three of the children, their spouses, and seven grandchildren set time apart to celebrate with them, so Cal and Mimi took the whole family to Cancun, Mexico for a week. It was a marvelous time of pure fun, especially given the options available at the all-inclusive resort that they selected near Tulum. Mimi and Cal were not necessarily up to jet skiing or scuba diving, but some of the children were. They all spent time in the water, visiting old Mayan ruins, and engaged in some wonderfully deep talks. They made a point to gather every afternoon and choose a topic of conversation that encouraged each family member to think deeply, especially in discussing the impacts on their lives of some of their shared experiences, such as growing up in a doctor's family or moving to Ecuador.

As a result of their experiences growing up, living outside the US and engaging in countless mealtime conversations, the adult Wilson children grew very comfortable interacting with people from other cultures. They can talk easily with anyone. Mimi took great pleasure in observing that all three children, and the older grandchildren as well, had become comforting and understanding hosts to anyone who felt like they were from the "outside." They often alluded to the different worldview they have, compared to many of their peers and colleagues. In their own transitions, such as moving to Grand Rapids, where they were searching for new friends, their upbringing presented a bit of difficulty because of their greater interest in global occurrences, politics, and tragedies, and not just local events and politics. In raising and training their own children, all three made a point of including frequent international trips and exposure to other cultures, which they did as intentionally as Cal and Mimi had done with them.

At this season of their lives, Cal asked their children one by one to reflect on the question, *"Was there anything about our family's international life that you regretted?"* The one thing Kurt, Kyndra, and Kevin all agreed upon was that as parents, Cal and Mimi were perceived to be relatively out of reach during much of that time, specifically when they were working in Jordan or Rwanda. They indicated they had longed for them to be more accessible as grandparents. Cal and Mimi had not interacted with their grandchildren as many grandparents might have; they were simply gone, and that fact at times produced some sadness.

In terms of their own formation as adults, Kurt, Kyndra, and Kevin all felt absolutely that they did not have any regrets. They credited the international travel the family did before and during their time in Ecuador as a key element in their formation, and they saw only positive benefits from it, in terms of understanding other cultures and their ability to be flexible with their lives, time, diet, and development of relationships. And they very much wanted to pass these lessons on to their children. For example, Kurt and Lori moved with their two children to London for a year to allow Lori to obtain a master's degree in theology. As their two children matured, it became evident that the value of a global perspective had been well taught. Pierce, their oldest, began to develop skills in video editing and production, and ended up moving back to London for a couple of years to continue this work, without any qualms whatsoever. His sister Miriam, after obtaining her bachelor's degree in philosophy at Denver University, intentionally moved to Amsterdam to begin her master's degree, again, with great excitement and anticipation.

There were times the children had wished Cal and Mimi were closer, especially when they were apart during many holidays. Interestingly, the holidays became one of the major flashpoints for Cal and Mimi as they returned to the US. They had so many memories of holidays spent apart from their children that they knew they had a lot of catching up to do. And so, they happily began making plans to have the whole family together for Thanksgiving and Christmas, perhaps rent a VRBO together. This succeeded once or twice, especially when their sons and families were in Michigan, and they brought Tom, Kyndra, and their children with them to a large VRBO home on Lake Michigan, sharing a wonderfully happy and reflective Christmas together.

But they also discovered that during the years of holidays when they were not able to be together the individual families had developed their own traditions, their own ways of celebrating, and their own friends with whom to celebrate, and in general their children wanted to continue these traditions.

They usually managed to get together within the general time frame of a holiday, and still had fun together, but it was not the same traditional family-centered holiday that Cal had experienced growing up.

Mimi, however, understood, because this is exactly what she had experienced in her later youth; celebrating the holidays with kindly friends or families, but not with her parents. Early in her married life, Mimi had hoped that in her family the celebration of holidays would be different, and she worked to make them special in the early years with uniquely special traditions. In the end, she also knew that in making the decision to follow God's leading to Ecuador and beyond, that this aspect of family life was going to inevitably change as the family matured.

CHAPTER 58

Durable Relationships

*P*art of the value of a relationship is reflected in the hard work to keep it as a lasting, durable relationship. Cal and Mimi knew that to carry on relationships with the large number of individuals in their lives was going to require a great deal of their time, energy, and finances. This meant that even when they were not physically present in a country, they continued regular contact through letters, email, text messaging, phone calls, and more recently WhatsApp. They took the time and allocated the money to do this. They both thrived on seeing a relationship grow and deepen, not only with others, but also between themselves, as they continually worked on the evolving relationship between the two of them. As they watched this happen with other people, focusing on them and watching them blossom, and especially learning to rely on the Lord in every part of their lives … the joy they experienced was incredible.

In their retirement, Cal and Mimi committed themselves to visit each of their former lives on a regular basis. They visited each of the three continents on which they had lived and worked at least once annually over the first few years, and sometimes more often as the situation dictated. Then, as events and life interruptions intruded, they began to miss a year with one or two countries, but their goal continued to maintain those relationships.

Relationships in Shiprock

Within two years of moving on to private practice somewhere in the US, the doctors who had worked together on the Navajo Reservation in Shiprock, New Mexico, planned a return visit to the southwest desert to go camping together. And following that visit, they continued to meet every few years. Since all had begun a private practice and were enjoying a better income, they moved from camping to small resorts, then to upscale resorts. As the years advanced, Cal and Mimi tried to attend at least some of the weddings of their colleagues' children just to share the joy. At the most recent gathering in Santa Fe, New Mexico, in 2018, at least nine of the ten original families were able to attend and reminisce about the "early years." Obviously over the years many changes had occurred; the children were now establishing their own families, at least two of the doctors had lost their wives, and most were either beginning or contemplating retirement. But they all respected the tight bond that united them and the value of friendship stretching over the decades.

Relationships In Ecuador

Each time Cal and Mimi returned to Ecuador, they were invited to stay with Nestor and Susana Romero, the first couple active in the weekly Bible study group that Cal and Mimi had started years before. The spiritual growth in both of them had been wonderful to observe, and Nestor became a very capable Bible study leader, eventually assuming the leadership of the original group after Cal and Mimi left, as well as two other groups that he had personally begun. Over the years Nestor and Susana, as well as their youngest daughter Silvana, have visited the Wilsons in Colorado where they fished and traveled together, and most of all just chatted about absolutely everything and especially the Scripture. Periodically, Nestor would have a question about one of the more difficult passages in the book of Hebrews or in Revelation and would send Cal a WhatsApp message outlining his question. It was usually so complex that Cal could not simply reply to the message but had to call Nestor to discuss the issues over an extended period of time. Often Cal did not have an immediate reply, but had to research the topic first, and then share his findings with Nestor. It was truly a mutually edifying relationship, even if it was long-distance.

On visits back to Ecuador, Cal also wanted to continue to encourage the development of the individual family physicians he had trained. He particularly wanted to encourage them in their training of others, in their own multiplication within the field of Family Medicine. A significant event occurred 20 years after Cal and Mimi had left Ecuador that greatly stimulated this growth. A new administration was elected in Ecuador that was very leftist leaning, similar to other administrations in the surrounding Andean countries of that time. They aimed to bring services as close as possible to the people in the villages and to focus on the poorer people in need in their country, and one of their chief priorities was health care.

Being very leftist-oriented, these national leaders had learned from and admired the health system in Cuba, which trains and places a general physician in every village of more than 80-100 people, with their own clinic and a referral network system. The new Ecuadorian president began working to develop a similar community-oriented health focus.

Cal first heard about this change of events at a national global health conference where one of his first family physician graduates, Dr. Susanna Alvear, had been invited as one of the guest speakers. She was known as an outstanding medical educator, and well recognized for her scholarly work. During her talk, she announced that shortly after the new administration had taken power, she had been called in to talk to the new Minister of Health. She was told, "We want primary health care in Ecuador during our administration to be delivered by capable, trained family physicians and not just doctors straight out of medical school. Our goal is to have at least 3,000 trained family physicians in the country before this administration ends. How are you going to do that? We have already budgeted (millions of dollars) to work toward this goal. We want you to think about it and tell us how it can be done."

This had happened only shortly before her arrival at the conference, so she asked the entire conference for their thoughts. At the time, there were only a few hundred family physicians in Ecuador. To Cal that represented great growth, having started from only five family physicians 20 years before, but now they wanted 3,000. Back in Ecuador, the potential logistics and methodologies were hotly discussed, and they asked for Cal's thoughts, but he knew they had to solve it themselves. Ultimately, several plans were proposed, and within three years, the Ministry of Health and the senior family physicians settled on a program that trained at least 800-900 new family physicians a year. As of 2021, there are now well over 2,000 family physicians in the country.

Cal and Mimi visited Ecuador as this new training was starting. It was amazing to see it happen, and even more wonderful to see how the family physicians whom Cal had trained were recognized as the authorities and leaders in this new program, now some of the most respected doctors in the country. Of the first two graduates, Dr. Susana Alvear was now the director of all postgraduate residency programs for the Catholic University of Quito, and Dr. Jose Eras became the president of the Quito College of Physicians and the following year President of the Ecuadorian Medical Federation.

One of the key elements of the new training programs was that despite wanting to train a large number of doctors in a rapid period, they didn't want to sacrifice the quality of the education. It was a question of training quantity versus quality, and they ultimately came to a good compromise for the development of a high quality family physician over a two-year program, rather than the usual three. Many of the major universities in Ecuador had already developed full Departments of Family Medicine, so the new Family Medicine trainees were part of a university-supervised training.

On these trips to Ecuador, Mimi's involvement assumed a typical pattern. She was usually asked to give a conference, and in Ecuador gave two conferences each visit, one in Spanish with a translator and one in English. She taught the women what she'd been learning from her personal study, and she always brought a craft for them to do, which they loved. Also, she taught them how to cook one recipe. Mimi had fun watching because it was hugely important to them to get it right. Many recipes can be adapted here or there, but for these women, it had to be perfect. Mimi loved the fact that after the conferences she now had new friends, and more relationships to continue and develop.

On a visit to Ecuador in 2017, Cal found it mindboggling to see how the jungle communities on the Onzole River where he had worked had absorbed what he had offered, and had continued to develop themselves in a variety of ways. Before leaving Ecuador, Cal had introduced his missionary mentor,

Lloyd Rogers, to several of the jungle villages on the Onzole River a couple of times just to get his thoughts on further work with these villages. That was Lloyd's strong point; he had spent most of his missionary life of at least 35 years living on the edge of the Amazon basin and working with jungle communities, helping them develop schools and community churches. Cal had learned much from Lloyd's experience.

After the Wilsons left Ecuador, Lloyd had begun making trips on his own up the river with a primary focus of improving the children's school education. In the eastern jungle in the Amazon basin, he was instrumental in setting up a comprehensive network of schools, from primary schools through high schools, helping to train the teachers, at times paying the teachers, providing them with necessary supplies, and in several cases helping them build a school building. As Lloyd visited the villages where Cal had been working, he noted that these communities desperately needed something that would help to retain the young people within the villages, rather than forcing them to migrate elsewhere. He discovered that one of the fundamental problems in the eastern jungle, as well as on the Onzole River, was that the brighter young people of the community could only get an eighth grade education. They were forced to travel outside the area for a high school education, a transition that greatly reduced their chances of returning to the community. Lloyd coordinated with the leaders of the community and offered to help them build a high school and to help make it operational, which he did.

The villagers supplied most of the materials and the labor, while Lloyd provided some of the more expensive materials like the roof and the more sustainable concrete block. Then he intervened with the Ministry of Education to get teachers assigned there. He had been through that many times before, so he knew how to work with the Ministry of Education.

A high school was formed and thrived, and because of that the entire region grew and continued to develop. Instead of young people leaving the communities, they stayed and began to raise families in their home village. The community numbered a steady 250-300 while Cal was working there, but when he returned to see the school in operation, the community had grown to 500 people, almost double in size. The streets between the houses that had previously been dirt that washed out when it rained were now cement walkways. Almost every home had its own personal latrine, and they were being used. They had developed a village trash dump that was monitored regularly to ensure none of it would contaminate the river.

What pleased Cal most was that because the village was developing and now had a high school, the Ministry of Health had finally established a permanent health center in the village that reached out to neighboring communities. It was staffed by a nurse, a midwife, and a physician from the Ministry of Health. He was overjoyed to hear that both Sixto and Lindon, the two young men Cal had trained, were both still actively working there. Sixto visited periodically, but since completing seminary training in Argentina, he was now working with Cal's mentor, Lloyd Rogers, in ministry in the Amazon basin, as well as continuing to develop churches on the Onzole River. Lindon had been named the community health worker in the village by the Ministry of Health, and when the clinic was established there, he was accepted on the clinic staff. The physician was gone when Cal visited, but he talked with a nurse who could not say enough good things about Lindon. She said, "He is not only one of the best health care workers I have ever worked with, but he's conscientious, and he knows the community. He is the axis around which this entire health center revolves; it's not us, it's Lindon who is the center of this health center!" Lindon was a very humble guy, and when Cal mentioned this to him, he looked down and shrugged.

The church that Cal had started in the village, basically a small group when he had returned to the US, had grown significantly under Sixto's direction. They had built their own church building and were at the time 80 or 90 in attendance, out of a village of 500. Two other Pentecostal churches were active in the village as well. In a phone conversation with Sixto in 2021, Sixto wanted to let Cal know that the church building had become too small. They were tearing it down and building one twice the size because the congregation now numbered well over 100 and continued to grow. This new church building was being built out of cement block with a plaster finish and with a metal roof, which meant it was built to last.

Knowing there were still active groups of Christian believers in several of the Onzole River villages, Cal planned to hold a conference of all the Christian groups on the river. This was quite an undertaking because communication was by word of mouth up and down the river. It took a lot of logistical planning, but close to 80 people attended the conference held in one of the smaller villages, Sancudo.

They came in the morning, and many of them spent the night before going home the next day. Cal gave a couple of talks and several of the others, like Sixto, taught as well. At midday, they ate a meal together that the women of Sancudo put together. They gathered under a makeshift shelter because one never knew when it was going to rain in the jungle.

As they ate, Cal was reminded of a similar conference years earlier in the village of Santo Domingo, just prior to his permanent departure from Ecuador. A long table and benches had provided seating for 80 people: 40 on one side and 40 on the other. They were having a great time with lunch with Cal sitting at the far end. Suddenly Cal noticed that at the far other end of the table the men were suddenly jumping up and then sitting down. It progressed in a wave-like fashion up the long table—a jump and sitting down again. Cal thought somehow they had learned to do the wave, like at a football game. He had never seen that on the river before, but he sure didn't want to be left out. So when the wave came to Cal, he jumped up and sat down, very pleased with himself that he had noted and participated in the wave. And then he saw the reason for it. A six-foot-long green snake had appeared under the table and was slithering its way up the entire length of it, underneath everybody's feet. As they saw this thing coming, they jumped up out of the way, and as the snake moved on, they sat down again. Cal watched as the snake slithered very close to him and then exited the shelter. Two or three guys who had come prepared with their machetes immediately leaped up, went after the snake, and turned it into guacamole.

Just before the conference in Santo Domingo ended, they held what was probably the first communion service on the river. The question was what were they going to serve? Fortunately, the town of Santo Domingo had a couple of little clay beehive ovens and both Sixto and Lindon had learned how to bake bread. So Sixto was put in charge of bread and made multiple little individual rolls for the service.

The communion cup was a little more problematic. There was no grape juice deep in the jungle, and wine was out of the question. As Cal considered this, he asked himself, "Why was wine part of the first communion service?" The simple answer was that it was the most common drink of the day, a soured grape juice. In these jungle villages, the most common drink used was coconut milk, which the people drank regularly because it was clean and uncontaminated. So, they used coconut milk for the communion drink, in several shared cups. Although Lloyd Rogers was not at that conference, after Cal's visit he held several other conferences very similar to Cal's snake-infested river conference—without the snake.

Relationships In Jordan

Cal and Mimi's visits to Jordan were different in that Cal had been more involved in training the entire spectrum of primary health care providers in Jordan, 650 doctors, and 2,500 nurses and midwives. His closest relationships were with the doctors and nurses whom he had trained to be master trainers in that country. When he and Mimi returned for visits, Cal could not meet with all of the more than 90 trainers, although they had developed close relationships with many of them. The Wilsons would give advance notice that they were coming and that they would love to get together. And of course, it was almost a given that they would be invited to their homes. This was the case not only with some of the more well-known physicians in the country, but they were also invited to some of the nurses' homes, which was always very enjoyable. The entire extended family and often some of the neighbors would be there, so it was a big group. Again, the warmth and the welcome in Jordan were almost overwhelming.

Mimi held conferences in Jordan as she did in Ecuador. She would lead a conference for the group of mostly Jordanian women she had previously led in a regular Bible study, followed by a conference for the English-speaking women. She was always happy to be part of these groups again.

They had become especially close to one family in Jordan, the Dababneh family, especially Sana. While the Wilsons lived in Jordan, Sana had taken Mimi under her wing in working with orphans and handicapped children in Amman. Their initial bond has continued to this day as a solid relationship. Sana's husband died abruptly in their home of a heart attack shortly after the Wilsons left Rwanda, leaving Sana as a widow with two young children. Several years after her husband died, Sana decided to move with her two children to Colorado Springs for one year in order to expose her children to the broader world, much as Cal and Mimi had done with their children. The children agreed, although with some hesitation. Even though the family had means, she wanted them to live as typical middle-class Americans, not as wealthy visitors.

Sana found a realtor in Colorado Springs, and she rented an average middle-class neighborhood house. Mimi helped her furnish it from thrift stores. Then Sana enrolled the two children in a public high school in Colorado Springs. The children had been quite favored in Jordan, but here they were just visitors, and they had to learn how to develop new relationships. Fortunately, they both spoke English perfectly, and absorbed American culture with little difficulty. They got into the idea of living like an average American, and they loved it. Sana got to know her neighbors and would take food over to them for special occasions, and the neighbors would bring food to her and shovel her walk. They made some short trips around Colorado and the neighboring states to get acquainted, and Cal and Mimi had the pleasure of seeing her much more frequently than if she were in Jordan.

This turned out to be pivotal in the development of Sana's

children and proved her wisdom in making this effort. Her children are both in New York now, the daughter working for the Red Cross, and the son with his own lucrative business, selling miniature fruits and vegetables to upper-level restaurants and big cocktail parties. Sana is still in Jordan, still doing well, and still very active, especially with other women. Cal and Mimi love being with Sana, appreciating her wisdom and profound experience in trusting her God through very difficult circumstances.

Relationships In Rwanda

It was always hard to leave each of the places where Cal and Mimi had lived, so to return and experience the welcome of those they had come to love was extremely heartwarming. They often wondered if the relationships meant as much to the other people as they did to Cal and Mimi, so it encouraged them to see they still meant a lot to these individuals. They rarely ate by themselves, but were invited to the homes of others for most meals.

In Rwanda they loved to visit with Peter and Katie Cartledge, the young British couple who had stayed with them for six months while they were getting settled there. The couple had been accepted as part of the teaching staff of the primary teaching hospital in Kigalil, where Peter, who was a qualified British pediatrician, taught pediatrics to the residents. By the time the Wilsons visited, they had been absorbed into a USAID-funded program (Human Resources for Health Program) that hired expatriate specialists to stay for a year or more and teach the residents. The Cartledges stayed for the full five years of that program, with Katie also finding work as the doctor for a local embassy. By that time, they had three young children as well, and to Mimi's great joy, hired Grace, who had previously worked with Mimi, to be their nanny for most of those five years.

Cal and Mimi stayed with them for one visit, in a sense turning the tables, and thoroughly enjoyed being with them, as well as being included in Peter and Katie's circle of friends. They made the rounds of visiting those who had been involved in the Bible study through the Anglican church. Most of this study group were the same people whom they had come to know, so this was a great way of continuing the relationships there as well.

Forgiveness entered into their visits to Rwanda, because Cal found that for his own sake, he had to forgive the Minister of Health who had shut down the Family and Community Medicine program and appropriated the funding designated for it. It was difficult when they returned to visit because she had continued as Minister of Health far longer than most expected. Most ministry-level officials in Rwanda changed about every two years, but she continued for six to seven years, through the entire Human Resources for Health program of training new specialists while excluding family physician training. Cal had hoped for a change and that the new Minister would be more tolerant toward training family physicians, but she stuck around, and became more hardened in her views over time. So every time the Wilsons visited, Cal had to forgive her all over again. Even when she left the Ministry of Health, she continued to stay in the country, and became the chancellor of a newly-formed university and medical school.

Eventually a new Minister of Health was appointed, and the system returned to the usual pattern of a change every two years. With this change, Cal's role on their visits to Rwanda was to meet with the nine family physicians who had been trained, to encourage them to form a professional society of Family Medicine, and to continue to keep the concept of Family and Community Medicine alive in the country. When possible, he encouraged them to continue to be active in training students in the medical school in Family and Community Medicine principles.

At some point, Cal believes the medical authorities in Rwanda will realize the country needs a higher level of primary care out in the communities, delivered by trained physicians. As with Ecuador, it will be a long time before a physician can be placed in each of the communities, but the basic elements for forming family physicians are still there.

One of Cal's great joys on return visits was to watch and participate in the ongoing development of one of the family physicians who had graduated in 2013, Dr. Vincent Cubaka (the Rwandan pronunciation of his surname is Chu-baka as in the Star Wars wookie, which he readily embraced!). Vincent had developed into an empathetic, kindly, and highly-skilled family physician, with a deep faith in God that permeates his interactions with others. Two visiting professors of Family Medicine from Denmark, Dr. Per Kallestrup and Dr. Lars Boenloekke, saw in Vincent a diamond who only needed a bit of polish, and they arranged for him to be admitted to Aarhus University in Denmark to complete a Doctorate in Family Medicine. In addition, they appealed to the Society of Family Physicians of Denmark and succeeded in raising enough money to pay for his airfare, lodging, and living expenses during the four-year program. Although it was challenging for Vincent to leave his wife and children behind, he recognized in this offer a tremendous opportunity. This education would allow for quick advancement in the Rwandan university system to the level of professor.

Cal kept in touch with Vincent's two mentors, Drs. Kallestrup and Boenloekke, and with Vincent during his training. They paired Vincent for his thesis with a Danish family physician who was also studying for a doctorate. The thesis partners chose to study several community health centers in Rwanda, meaning that some of the time Vincent could return to Rwanda for field work. He and the Danish physician formed a great team together.

Cal made a point of visiting Denmark for Vincent's thesis presentation and graduation. They couldn't miss this crowning achievement for a young doctor from Rwanda. When Vincent returned to Rwanda, he was immediately given a position in the School of Medicine and began teaching Family Medicine principles to the medical students and revising their curriculum. More recently, Vincent joined Dr. Paul Farmer's group (Partners in Health) in community health research.

Relationships in the US and the Time of COVID-19

The Wilsons had already developed an entire network of relationships in Colorado prior to leaving for Ecuador, and tried diligently to maintain these friendships during the years spent overseas. They generally returned to Colorado at least once yearly to reconnect with as many as possible, returning to the same church where Cal had been a member since his childhood. In some cases, they had enjoyed extended visits from some of their American friends in Ecuador, in Jordan, and in Rwanda, such as John and Kathy Pitzer, who visited Rwanda during the first few weeks to help them settle, and again at the end to help them prepare to return to the US. On another occasion the Van Ryns and the Matthews came to Rwanda for six weeks to cover the innkeeping duties of their large house while Cal and Mimi briefly visited the US. These same two couples, together with several more from their church, visited Jordan in 2017. Cal and Mimi took them to many of their favorite locales and introduced them to friends they had come to appreciate while there. They have also been able to deepen many of their previous US relationships of many years, such as with Glen and Shelly Volkhardt, with whom they worked in Ecuador, Mimi working with Shelly as co-authors on two books. The Volkhardts now live close by in Colorado Springs.

As Cal and Mimi look back on the recent experience of being semi-quarantined during the COVID-19 pandemic, they have not felt like they suffered. The only thing they really missed was not being able to travel as they had before. They had traveled internationally at least three to four times per year for the previous six years, and had become accustomed to that lifestyle of regularly planning to reconnect with friends and colleagues in other countries, continuing to support them in what they were doing and participating in their ongoing development. They were no longer initiating new projects but wanted to assist those they had previously mentored to continue enhancing their professional skills and their relationship with God.

The benefits that they enjoyed during the time of COVID included a quieter pace of life. Given the fact that most of their previous life had been extremely active and full, they began to enjoy the idea of staying quiet until 9:00 in the morning to simply be together, reading and discussing.

They discovered that almost everyone else in the world was experiencing the same sense of dislocation, isolation, and of feeling confined. People had to adapt to working from home and/or teaching the children at home, and most anyone they contacted was eager for companionship. So they began reaching out to a variety of people, their friends in the States and Denver as well as internationally, just checking on them, hearing what their life was like for them.

In many respects, their vast relationships were deepened during the pandemic, due to a mutual sense of longing for companionship and discussion of deeper issues. Women at home, both working from home and trying to teach their children, were desperate to talk to another adult about adult things. The isolation was even worse in countries like Ecuador or Jordan or Rwanda, where people were prohibited from even going out in the street; they were required to stay in the house in many countries except for once or twice weekly visits to the closest market. So, Cal and Mimi enjoyed some amazing conversations. As with many in the US, they increasingly used virtual videoconferencing to simply hear the events of the previous days rather than only the crisis events. The sense of connection improved for all involved.

CHAPTER 59

A Perfect Part-time Employment

*I*n considering retirement, Cal knew he would miss not having the intellectual stimulation of being an active part of a university department and participating in hallway discussions, in the conferences, and in the planning of programs and events. But it was time to move on. Dr. Frank DeGruy, the department chair, has been very gracious and more than willing to allow Cal to continue as a volunteer faculty member.

Cal continued giving some lectures and teaching a few classes, both in the Department of Family Medicine and the School of Public Health, on an intermittent basis. The volunteer position was not at all a burden, and it kept him in occasional contact with colleagues at the medical center, especially those involved in global health activities and interests.

Shortly after formally retiring, Cal received a surprise call from an organization called the Center for Personalized

Education for Physicians (known as CPEP), asking him to join the organization. He had followed CPEP since its inception 30 years earlier and very much appreciated what they were doing. Specifically, the Colorado State Board of Medicine established CPEP as a way of evaluating and hopefully rehabilitating doctors who had gotten into trouble with the medical board. Very often it was older doctors who just had not kept up with current scientific advancements and had committed some errors with patients because of it.

Over the years this organization continued to expand and was now evaluating and proposing rehabilitative measures for doctors from all over the US and parts of Canada. CPEP uses a multi-faceted approach to evaluate referred doctors in a comprehensive manner, looking at their medical knowledge, their clinical judgment, their documentation skills, their interaction with patients, and their communication skills; as well as their current level of cognition, health, and professionalism with patients and colleagues. The completed report identifies both the strong and weak skills of the physician, and when feasible offers a personalized rehabilitative process for improving the identified weak areas.

Cal joined the organization as an associate medical director, with the primary role of observing and participating in the evaluation sessions, reviewing all the information gathered, and compiling it into a coherent report that in a balanced fashion summarized the identified strengths and weaknesses, and proposed appropriate rehabilitative measures. He would also participate in a day-long course teaching some of these doctors how to improve their medical recordkeeping in the age of electronic medical records.

The work with CPEP is extremely fulfilling for Cal for several reasons. Many of the doctors referred for evaluation practice in relatively rural, underpopulated areas or underserved areas, and are often overwhelmed by the demands placed on them. Many times these doctors are the only source of medical care for a large area, and a simple disciplinary revocation of their license would deprive an extensive population of their only accessible source of medical care. CPEP offers the opportunity for these doctors to understand where they need to improve, and a program to help them learn, all with the blessing of the Medical Board.

The other aspect Cal enjoys about this work is the development of a working relationship with these doctors. By the time they arrive for evaluation, they've been through multiple hearings that focus on their failings, and many feel beaten down. At the same time, most of these doctors also concede they are lacking knowledge or judgment in certain areas and are willing to participate wholeheartedly in the learning process. In spite of Cal's limited contact time with these physicians, he finds it very rewarding to take some time to encourage them and give them hope for their future.

CHAPTER 60

The Innkeeper Living with Parkinson's

The first few weeks back in the US upon returning from Rwanda were overwhelming for Mimi, because she discovered that extending hospitality in the current cultural milieu was not the same as she had experienced in Rwanda or Jordan. She had become accustomed to a casual "come over and let's eat" type of invitation. But now in Colorado she found that most people planned far in advance to accommodate their busy schedules, and that simple companionship was not as valued as in a cross-cultural situation. "When I asked an old friend or neighbor to come for dinner tonight, they would look at you like you were daft," Mimi said, "because it took three weeks for them to get an idea of who's playing soccer where, and then they might question the value of such an effort, because they could only come for an hour and a half. Of course, there was no thought of spending the night, which I would love. I *love* overnights!"

Mimi and Cal eventually adapted, but they would put dates on the calendar and then forget them because it had been so far in advance. In addition, many individuals now had dietary restrictions that had not previously been an issue. For example, one guest walked in the door for a dinner party and announced that he was a pescatarian. Cal jokingly tried to clarify, "You mean Presbyterian?"

"No, no," the guest said. "My diet is limited to fish. I don't eat anything that has legs." This, of course, was after Mimi had prepared a great beef stew.

But overall, they have been pleased to have a home where they feel comfortable to invite people to visit. They originally designed their Lakewood home anticipating the possibility of needing to assume care of Cal's mother. They designed the walkout basement as a small apartment where she could live in comfort. Cal's mom took great pleasure in that, often visiting as they were renovating and enjoyed making it her own. As it turned out, Cal's mom died 12 years before his father did, so the apartment was never used by her. Instead, the cozy basement apartment became a way-station for myriad couples and families, especially young couples who were in transition and needed a place for a month or two.

However, beginning in 2018, Mimi's Parkinson's disease now began to impact their lives more significantly. Up to then

Mimi had been able to do whatever she wanted to do, only minimally slowed by Parkinson's. That was different now. She and Cal had to consider its effect on their plans and activities on a regular basis. They were forced to recalibrate their expectations of each other, their life together, and the future.

At times they felt depressed, as they realized there were elements of their life that either now or in the near future they were going to have to change, such as international travel. The nature of the travel experience is very difficult for someone with Parkinson's unless it's well controlled. For example, in getting off a plane at her destination, everyone is in a rush, pushing Mimi along, and if she cannot go as fast as the crowd might want, she feels like an obstruction. At the present, Mimi does not want to be one of the wheelchair passengers, because she can still manage to get off a plane in a dignified manner; she is simply a bit slower than many of the other passengers in that narrow tube.

Cal remembers a time when they had a very tight plane connection in Detroit. Their flight into Detroit was late, and they had a tight connection to catch to Denver. The incoming plane and the outgoing plane were on opposite ends of the airport, and in Detroit that's one long hall, at least half a mile long. Usually a train shuttles passengers quickly, but they arrived at the train to discover it was closed for maintenance. And because a train was usually available, the Detroit Airport has no shuttle carts available. The two of them had to run to the far end of the airport, which Mimi simply cannot do. It just doesn't happen. It was comical, but they thanked their Lord when the gate agent held the plane a few additional minutes for them to make it.

Mimi was faced with the reality that this was not going to improve; it was only going to get worse. Even worse, her reflexes slowed to the point that she felt unsafe in driving and decided to give up driving. This was a real loss.

Still … Mimi loves to have guests; she is still an innkeeper! She can still fix an elegant dinner for any number of people if she has an appropriate amount of time to prepare it, but it is now a slower process. The days of cooking one day for the month are gone, although she can still manage to complete three to four meals in a day using the same methodology. Everyone who comes into the house understands it's going to take longer, but they don't care, they still love the deep conversations with Mimi.

Mimi dearly misses speaking to groups. She loved to teach and was always collecting illustrations and organizing her thinking. She tries to replace this by continuing to mentor young women who are willing to spend one-on-one time with her. The mentoring started when Mimi was newly married and women wanted to know how she did certain things, like cook once a month. In those days, when Mimi was mentoring someone, she would make sure they were making a meal together as they were talking, regardless of the topic of the discussion. That way this young mother could take home a meal after some deep discussion, because Mimi knew she would be behind schedule for days if she gave up three hours to spend with her.

Mimi knows that one key attribute can contribute to the spiritual development of others, and that is a contented heart, an attitude of peaceful dependence on our Father God. That means intentionally choosing contentment in advance of a stressful situation or crisis. She continually prays for the ability to put contentment into practice in her own heart, and to be able to demonstrate it to others.

CHAPTER 61

Life Lessons

"What I miss now more than anything else is the uncertainty of living in another country," said Cal. "It is a great adventure—you never know what the day's going to bring." In Ecuador, Rwanda, and to a certain extent in Jordan, the culture does not consider or encourage long-term planning in the same way Americans do. It is not at all unusual for a friend to pop over to your house just to say "Hi," which in their mind is one of the hallmarks of being a friend. They often happen to show up right at a mealtime, and their culture expects you to graciously invite them to sit down and join you for the meal. They love sitting down over mealtime; it is often quite spontaneous, and they never care what's being served. Mimi would always cook more than enough food for a whole other family for every lunch and dinner to encourage these spontaneous visits. The most rewarding part of this spontaneity was that these "interruptions" were often when the most important conversations took place, when the real issues of their life and relationship with God could be discussed.

In addition, Cal welcomed the uncertainty inherent in his life and work. He thrived on the challenge of solving an issue on the fly, on the spur of a moment. Multiple opportunities per day presented themselves for unexpected problem solving in international work.

Cal and Mimi both miss the people and the depth of the relationships formed. When a group of Latin Americans or Africans gather together, they generate unimaginable energy; they are moving and dancing all the time. "They're so into the physical," Mimi said, "and I just love all that. In fact, there are times I can't listen to Ecuadorian music because it makes me long for the warmth of the Ecuadorian culture." Mimi misses the work with handicapped children, which she found to be very rewarding over many years, even though the opportunities to work in this area came suddenly and unexpectedly.

When Cal and Mimi settled into a new continent and a new life, consistently the relationships that formed over their time in another country progressed much more rapidly and to a greater depth than many of their US relationships. This occurred both with fellow expatriates, such as Peter and Katie Cartledge or Michael and Amy Miller; and with local nationals, such as Sixto, Nestor and Susana, Remberto and Marta, Alfonso and Ines, Susana Alvear and Pepe Eras, Grace, Nicholas, or Sana Dababneh. In most cases, the depth of the relationship grew as Cal and Mimi recognized the beauty of the character and inner life of these friends, together with clear evidence that these friends were allowing God's Holy Spirit to mold their lives and personality toward a genuine expression of love and caring, and ultimately worship.

Cal describes one of the first lessons he learned: "For most of my life I've been very ambitious, wanting to take advantage of every opportunity that presented itself," said Cal, "particularly in a situation like Ecuador with multiple possible directions and many people who were willing to help make the most of those opportunities." One of the byproducts of limitless opportunities was that he became so involved in multiple simultaneous projects that he really didn't have much time for his family or for personal reflection. It took everything he had to keep up with the demands of all the projects, and it drained him emotionally and left nothing for the family. On the day Mimi told him she felt like she was caught in the wake of a speedboat and couldn't get out, he took her words to heart. "Since that time, it's been a struggle, but at least we both recognize the signs and the symptoms of overcommitment," Cal said.

One of the big things both Cal and Mimi have grappled with is the possibility of bitterness—what do they do with the bitterness of disappointment? Do they blame the people responsible, or do they work with it? They have witnessed bitterness in others, triggered by misfortune or accident, destroy too many relationships. They did not want to fall into that trap.

Yes, it was very disappointing to have the Minister of Health cancel a postgraduate program in Family Medicine that was certain to benefit the entire country of Rwanda, simply because of a different philosophy of medical development. However, both Cal and Mimi knew that anger and subsequent bitterness over the cancellation was not going to reverse the situation, nor would it allow them to watch for God's sovereign hand in bringing good out of it. They had to be content and willing to forgive the ones responsible. Cal noted that it was easier to think kindly of the responsible Minister of Health after a couple of years of applying this discipline.

Thinking back, Cal had not anticipated spending a full ten years in private practice before immersing himself and his family into mission work, but he has seen in retrospect that those ten years were extremely valuable in providing the background that he needed, both in medical skills as well as in teaching, before applying those skills to a different environment and culture. The period of private practice also allowed Mimi and him to set the family culture and expectations in place with their children before taking them into another culture. His counsel to young physicians who are interested in international work is that the years they spend honing their skills as a physician in their home environment are never wasted, as those years were not wasted for him.

Another thing they've become convinced of is the importance of avoiding, particularly in less developed parts of the world, creating a dependence upon themselves. This principle must be applied early in the development of a new project, activity, or relationship, and it has to be continued throughout their involvement with it. There's a subtle pull, a sneaky tendency to enjoy having other people dependent upon them, with all of the emotional benefits that brings. This pull must be resisted. The efforts need to focus on enabling the local people to become not only skilled in new areas, but also become local reproducers of those skills. To empower them to take over the project or ministry, to make it their own, outsiders must get out of the way.

It is certain there were great spiritual forces at work the day Cal glanced around at a Missions Conference and spied red-haired Mimi Spees. They discovered early a shared commitment and desire to participate in international missions. Mimi's motivation came from a longing to provide a welcoming home environment for the lonely and isolated, drawing on her long experience as a child in boarding schools where she was dependent only on her Heavenly Father. Cal's interest in international missions was soaked in the opportunities inherent in uncertain circumstances, and the adventure of pioneering new directions in medicine and spiritual development.

Cal was looking for a mate, for someone who had an equally pioneering spirit, somebody who was willing to take risks, to enter into situations that were dubious and vague and to love it. Many of his compatriots in the US appeared fearful of that kind of attitude, but Cal saw it in Mimi. She had grown up with risky uncertainty, and she was still open to that kind of lifestyle.

Mimi imagined a lot of play or fun in a mate. Her father was a gentle man, and he loved a good joke; humor was easy with him. Mimi was interested in somebody who was deeply spiritual but not … stuffy. "I just was thrilled with Cal," Mimi said. "I don't know why. I was dating other people, but I was intrigued by what Cal could offer in a relationship, and I was right." She was absolutely folded into his large family, and Mimi loved being a part of that as well.

They can look back at almost every relationship and every event and in retrospect see God's hand orchestrating it, guiding them through it, and providing the ability to see some of the potential results of it. The accumulated weight of so many events and circumstances with clear evidence of Divine direction makes them feel incredibly loved by God, and increasingly able to trust Him with what appears to be chaos. This is seen even in simple things like the new, incredibly deep relationships that formed. They can see in retrospect that these relationships often occurred at a crucial point for the other person or for Cal and Mimi, and that they often resulted in real transformation of mind and spirit and family over time.

Their greatest joy as they have come to this stage of their lives has been the clear evidence of God's active presence in guiding and directing their work; in allowing them to be actively involved in the lives of so many individuals, including their own extended family; and in providing for their emotional, spiritual, and financial needs along the way. They can clearly see God's hand in protecting and developing their children, particularly when they left the home nest, and Cal and Mimi weren't as available as they had been earlier in their lives. God was clearly developing them into capable and Spirit-sensitive individuals while Cal and Mimi were working in the same capacity with others.

As with most people, they could not see or predict the outcomes of many of their choices or directions in life, but they feel privileged to be able to watch, over the years, how God opened many opportunities for the good of others and His special blessing, such as the development of over 2,000 well-trained family physicians in Ecuador from a nucleus of 5 committed doctors, or the joy of watching young people such as Sixto, Remberto and Marta, Nestor and Susana, Pepe Eras, Sana Dababneh, or Nicholas, and Dr. Vincent mature and be used by God in the lives of hundreds of others. They could not immediately envision why God appeared to close other attractive opportunities, such as the continuation of the Rwandan Family and Community Medicine training program, but with time they have come to accept that this may have spared them from distraction and a potential lack of real transformation.

Given all of these adventures, relationships, achievements, and disappointments over the course of nearly 55 years, Cal and Mimi can confidently say that God can truly be trusted with their lives and the lives of others, and that He is good. In C.S. Lewis' magnificent fable *The Lion, the Witch, and the Wardrobe,* he includes a dialogue between a pair of talking beavers and a young girl named Lucy in the mystical land of Narnia, about the Lion Aslan, a figure of God Himself.

"'Ooh!' said Susan, 'I'd thought he was a man. Is he - quite safe? I shall feel rather nervous about meeting a lion.'

"'That you will, dearie, and no mistake,' said Mrs. Beaver; 'if there's anyone who can appear before Aslan without their knees knocking, they're either braver than most or else just silly.'

"'Then he isn't safe?' said Lucy.

"'Safe?' said Mr. Beaver; 'don't you hear what Mrs. Beaver tells you? Who said anything about safe? Course he isn't safe. But he's good. He's the King, I tell you.'"

"Our God is not safe." Cal notes, "He has led us into multiple adventures, each surrounded by great unknowns regarding our own security and that of our family, and the outcomes of our intended work. But He has proven to us that He is good; His leading has led to transformations in our lives and the lives of many who appeared on our path, and even national outcomes that we could never have foreseen. Mimi experienced how our Heavenly Father developed and used every talent and skill she possessed in helping to encourage and develop hundreds of young people and women along her path. "We placed our lives and our future in God's hands," said Mimi, "and have seen that He can be trusted for our good, and the good of others. He is trustworthy, and loving, and good!"

About the Authors

Dr. Calvin Wilson is an early advocate for the efficacy of the principles of Family Medicine to provide effective medical services globally. He has developed training programs that have impacted thousands of medical practitioners throughout the world, facilitating the spiritual development of many people along the way. Among other awards he received the Humanitarian of the Year award from the American Academy of Family Physicians.

Mimi (Marilyn) Wilson is the daughter of missionary parents and grandparents who worked in the Democratic Republic of Congo. She is an international speaker, co-author of five books, and a beloved mentor of young women, focusing on their development as women and their relationship with their Father God. Mimi initiated services to help the handicapped function to their highest capacity in many of the countries where she and Cal lived. She is best known for her warm hospitality.

Cal and Mimi live in Lakewood, Colorado. They have three married children and seven grandchildren, all of which they absolutely adore and cherish!

Made in the USA
Coppell, TX
29 September 2022

83801065R00277